D0768702

WHY PRESIDENTS SUCCEED

353.03
S611

◆ WHY PRESIDENTS SUCCEED ◆

A Political Psychology of Leadership

DEAN KEITH SIMONTON

DISCARD

SANTA CLARA PUBLIC LIBRARY
2635 Homestead Road
Santa Clara, CA 95051

Yale University Press ◆ New Haven and London

In: Public Library Catalog

Copyright © 1987 by Yale University. All rights reserved. This book may not be reproduced, in whole or in part, in any form (beyond that copying permitted by Sections 107 and 108 of the U.S. Copyright Law and except by reviewers for the public press), without written permission from the publishers.

Designed by Nancy Ovedovitz and set in Baskerville type by Keystone Typesetting, Orwigsburg, Pa. Printed in the United States of America by Vail-Ballou Press, Binghamton, N.Y.

Library of Congress Cataloging-in-Publication Data

Simonton, Dean Keith.
Why presidents succeed.
Bibliography: p.
Includes index.
1. Presidents—United States. 2. Political leadership—United States. I. Title.
JK518.S56 1987 353.03'23 86-28088
ISBN 0-300-03836-4 (alk. paper)

The paper in this book meets the guidelines for permanence and durability of the Committee on Production Guidelines for Book Longevity of the Council on Library Resources.

10 9 8 7 6 5 4 3 2 1

To Melody and Mandy

◆ CONTENTS ◆

◆ TABLES AND FIGURES ◆

TABLES

FIGURES

# ◆ ACKNOWLEDGMENTS ◆

I am indebted to the many research assistants who contributed to my efforts to study presidential leadership from a scientific perspective: John Bayliss, Melisse Bouziane, Kimiko Burton, Maia Chang, Ron Day, Niki De Santo, Melissa Ewen, Alphonso Ford, Kari Hansen, Howard Hines, Elizabeth King, Jon Landsworth, John Lucas, Rob Messerli, Alan Morris, Lisa Rogers, Susan Slager, William Spahr, Cindy Stein, Ted Sullivan, and Brent Treichler. Much of my research was also made possible by a series of generous grants from the University of California at Davis.

I thank as well the colleagues whose conversations and correspondence have stimulated my thinking in ways that they may never know: Kenneth Craik, Lloyd Etheredge, Joel Johnson, William McKinley Runyan, Lee Sigelman, Philip Tetlock, Hans Wendt, and David Winter. I am also grateful to Ken Craik for the opportunity to polish the manuscript while I was Visiting Research Psychologist at the Institute of Personality Assessment and Research at the University of California at Berkeley. The readers for Yale University Press deserve credit, too, for helping me substantially improve the book's content and style.

Finally, I immensely appreciate the patience of my wife, Melody, and my stepdaughter, Mandy, who tolerated my inert presence in front of my computer during hundreds of hours of statistical analyses and word processing.

ACKNOWLEDGMENTS

◆ 1 ◆

INTRODUCTION

Thirty-nine men have held the office of President of the United States in the past two hundred years. Unless some military holocaust or political disruption radically alters the fundamental basis of American government, we can expect this list of chief executives to grow every four or eight years. The American people take their presidents so seriously that suicide rates drop temporarily during election years (Boor and Fleming 1984; compare Wasserman 1983). The impending November election may foster closer social integration that brings even the alienated and forlorn into the fold for a short time. The resident at 1600 Pennsylvania Avenue also takes himself seriously, perhaps too much so, for the stress experienced by an incumbent may be sufficient to shorten his life expectancy (Barry 1983–84; compare Sorokin 1926). The presidency is in any event a hard job and an important one, and as a consequence frequently an unpleasant experience (Buchanan 1978). While the difficulty of governing the United States has always been immense—Jefferson looked forward to leaving office with the words "Never did a prisoner released from his chains feel such relief as I shall on shaking off the shackles of power"—the burdensome responsibilities have expanded tremendously over the years. For complex reasons, the scope of American government has greatly enlarged (see Lewis-Beck and Rice 1985; Lowery and Berry 1983), the duties of the office necessarily following suit. More important, the President of the United States of America has become the most powerful leader in one of the most powerful nations the world has ever seen. Because the repercussions of even a seemingly trivial mistake can be immense, the president is under extreme pressure to do well. He must stay on top of things, stay in charge, or else face, and make the American people suffer, the consequences. Harry S Truman said: "Being a President is like riding a tiger. A man has to keep on riding or be swallowed."

Some American chief executives have ridden the tiger more successfully than others. On the one hand are the classic successful presidents like Lincoln and Franklin D. Roosevelt, and on the other hand are the failures like Grant and Harding. It is not easy to state outright what it means to achieve success in the White House, for reasonable criteria of presidential adequacy are both numerous and varied. We can speak of the president's ability to inspire voters to cast their ballots on his behalf. We can scrutinize the results of polls, such as the Gallup poll, to discern how many Americans approve of the incumbent's handling of national affairs. We can more specifically study how well the president performs his duties as legislator, administrator, diplomat, and commander-in-chief. Finally, we may inquire how the president will stand in the eyes of posterity, or at least in the critical minds of historians. Will this or that president be counted among the great presidents of all time?

I have just described the outline of this book. Chapter 2 examines success in presidential elections, chapter 3 popularity in the polls, chapter 4 performance in the Oval Office, and chapter 5 presidential greatness. For this book is about presidential success. How are presidents evaluated by these four standards of success? What must a president do to be considered successful? Can we predict which candidate for the office will most likely succeed after inauguration day? To what extent is presidential success dependent upon forces beyond the incumbent's direct control? When Benjamin Disraeli became the prime minister of Great Britain in 1868, his response to a friend's congratulations was "I have climbed to the top of the greasy pole." Are there such hazards on this side of the Atlantic?

A huge supply of books on the presidents and the presidency already crowds library shelves. Indeed, so many volumes have been published that it is rather difficult to conceive a book title that has not been used at least once before. Titles already claimed include, with no attempt whatsoever to be exhaustive, *Presidential Greatness* (Bailey 1966), *Presidential Leadership* (Edwards and Wayne 1985; Hargrove 1966; Herring 1940), *The Presidency* (Finer 1960; Heller 1960), *The American Presidency* (Brown 1966; Laski 1940; Page and Petracca 1983; Rossiter 1956), *Presidential Power* (Neustadt 1960), *The Chief Executive* (Koenig 1975), *The American Chief Executive* (Kallenbach 1966), and so forth. Although few of these books concentrate on the problem of presidential success, virtually all devote substantial space to the topic. So why do we need one more volume, yet another title to add to the bibliography?

My reply is that this book takes an altogether different look at the four criteria of presidential success. The difference is both substantive and methodological. Substantively, I examine presidential success primarily from the point of view of the political psychologist (see, for example, Hermann 1977, 1986; Knutson 1973). Here I am concerned less with the institutional and historical substrata beneath presidential acts than with the psychological processes underlying the exercise of political leadership. A political psychology of the presidency concentrates on the development and manifestation of personal attributes that may contribute to effective leadership, the general situational constraints on the realization of a leader's potential, and the attributions that followers and observers make when judging a leader's performance. Unlike the pure political scientist, the political psychologist considers such factors as motivation, cognitive style, intelligence, childhood experiences, age, attitudes, and environmental stimuli; unlike the pure psychologist, the political psychologist is also concerned with significant acts of political leadership—winning an election, initiating and carrying out legislative programs, or serving as a wartime commander-in-chief. Political psychology is personality, developmental, and social psychology applied to political phenomena. The presidency is adopted merely as one example of political leadership; I could have scrutinized prime ministers, dictators, or monarchs without inhibition (see Simonton 1984d; Sorokin 1925, 1926; Woods 1913). From time to time throughout this book I compare the etiology of presidential success with that of leadership generally. In line with my concentration on presidential leadership written with a small *p*, this book pays somewhat less attention to the characteristics of the American public (whether as voter or as survey respondent), a topic that has attracted a considerable amount of high-quality research, especially from political scientists (for example, Fiorina 1981; Kiewiet 1983; Monroe 1984). Leaders, not followers, are the center of attention, and accordingly I mention the public only insofar as such discussion, in my view, clarifies some aspect of political leadership.

The restriction to a political psychology of presidents is narrowed all the more by the methodological contrast between this book and most others on the same subject: I review the empirical research on the four criteria by which a president can be judged. Admittedly, *empirical* is a word of diverse meanings, not all restrictive. If it is employed in the sense of "depending on experience or observation," then certainly all works written on the presidency are empirical. Nonetheless, in the behavioral sciences the usage is often more narrow. In this book, we will impose two restrictions on this adjective (see Simonton 1981a, 1984b).

First, *empirical* means *quantitative*. Measurements are made of variables, that is, of attributes that vary over time or across individuals. A president's performance may fluctuate over time, and different presidents may vary appreciably on any given criterion of success. For example, a given president's use of the veto power may change from Congress to Congress or even from session to session, and some presidents veto more bills than others. Veto behavior thus becomes a variable that can be assessed in terms of concrete numbers, such as the number of vetoed bills per Congress or per president (see, for example, Copeland 1983; Lee 1975; Rohde and Simon 1985).

Many advantages accrue from variable quantification, but by far the most crucial advantage comes from the ability to use sophisticated statistical techniques. It is unnecessary to describe here all that can be accomplished by applying these mathematical tools (see, for example, Kessel 1980; Simonton 1984b, chap. 1). Suffice it to say that, among other assets, statistics tell us how strongly two variables are related, and whether that relation is positive or negative. A common instance is the Pearson product-moment correlation coefficient, usually signified by r, which ranges from -1 for a perfect negative relation to $+1$ for a perfect positive relation, with 0 representing an utter lack of linear association between two variables. With this coefficient we can answer questions such as: Is an incumbent less likely to resort to the veto when his party dominates the two houses of Congress? Are inflexible chief executives more disposed to fall back on the veto power to curb undesirable legislation than they are to bargain and negotiate deftly as a bill works its way from committee to floor vote?

Purely qualitative treatments of presidential leadership, no matter how astute, cannot answer questions like these with any precision and confidence. Only statistical analyses permit us to specify what percentage of the variance can be explained using one or more predictors. The square of the correlation coefficient (r^2), for example, indicates what proportion of the variation in a given criterion can be accounted for using a particular predictor variable. Moreover, whereas qualitative discussions will frequently lean on expressions like "all other factors held constant," a multivariate statistical analysis can elevate such qualifications from equivocations to mathematically forthright assertions. Commonly, multiple regression is exploited to obtain coefficients similar to correlations (beta weights, or βs) which indicate how one variable affects another after controlling for or partialing out the effects due to other variables in the equation. Quantification can accordingly support accurate and secure predictions. We cannot claim to understand the roots of presidential success without acquiring the capacity to generate at least approximate forecasts or projections. Thus, I will show how we can predict almost without error the victor in the presidential general election (chapter 2), explain over two-thirds of the fluctuations in the president's approval rating during the course of his administration (chapter 3), anticipate at least half of the variation in certain aspects of an incumbent's legislative performance (chapter 4), and account for over three-fourths of the president's ultimate standing with posterity (chapter 5).

Second, *empirical* means *nomothetic*. A nomothetic investigation searches for laws, principles, patterns, or regularities that transcend the idiosyncrasies of name, time, and place. In this book I concentrate on those correlations among variables that should hold for all occupants of the White House. A nomothetic analysis properly treats such issues as: What do great presidents share that sets them head and shoulders above inferior presidents? The response necessarily evokes generalizations that ignore the uniqueness of each president. The nomothetic question of this book is the relative importance of individual and situational factors in the determination of successful political leadership. Are certain personal attributes consistently correlated with presidential success in any of the four categories? What circumstances, whether political or economic, most favor the appearance of superior leadership in office?

The nomothetic approach is quite distinct from the idiographic method favored by psychohistorians and psychobiographers (Simonton 1983c). The practice of psychoanalyzing (at a distance) specific presidents in a case-study format goes back as far as Sigmund Freud himself, who launched a vitriolic attack on the psyche of Woodrow Wilson (Freud and Bullitt 1967). These studies have continued to the present day, albeit from theoretical positions not always faithful to orthodox psychoanalytic theory. Wilson (George and George 1956, for example), Eisenhower (Bruhn and Bellow 1984), Lyndon Johnson (Kearns 1976), and Nixon (Chesen 1973; Mazlich 1972), among others, have all been favored with this treatment (see Elms 1976, chap. 4). Even though inquiries such as these will no doubt persist for as long as there exist enigmatic presidents, we cannot too boldly underline the fact that these case studies emerge from an enterprise utterly separate from the nomothetic. The psychohistorian or psychobiographer is dedicated to deducing the peculiarities of a single case from general psychological (normally psychoanalytic) principles. In contrast, nomothetic research is inductive in nature, proceeding from the particular to the general by abstracting laws from the whole set of chief executives. Idiographic analysis attempts to apply science to explicate history, whereas nomothetic analysis exploits history to advance the cause of science (see Langer 1958; Simonton 1983c).

James D. Barber's *Presidential Character* (1977), which has become something of a classic in political psychology, is a nomothetic treatment of presidential success. His explicit aim, as announced in the subtitle, "Predicting Performance in the White House," was to formulate the universals that decide the ultimate success of a president. Barber's two-dimensional personality scheme—active versus passive and positive versus negative—yields a fourfold typology of presidential character that serves as a guide for predicting how a president will behave after stepping over the White House threshold. Although we cannot challenge Barber's nomothetic intent (mixed though it is with some idiographic ways), his orientation is definitely qualitative. Numbers, tabulations, statistics have no place in his lengthy treatise (compare Barber 1965). The same may be said of James MacGregor Burns's *Leadership* (1978). Although known primarily for his insightful studies of individual presidents, here Burns advanced a theory of political leadership centering on the nomothetic distinction between "transactional" and "transformational" leaders. The former "approach followers with an eye to exchanging one thing for another: jobs for votes, or subsidies for campaign contributions" (p. 4); the latter form of leadership "occurs when one or more persons *engage* with others in such a way that leaders raise one another to higher levels of motivation and morality" (p. 20)—clearly a higher grade of president. Burns, like Barber, supports his provocative thesis with qualitative and idiographic illustration rather than by confronting systematically collected data. As I will show in chapter 5, neither Barber nor Burns, insofar as their ideas can be translated into verifiable propositions, have offered theories that survive empirical scrutiny.

Yet we have witnessed in recent years a striking upsurge in quantitative *and* nomothetic studies of past and present White House residents. One reason for this increase is that the complex mathematical procedures long used by economists have infiltrated the research appearing in political science journals (see, for instance, Monroe 1979). Certain adventurous historians, too, have begun to use quantitative methods, mostly in the guise of cliometrics (for example, Aydelotte 1971; Fogel 1975). Many psychologists have shown an interest in extending psychometric methods to political leaders, presidential and otherwise (see Simonton 1981a, 1984b). Even though not all quantitative studies are equally nomothetic—many researchers continue to focus on singular events such as specific elections—enough are so that the empirical approach to explaining and predicting presidential success has become an interdisciplinary activity. Such professional journals as *Political Behavior*, *Micropolitics* (now defunct), *Presidential Studies Quarterly* (at least in more recent issues), and *Political Psychology* (the official publication of the International Society of Political Psychology) have facilitated the communication of results beyond the specialized audiences reached by journals in the disciplines of psychology, political science, history, and, to a lesser degree, communications, journalism, and geography.

A careful reading of this extensive literature, however, reveals that researchers in one discipline often remain quite ignorant of similar, sometimes nearly identical, work already published by researchers in another discipline. Political scientists and historians, for instance, have affirmed generalizations about presidential leadership that have already been contradicted or qualified by articles published in leading psychological journals, and psychologists have been no less guilty of comparable lapses in scholarship. This lack of full scientific exchange is not conducive to a well-rounded appreciation of political leadership. The primary purpose of this book, therefore, is to bring all this interdisciplinary work together in a single volume. The next four chapters treat the principal criteria of presidential success—election victory, popularity in the polls, administrative performance, and historical greatness—from the standpoint of the empirical literature that has accumulated. Though I focus on quantitative efforts, I do not delve into the statistical analyses in any detail. That has already been done in the original articles and books. Even results that are reported here for the first time represent mostly extensions of previously published work. Consequently, my emphasis is on providing an inventory of nomothetic conclusions, some tentative, others securely established. Only when an empirical study is taken to illustrate a particular type of methodological approach will the technical aspects be recounted at all. Accordingly, extensive knowledge of statistical methods is not a prerequisite for benefiting from this book. Its intended readers are not just social and behavioral scientists, but intelligent voters and even practicing politicians. To increase the book's usefulness, the last chapter evaluates the progress that has been made in the scientific study of presidential success. After summarizing what we know about the comparative significance of individual and situation in the determination of presidential success, chapter 6 sketches a theoretical framework that draws the diverse facts together into a single perspective on political leadership, presidential and otherwise.

Because of the substantive and methodological requirements, this volume is thinner than many books on the presidency. The numerous advantages of empirical inquiry notwithstanding, many questions are simply not amenable to empirical treatment. In a way, science has achieved its phenomenal success in the acquisition of knowledge not by addressing the truly big questions but rather by concentrating on those questions that are capable of being answered. At times this means that the scientist may prefer a trivial but answerable problem to an enigma profound but elusive. Some skeptics have gone so far as to suggest that the product of rigor times significance is a constant—that an inverse proportion exists between scientific precision on the one hand and broad philosophical importance on the other. This notion of an inverse connection, of course, is misleading. Numerous "trivial" issues in science, about which the average individual on the street could care not an ounce, have yielded weighty implications: atomic energy, computer electronics, and genetic engineering are a few examples. Nevertheless, a germ of truth hides in the idea that something is lost as well as gained in the scientific enterprise, that some regions of genuine import cannot be reached with acceptable empirical rigor. This limitation certainly applies to any political psychology of presidential leadership, a subject challenging to approach from a purely quantitative and nomothetic perspective. That is why this volume supplements rather than replaces other treatises on the presidency.

Yet I should not lower the reader's expectations too much. Although a whole array of provocative subjects, from constitutional provisions to presidential psychodynamics, are not considered between these covers, I have brought together a considerable amount of material never before assembled in a single volume—material that significantly advances our understanding of presidential success. Certainly sufficient empirical work has been completed to permit some response, albeit preliminary, to the persistent question of the relative impact of person and context in the realization of political leadership. As a personality, developmental, and social psychologist who has devoted over a dozen years to studying the foundation of truly exceptional personal influence, I cannot but see this issue as one that must be addressed by any political psychology that seeks comprehensiveness. The question is absolutely fundamental to our understanding of all types of historical figures, including those leaders and creators considered geniuses (see Simonton 1984b). And even if by the end of this book we will not by any means have all the answers, we will at least know most of the key problems—as well as some of the means available for their empirical resolution.

◆ 2 ◆
ELECTION SUCCESS

American history is full of notable leaders who might also have been noteworthy presidents if it were not for their failure to be elected to the Oval Office. Stephen A. Douglas, James G. Blaine, William Jennings Bryan, Charles Evans Hughes, Thomas E. Dewey, Adlai E. Stevenson, and Hubert H. Humphrey are just a few distinguished politicians who might have made good presidents, perhaps even great ones, had they only been more popular in the voting booth. Of course, there have been a number of politicians who have put into practice the saying "if at first you don't succeed, try, try again": Thomas Jefferson, Andrew Jackson, Richard M. Nixon, and Ronald Reagan are perhaps the most conspicuous examples. Yet the fact remains that any assessment of presidential success must await victory on election day.

Hence, I must begin by discussing the factors that contribute to winning the nomination. Because the nomination process has changed quite drastically over American history and, in any event, is a rather indirect indicator of presidential election success, my discussion of nomination will be brief, limited to considerations of the most general relevance. I will then proceed to a far more detailed study of several factors that make for success in the general election. The chapter will conclude with a treatment of the additional factors, both individual and situational, that contribute to a president's reelection—clearly the most direct guide to assessing presidential success by the criterion of the voting booth.

NOMINATION

Modern aspirants to the Oval Office must win nomination by a major American political party before they can be considered serious contenders. No contemporary politician running as an independent candidate, like Congressman John Anderson in 1976, has attained the nation's highest office. Third-party candidates seldom even get the attention in the mass media that is necessary to mount a highly visible and hence credible campaign (Stovall 1985). But to capture the nomination of a major party now requires that the candidate accumulate delegates, and this forces the many hopefuls to run the presidential primary gauntlet. Once a candidate has captured the nomination, it is customary for him to deliver a rousing acceptance speech that, presumably, unites the rank and file behind the party's standard-bearer and platform. This address is not always successful in healing the wounds caused by the primary free-for-alls and convention floor fights, as George McGovern learned in 1972 (see Stone 1986). McGovern's failed candidacy also reveals another facet of the nomination process: the candidate must work with the convention delegates to choose an appropriate running mate. This choice is often crucial for mending the strains of party dissension and faction, and it is the final step in establishing the ticket to be presented to the voters in the general election. McGovern's slip-up over the selection of a vice-presidential candidate—needlessly creating the "Senator Eagleton affair"—did irreparable damage to the Democratic presidential ticket.

Admittedly, the nomination process entails much more than winning competitive primaries, delivering acceptance speeches, and carefully picking running mates. However, these three requirements have been the subject of research that best satisfies the substantive and methodological restrictions imposed in chapter 1. Moreover, that research exemplifies three varieties of empirical inquiry. The work on primaries exploits historical data regarding election results; that on nomination speeches uses content analytical methods; and that on running mates takes advantage of biographical data about presidents and vice presidents.

Presidential Primaries

In the early days of American democracy the selection of the chief executive was a relatively simple affair. A political caucus made up of national party notables might have a casual meeting to decide who was to head their party's ticket. Only slightly more democratic was the nomination of candidates by state legislatures, frequently a source of "favorite son" candidacies. Nor should these elitist procedures amaze us, for in the formative years of our nation most leadership positions of any consequence were not allowed to be filled by the choice of the uneducated masses. State legislatures chose their United States senators (until the Seventeenth Amendment was passed in 1913) and, in many instances, their own state governors, while the framers of the Constitution deliberately arranged for an electoral college to intervene between the popular will and the actual appointment of a president.

The political scene is very different today. The popular vote now directly decides who attains high office; the electoral college is viewed as a vestigial organ of government, an awkward encumbrance to the expression of the people's choice. The first election that a presidential candidate has to face is no longer the general election in early November but rather the early New Hampshire primary, the first of a long trial period of statewide primaries that only a few presidential candidates survive. Moreover, it has become the rule rather than the exception for one candidate to accumulate enough delegates to obtain a first-ballot nomination by the time the convention comes around; since 1936, when the Democrats dropped the two-thirds rule for nomination, only three conventions of either major party have had to resort to more than one ballot to pick the nominee (Kessel 1980). Because the magnitude of a candidate's success in the primaries determines the degree of party harmony in the nominating convention, the primary system also contributes indirectly to the candidate's chances in the general election. Indeed, in the case of such dark horse candidates as Jimmy Carter, the primaries are the chief means of earning national attention. Therefore, the factors that affect success in the primaries are well worth knowing.

In *Before the Convention* (1980), John Aldrich inventoried the numerous factors that contribute to a politician's decision to run (such as a demonstrated willingness to take risks) and those that determine the probability of winning the primary campaign (such as the establishment of momentum early in the primary series). Aldrich showed as well, albeit on a more logical than empirical basis, that the more aspirants there are, the more unstable the competition, so that some candidates quickly begin to accumulate momentum at the expense of rivals. From our perspective, what is omitted in Aldrich's otherwise comprehensive account is an effort toward a quantitative estimate of the relative significance of the diverse factors. It is for this reason, I believe, that a paper by Joseph Grush (1980) stands out.

Grush's specific goal was to evaluate the comparative influence of three distinct variables, namely, campaign expenditures, past performance in previous primaries, and regional exposure. Like Aldrich, Grush turned to the 1976 presidential season for data, but examined only the Democratic primaries, in which a large number of candidates ran. All told, there were twenty-five primaries in which three or more aspirants competed, the competition lasting fifteen weeks. Eighteen candidates competed in at least one primary, and six (Carter, Harris, Jackson, McCormack, Udall, and Wallace) competed in seventeen or more. The dependent variable in each primary was the candidate's voting outcome, defined as the percentage he received of the total vote for all candidates. Campaign expenditures were also expressed as a percentage of the expenditures of all candidates in the primary. Each candidate's past performance was defined as the simple average of the voting outcomes in all previous primaries. Regional exposure, finally, was defined in terms of whether the candidate held an elective office, such as governor, senator, or representative, that would make him familiar to the voters of the region in which the primary was held. Carter was considered to enjoy regional exposure in Florida, North Carolina, Georgia, and Tennessee, while Brown had such exposure in Nevada and California.

Around 80 percent of the variance in voting outcomes can be

predicted using the three variables of campaign expenditures, past performance, and regional exposure. Although overall these three factors carry about equal weight (β equal, respectively, to .40, .40, and .36), their relative impact changes as the primary season progresses. In the first half of the primaries, campaign expenditures (β = .51) have almost twice the weight of regional exposure (β = .27), past performance falling in between. In contrast, in the second half of the primary season, past performance carries as much weight as expenditures did before (β = .52), regional exposure is nearly as important (β = .48), and campaign expenditures drop to less than half the impact of either (β = .22). This shows the significance of gaining momentum early in the primary series, for once a winning streak is begun the necessity of heavy outlay for political advertising shrinks considerably (Norrander and Smith 1985). The bandwagon effect eventually takes over (see Aldrich 1980; Bartels 1985a). Another finding is that the predictive equation improves slightly with time; 76 percent of the variance in voting outcomes is predicted in the first half of the primary season, 85 percent in the second half. Less is left to chance, to the luck of the draw, as time goes on. Overall, the predictive equations do an excellent job of specifying the winning candidates in the primaries. The three leading vote-getters were identified nearly 90 percent of the time, and almost 70 percent of the rank orders were anticipated.

Grush (1980) presents an intricate model of the 1976 Democratic primaries to try to explain how the three variables operate together to affect the voting outcomes. A central component of this model is the role of repeated exposure in changing public opinion about the candidates (see also Grush, McKeough, and Ahlering 1978). Our fundamental concern here, however, is what these empirical findings suggest about the role of a candidate's leadership skills in his victory in the primaries. One might rashly infer, on the basis of the data, that a candidate can buy a nomination. Given how important campaign expenditures are in the early phases of the primary season, it looks as if a rich candidate need only purchase the first set of primaries and then coast the rest of the way to the nomination on the momentum thus established.

But reality is a bit more complex than that. Regional exposure and previous primary victories can overrule the flow of cash. Moreover, regional exposure and prior successes contribute directly to the availability of campaign funds. Finally, we must acknowledge that the better candidates are more likely to elicit campaign contributions than the lesser candidates, even if the latter are independently wealthy (see Aldrich 1980). In fact, it can be argued that all three variables to some extent merely reflect a single underlying factor—the quality of the presidential candidate. To obtain regional exposure the candidate must not only have attained a significant elective office, but, we must assume, have done a good job in that office. It is doubtful that regional exposure would have been of any value to Carter in the southeastern primaries if he had been perceived as an inferior governor. (Carter's gubernatorial prowess earned him a cover story in *Time* magazine about three years before he announced his decision to run for president.) Likewise, the initial victories that can start the bandwagon rolling are very likely built upon earlier successes as both a campaigner and a government official. Therefore, though it may be useful to divide the predictors of primary success into the three examined by Grush, it may be equally instructive to think of these three influences as mere effects of the candidates' leadership attributes.

The 1980 primaries have inspired additional investigations which round out our discussion of the primary process, and which have implications for the general election as well. These empirical inquiries all concern the kind of image that should be displayed to the voters, especially as conveyed by campaign oratory and by media presentations of the candidates. For example, Shyles (1984a) scrutinized televised political spot advertisements to show what kind of image was projected by each candidate. Though differences exist among the rivals, most candidates try to convey experience and competence among their prominent assets. This result is linked with Grush's notion of regional exposure, for such exposure would likely stress the same attributes to prospective supporters. Earlier, Shyles (1983) had examined political spots to discern the dominating issues of the 1980 primary season. Again, contrasts among the candidates were detected, but one position was universally favored, national well-being (as in the pursuit of the American dream). Given how uncontroversial such a position is, each candidate's strategy was apparently to avoid alienating voters by adopting unequivocal stands on divisive issues.

Compatible with this conclusion is the chief finding of a content analysis of campaign oratory in the 1980 primaries (Stiles, Au, Martello, and Perlmutter 1983). Using a taxonomy of verbal response models, the investigators found that the candidates favored "confirmation forms," or "we" statements, such as "We believe in a strong America" and "We are a peaceful people." Any politician's inherent inclination toward such innocuous formulas may be enhanced in the primaries even more than in the general election. Because during the primaries the candidates may have to appeal to an ideologically narrower band of voters (except in those primaries permitting crossover voting), differences among the candidates may be underplayed. The only workable alternative may be broad and bland appeals to the great American consensus (see Norrander 1986b).

A narrow band of opinion in the primaries may be responsible, in part, for another conclusion drawn from the 1980 presidential year: the perceived personal qualities of the candidates, especially their respective capacities for leadership, have a tremendous influence on voter choice (Marshall 1984; Norrander 1986a). Indeed, no factor, not even positions on the issues, exerts more influence on primary election day, at least judging from responses to exit polls. The people, given a limited choice of ideologies, may fall back on a very subjective criterion, namely, a candidate's ability to project an image of effective leadership. Augmenting the consequence of personal qualities, perhaps, is the fact that the candidates in the primaries, unlike those in the general election, differ immensely in name recognition, many of the hopefuls being virtual nonentities to the public (Aldrich 1980). In any event, this factor also ties in nicely with Grush's (1980) results, for regional exposure, campaign expenditures, and past performance all probably contribute to the successful portrayal of the personal qualities favored by voters in the primaries.

It has become customary for the candidate chosen to head his party on the national ticket to make a nomination acceptance speech before the convention. This speech sets the tone for the coming campaign just as much as the inaugural address sets the tone for the president's administration. In a sense, the speech signals the transition from the nomination to the election campaign, a symbolic meaning evidently appreciated by the 1976 Democratic candidate when he opened his speech with the very words with which he had begun his quest for the nomination: "My name is Jimmy Carter and I'm running for President." Consequently, it is of value to inquire if we can learn anything about the candidates and their parties from these often dramatic addresses.

One pioneer investigation applied content-analytical computer programs to the twenty acceptance speeches delivered by candidates of both major parties between 1928 and 1964 (Smith, Stone, and Glenn 1966). These programs, in essence, were used to tabulate the frequency with which various key words occurred, the tabulations then being grouped into larger content categories. Though the techniques are crude, they can be applied to large batches of text with perfect reliability and objectivity. After discerning the principal content categories in the acceptance speeches, these researchers proceeded to make two types of comparisons.

The first comparison is temporal. Is there any systematic change in the content of the speeches over the thirty-six years covered? Have political values and goals shifted over time? The answer is yes. As we pass from the earlier to the later speeches, references to power, strength, and authority tend to diminish in frequency. Also declining are references to normative modes of behavior and moral imperatives, and words and phrases indicating concern with economic issues. In contrast, references to goal-directed behavior and to needs and desires have increased over the years. But perhaps the most important shift is that the issue orientations have become ever more diffuse, the number of domestic and foreign policy issues noticeably increasing. Each successive presidential election forces the nominees to cope with a growing complexity of problems, whether economic or diplomatic, budgetary or military. The time when a nominee could address a few well-defined issues—as William Jennings Bryan did in his 1896 "Cross of Gold" speech—is long past. The candidate these days must aim a shotgun rather than a dueling pistol.

The second comparison is political. Is there any contrast in content between Democratic and Republican acceptance speeches? Again, the answer is yes. The Republicans exhibit a strong tendency to make references to traditional authority and moral imperatives. On the other hand, the Democrats are prone to emphasize pragmatic means of exercising control, with more stress on power than on authority. Another contrast concerns how the nomination speeches have changed over the years in each party: Republican nominees have been slower than Democratic nominees to give up appeals both to domestic economic issues and to the use of the traditional authority structure for the solution of problems. It appears that the Democrats are at the leading edge of the issues, the Republicans following behind, at least for the period 1928 to 1964. The nomination of Ronald Reagan by the 1980 Republican convention in many respects represented a return to classic party preoccupations.

All this is not to say that there are no departures from historical trends and party differences, for there are. Truman and Dewey in 1948, Eisenhower and Stevenson in 1952, and Johnson and Goldwater in 1964 all departed somewhat from the usual form. It would be interesting to learn whether the departure of two nominees from the norms of their respective parties has anything to do with their comparative chances of success in the voting booth (see Kessel 1980; Rosenstone 1983). If, judging by their nomination acceptance speeches, George McGovern was a less typical Democratic nominee in 1972 than Richard Nixon was a Republican nominee, would our knowledge of that difference have allowed us to anticipate their respective chances of victory in the general election? Conceivably, content analytical techniques may be developed to the point that we can more directly determine how much election success depends on the comparative match of individual and situation, that is, the degree of fit between the candidates' positions and those of their respective parties. At the moment, to be sure, the methodology is more promise than achievement, but the promise warrants pursuit.

Running Mates

The vice-presidential candidate is usually chosen to balance the ticket. Often this balance is either geographical or ideological in nature, and sometimes both. In Reagan's unsuccessful bid for the 1976 Republican nomination, for example, the unusual last-ditch step was taken to pick a running mate before the convention had even chosen the presidential candidate (although Ford's nomination appeared next to locked up by then). Reagan named Richard Schweiker, an Eastern seaboard senator (Pennsylvania), to balance his status as a former Pacific coast (California) governor. Schweiker's liberal credentials also contrasted with Reagan's old-style conservatism. To be sure, not all maneuvers to balance the party ticket are so blatant, but Reagan's surprise move illustrates how geography and ideology serve as useful criteria in selecting a running mate.

Are there other criteria? How do the presidential and vice-presidential candidates compare in biography, personality, and political experience? Little research has been done addressing this issue, unfortunately, and findings are scattered in tidbits here and there. Wendt and Muncy (1979), in an investigation that will be more completely discussed in chapter 4, observed that vice presidents had a much higher probability of being only children than did presidents, none of whom has been an only child. Thus, while both presidents and vice presidents tend to be first-born children, the vice presidents are less likely to have younger siblings over whom, presumably, they can practice dominance behaviors. The only child may also be more disposed to identify with authority figures (lacking any peers within the family), and accordingly the only-child vice-presidential candidate may get along better than others with the first-born presidential candidate.

Apropos of this last point, Herbert Barry III (1979) has noted the curious fact that presidents who were affiliated with their predecessors (in the sense of belonging to the same party) tended to be first-born sons who were paternal namesakes. Barry argued that such a child is far more likely to identify with authority figures than are later-born sons given other names. Sons so explicitly identified as a chip off the old block will, as mature politicians, adopt a position even closer and more submissive to their predecessors. Frequently this political subservience takes the form of accepting the invitation to occupy the vice-presidential slot. John Adams, Calvin Coolidge, and Gerald Ford are examples. In contrast, those chief executives who were later-born sons with a brother who bore the father's first name were presumably less firmly identified with authority figures, and, as a consequence, they were less prone to be linked with their predecessors. In fact, only one president in this category, Richard Nixon, served as a vice president before becoming president. Hence, vice-presidential candidates, if they are not only children, may be first-born sons who are paternal namesakes.

Besides any birth-order dovetailing, running mates may have complementary personalities. In a study to be discussed in chapter 4, presidents and their vice presidents seemed to balance their respective degrees of dogmatism (see Simonton 1981c). If the president is rigidly idealistic in his thinking, the vice president will be more pragmatic in orientation, while a flexible and practical president will more likely have a dogmatic vice president. The running mates behave like Mutt and Jeff, one member definitely standing for something while the other supplies the qualifications. The pairing of Ronald Reagan with George Bush may exemplify this curious complementarity.

Political experience may be a crucial criterion for selecting a running mate as well. Casual observation suggests that some sort of matching process takes place. A presidential candidate who is a Washington outsider often appears to select an insider as a running mate. In the 1980 campaign, for instance, Reagan chose former CIA director Bush, just as in the 1976 campaign Carter selected Senator Mondale. Nonetheless, it is just as easy to cite counterexamples. Outsider Governor Wilson ran with outsider Governor Marshall in 1912, and experienced insider Senator Kennedy teamed up with experienced insider Senator Johnson in 1960. So what is the truth of the matter? How do the running mates match up in fact? Do they tend to be similar or complementary?

A recent empirical study addressed this question (Simonton 1985b). All successful running mates in the forty-nine elections between 1789 and 1980 (inclusively) were examined. The president and vice president in each instance were assessed on a wide range of political experience variables, including years as state governor and as state legislator, years in the House of Representatives and in the Senate, total years in public office and in national office at the federal capital, and the age at which they first entered public affairs and national affairs. In addition, such background variables as education (college graduate or not), occupation (lawyer or other occupation), and military experience (years in service) were measured. There were seventeen variables in all. When the correlation between the presidents' scores and those of their respective vice presidents was calculated, little evidence appeared for matching of any kind, whether by similarity or by complementarity. The only correlations of any statistical reliability were those concerning the age at which each first attained public office ($r = .29$) and specifically national office ($r = .30$). However, as I will discuss later, the age at which politicians enter political office has gotten higher over the course of American history. Once we control for this temporal trend, the correlations become insignificant—the partial correlations are .15 for public office and .22 for national office.

Consequently, the best conclusion we can make is that in the past two centuries the victorious running mates have not been matched in political experience, nor even in educational or occupational background. It is conceivable that the other, more obvious criteria, such as geography and ideology, dominate the selection of a running mate to such a degree that little latitude is left for the influence of differences in political experience.

If there is no evidence that the presidential and vice-presidential candidates are matched in political experience, do they at least differ from each other? Why is one chosen to head the ticket while the other assumes the subsidiary role? To deal with this question it is necessary to study the successful running mates not as pairs but rather as individual presidents and vice presidents taken separately (Simonton 1985b). Because some of the vice presidents later became presidents, five different groups have to be distinguished. In thirty cases the vice president served only as a vice president, never as a president. Aaron Burr is the first example, and Hubert H. Humphrey and Nelson Rockefeller are among the more recent examples. Five vice presidents succeeded to the presidency upon the death or resignation of their predecessors, but failed to be reelected to the office on their own. The reelection bids of four accidental presidents were successful, while four former vice presidents were elected to the presidency without the advantage of an incumbency obtained via vice-presidential succession. Finally, twenty-six presidents, including George Washington and Ronald Reagan, never served as vice presidents. Sixty-nine leaders were studied altogether.

As in the study of running mates, a respectable number of variables were used to assess the comparative educational, occupational, military, and especially political experiences of these distinguished politicians. A discriminant analysis was then employed to determine whether the five groups differed from each other on any of the potential discriminators (almost two dozen in all). It turned out that only two variables differ across the five groups, and both of these discriminators regard military experience, namely, the number of years of military service and whether or not the politician in question was a former army general. (Not one president or vice president was an admiral, though Admiral George Dewey, the hero of the Spanish-American War, announced his availability for nomination in 1900 with the damning words: "I am convinced that the office of President is not such a very difficult one to fill.")

The only reason that length of military service is a discriminator is because it correlates so highly with being an army general (r = .64). Once we make allowance for the discriminating power provided by experience as a general, length of military service becomes irrelevant. We are thus left with the fundamental conclusion that the only way the five groups can be distinguished is their relative probability of having a general among their ranks. In concrete terms, just one of the forty-three individuals who served as vice president of the United States was a former general (George Clinton, a brigadier general during the Revolutionary War), whereas ten (or 38 percent) of the twenty-six individuals who served only as president were generals at one time. Washington was, of course, the first, Eisenhower the most recent. The remaining eight were Jackson, W. Harrison, Taylor, Pierce, Grant, Hayes, Garfield, and B. Harrison. All told, politicians who went directly into the White House are over sixteen times as likely to have been generals as those who served as vice presidents either as their highest office or as a prelude to the presidency. What are we to make of this contrast?

Most probably this preponderance of generals among the presidential candidates reflects the infatuation of the American people with the war hero. Almost all of the generals who attained the White House received national acclaim for their military accomplishments, this being particularly true for Washington, Jackson, W. Harrison, Taylor, Grant, and Eisenhower. Once a hero becomes a celebrity, with positive and universal name recognition, his being chosen to head the ticket becomes a foregone conclusion. Even those generals whose names did not become household words (brigadier generals by and large) could probably borrow a little of the luster that surrounded either the superior generals under whom they served or the battles in which they fought. Thus Pierce, a brigadier general, fought at the "Halls of Montezuma" under General Scott, the hero of the Mexican-American War and an unsuccessful presidential candidate. Garfield, another brigadier general, fought at Shiloh and Chickamauga, his gallantry in the latter battle causing him to be promoted to major general. On the other hand, war heroes, whatever the basis for their status, are not sought for the secondary spot on the ticket. Either a former general is not viewed by the nominating convention as a good push from the bottom or else a former general is unwilling to accept so lowly a position, having had so much glory on top.

Whatever the reason, one fact must be noted: the selection of the army general for the presidential spot does not imply that the candidate tends to have less political experience than his running mate, for there is no correlation between being a general and the amount of political experience attained. This result may seem surprising to those of us whose chief recollection of a general turned president is that of Eisenhower, an inexperienced, even, at times, naive politician. And from our history books we learn the consequences of the woeful inexperience and naiveté of Grant, who was so little involved in American politics that he was thirty-four years old before he cast his first, and evidently only, vote for a presidential candidate. Taylor never voted for a presidential candidate before his own election. Nonetheless, most generals had accumulated considerable political credits in various offices, both local and national, before assuming the presidency. Washington had served almost twenty years in public office, Jackson sixteen, W. Harrison twenty-nine, Pierce sixteen, Hayes thirteen, Garfield twenty; even the comparatively inexperienced B. Harrison had served one term in the Senate. Eisenhower, Grant, and Taylor were exceptional in that the presidency was their first elective office. Therefore, American voters, by preferring generals as presidential candidates, are not necessarily preferring celebrity to experience. Besides, as shall be seen in chapter 4, generals have many qualities that tend to be associated with charismatic leadership, especially the experience of having led their country to military victory. In chapter 5 we will discover, too, that war heroes have a high probability of earning high marks on presidential greatness.

Nonetheless, the American public has tended to shy away from generals in more recent times ($r = -.26$). In the first hundred years of our nation, almost every war produced a general who became president. The Revolutionary War gave us Washington, the War of 1812 and associated Indian wars W. Harrison and Jackson, the Mexican-American War Taylor and Pierce, and the Civil War Grant, Hayes, Garfield, and B. Harrison. No presidential prospect emerged from the Spanish-American War (Colonel Roosevelt entered via vice-presidential succession), and of the wars in this century only World War II yielded a presidential candidate, and then only one, Eisenhower. The Korean and Vietnam Wars have produced no presidential material, though Douglas MacArthur was several times pushed for nomination by the conservative wing of the Republican party. Actually, the trend away from nominating generals may say more about the increased professionalism of the United States Army than about attitudinal changes in the American voter. Generals Washington,

Jackson, and W. Harrison were all part-time military men who were otherwise engaged in business and politics. And all of the general-presidents from the Civil War were civilians at the time Fort Sumter was attacked, only Grant having had prior experience (in the Mexican-American War) and training at West Point. In fact, General Taylor was the sole career soldier before Eisenhower. By the time the United States entered World War I, the American army had become thoroughly professionalized; thus few generals from Pershing on have aspired to political office. An example of the change is the experience of Theodore Roosevelt, who had no difficulty raising a motley group of volunteers to serve in the Spanish-American War—so amateurish an affair that his Rough Riders arrived in Cuba without horses to ride—but was turned down by President Wilson when he suggested that the similarly laissez-faire " Roosevelt division" be sent to the trenches of France to engage in equally foolhardy acts of courage.

The trend away from the prominence of generals in the top slot should warn us that the criteria for selecting running mates may have changed over the course of American history. To acquire an idea of whether this is broadly true, let us return to the successful running mates between 1789 and 1980 (Simonton 1985b). How do the educational, occupational, and political experience variables vary over time? That is, how do they correlate with the year of the election? Looking at the vice-presidential candidates first, we find that their level of political experience has declined somewhat over the years. In particular, they are less likely to have been former state governors ($r = -.36$) or state legislators ($r = -.32$), or to have experience in such appointive executive offices as the cabinet ($r = -.30$). Finally, the age at which they entered their first public office has increased ($r = .36$). The presidential half of the team has altered even more drastically; besides being older upon obtaining their first public office ($r = .46$) as well as first national office ($r = .35$), those who head the winning ticket have become ever more likely to be college graduates ($r = .35$) and to have spent fewer years involved in public affairs ($r = -.39$) and national affairs ($r = -.30$) and in public offices ($r = -.44$), especially appointive executive offices ($r = -.31$).

The overall picture is that of decreased levels of political experience on the part of both members of the team, but with the decline being particularly conspicuous in the case of the presidential candidates. In the early history of our country, presidents entered office with considerably more experience in public and national affairs than is true today. In the case of appointive executive office, for instance, it was commonplace in the formative years of American democracy for presidents to have been diplomats and cabinet members—secretaries of state alone included such future presidents as Jefferson, Madison, Monroe, J. Q. Adams, Van Buren, and Buchanan—whereas in this century no president has been an ambassador and only Taft and Hoover served in the cabinet (the latter, ironically, as Secretary of Commerce). Hence, Reagan and Carter, neither of whom held national office prior to entering the White House, may be seen as typical of a historical trend.

Nevertheless, the fact that both the presidential and the vice-presidential candidates are becoming less politically experienced says nothing about the gap between them. The changes could occur to both running mates at the same rate so that their relative degrees of competence remain constant. To check this possibility the vice president's score was subtracted from the president's score to yield an index of superiority in the candidate who headed the victorious ticket. This index was then correlated with the year of election. Two important changes appeared. First, more recent presidential candidates have become increasingly likely to boast greater experience in elective executive office ($r = .35$), especially gubernatorial office ($r = .47$), than their running mates. This increasing differential is mostly attributable to a decline in the level of elective executive experience on the part of the vice-presidential candidates, especially at the state level. Former state governors may have become less willing over the years to assume the subordinate spot on their party's ticket. Indeed, the presence of a governor in the secondary spot is highly correlated with the amount of political experience enjoyed by the nongovernor who occupies the primary spot, for only a highly experienced and competent politician can take the top spot on the ticket from a former or current governor.

Second, the amount of legislative experience ($r = -.30$), again particularly at the state level ($r = -.32$), has become more equal for the presidential and vice-presidential candidates. Most of this change can be ascribed to the decline in state assemblies and senates as training grounds for future presidents. Washington spent many years in the Virginia House of Burgesses, and Lincoln was active in the Illinois legislature, but the only recent president to have even a modicum of experience as a state legislator was Carter (and the last one before him was F. D. Roosevelt). The findings may be summarized as follows: as we proceed from one election to the next, the two running mates become ever more different in executive, especially gubernatorial, experience, and even more alike in legislative experience, particularly at the state level.

Though the differences between the running mates have shifted over time, that is not to say that they differ overall. Certainly the presidential and vice-presidential candidates do not differ markedly from each other in either executive or legislative experience, whether at state or national levels. The only consistent contrast between the running mates remains experience as a general, and that contrast has tended to decline in significance over the years. We are thus left with the conclusion that, for the most part, the two politicians who are nominated by the convention to lead the party in the presidential election do not substantially differ from each other in political experience, nor are they matched in any reliable way in terms of complementary political backgrounds. This null effect turns out to be very important; in chapter 4 we will use it to explain why vice presidents who succeed to the presidency upon the death or resignation of their predecessors do not perform very well as chief executives.

We are compelled to observe that all the empirical research just reviewed on the matching of running mates—whether we are looking at birth order, paternal namesakes, inflexibility, or political experience—scrutinized only those teams that won the general election. Those teams that lost were ignored, usually because the focus of the study in question was on presidents and vice presidents rather than all candidates. Although it might in principle be worthwhile to inspect the losing teams, in practice this would often prove difficult for lack of data. It is one of the peculiarities of history that less information is recorded about the defeated than about the victorious (see *If Elected . . .* 1972). Nevertheless, the dependence of these inquiries on half the potential sample need not undermine the usefulness of the findings. For one thing, we can always posit that all contenders from the major political parties are selected according to the same criteria, no matter which party's offering is accepted by the American voter. Given that success in the general election is not the monopoly of any one party for any appreciable length of time, this assumption seems reasonable enough (Gans 1985). Furthermore, even if we are unwilling to assume that the victorious running mates are matched according to the same selection criteria as the defeated running mates, we are still dealing with the victors, and thus we may conclude that the matching patterns revealed in the above empirical studies show which team characteristics are most conducive to success in November. The first assumption appears the most secure, for a study to be discussed later in this chapter has shown that both winning and losing presidential candidates in the general election may be selected according to similar criteria (Stewart 1977). Nonetheless, both possibilities are interesting, and certain implications (concerning the vice-presidential succession effect, for example) do not require us to commit ourselves to just one alternative.

ELECTION VICTORY

The most reliable gauge of presidential election success is, of course, victory in the general election. In this section I discuss four factors that may contribute to that final decision: the personal attributes of the candidates, the campaign rhetoric the candidates employ, the campaign strategies they pursue, and the political zeitgeist behind the election. This sequence represents a rough ranking of the factors from those in which individual variables predominate to those in which situational variables prevail.

Personal Attributes

Somewhat surprisingly, relatively little research has been done on the personal characteristics that contribute to victory at the polls.

This dearth may be unfortunate, for tentative experimental evidence exists that the candidates' personal appearance can affect how voters perceive their leadership qualities and hence can affect which candidate wins (Rosenberg, Bohan, McCafferty, and Harris 1986). Two personal traits may show the most promise as predictors of election success.

Age. The trait that has perhaps received the most empirical attention is the candidate's age—a criterion that is frequently bandied about at election time. Ronald Reagan's advanced age, for instance, was among the issues raised during the 1980 presidential campaign. But how useful is this criterion?

Harvey C. Lehman, in his comprehensive *Age and Achievement* (1953), devotes some space to comparing the ages of successful and unsuccessful candidates. He specifically compared thirty-eight successful candidacies of twenty-seven different nominees with one hundred eight unsuccessful candidacies of seventy-three different nominees. There are more candidacies than nominees because a politician, naturally, may run more than once. Also, there are more losers than victors because only one candidate can win any given election, whereas more than one can be defeated. All elections up to 1936 were included, but Lehman omitted all vice presidents who only became president upon the death of their predecessors. Interestingly enough, the average age at nomination was about the same for both successful and unsuccessful candidates (57.0 versus 57.4, respectively, with medians of 56.6 and 57.0). The peak age for receiving the presidential nomination is between fifty-five and sixty-nine for both winners and losers. However, there is much less variation in the ages of the successful candidates than the unsuccessful ones (variances 31.4 versus 86.5, respectively). In more concrete terms, the age range of the unsuccessful candidates is over twice as wide as that of the successful candidates. The ages of the unsuccessful nominees span forty-nine years (from thirty-six to eighty-five), whereas those of the successful nominees span twenty-one years (from forty-six to sixty-seven). In Lehman's sample, the youngest president to be elected was T. Roosevelt (who assumed the office at forty-two upon the death of McKinley, but who was not elected until four years later), the oldest W. Harrison, who was elected at sixty-seven, inaugurated at sixty-eight, and dead thirty-one days later. With the election of Kennedy (forty-three) and Reagan (sixty-nine), the age span for successful candidates has increased to twenty-six years, but nonetheless it remains about half the range for the unsuccessful candidates.

Looking at the unsuccessful nominees, we can hardly expect the age range to enlarge. William Jennings Bryan was nominated to head the Democratic ticket in 1896 when he was only thirty-six years old, a mere year older than the Constitutional minimum of thirty-five for a president of the United States. At the other extreme, it is difficult to imagine a serious presidential candidate older than eighty-five, the age of Peter Cooper when he headed the Greenback Party in 1876. Reagan, the oldest president to date, was only seventy-three when he ran for reelection in 1984. Lehman surmises that the nominees may not be defeated on account of their being either too old or too young, but rather the converse: a party likely to lose to a popular incumbent may deliberately choose to run a candidate who is especially likely to fail. Either the nomination is given to honor the contributions of an old party regular (as a gold watch was once given upon retirement), or else a young, vigorous, new-blood candidate is granted the opportunity to prove himself in an act of political desperation, more mature prospects not wanting to risk their reputations and resources on a venture unlikely to bring worthwhile returns. In contrast, when a party appears to have a reasonable shot at the presidency, the competition is more likely to stiffen, and the age of the nominee to fall within the optimal 55–60 age bracket.

Lehman's interpretation probably has some truth to it; yet he also may be justified in suggesting that the very young or old candidate might be handicapped in his political campaign even if nominated by the stronger party. When George B. McClellan, the former Union general, was chosen by the Democratic Party to run against Abraham Lincoln, the commander-in-chief, who had relieved him from command in the East, it was not a foregone conclusion that Lincoln would be reelected. The Civil War was not moving as well as the North expected. Lincoln was the first president of the fledgling Republican party, and he had entered office with less than 40 percent of the popular vote. Under such conditions, the fact that the incumbent was fifty-five years old and experienced in office may have carried some weight with the voters when contrasted with General McClellan's thirty-eight years.

The notion that there may be an optimal age for assuming the presidency receives reinforcement from several studies of the age at which leaders become heads of state in other countries. Lehman (1953) himself showed that the same peak age range of fifty-five to fifty-nine holds for a wide array of leaders, including presidents of republics other than the United States, as well as British prime ministers and chief ministers. Jean Blondel's (1980) investigation of postwar world leaders found that of the nine hundred or so heads of state, 55 percent were over fifty at the time of their first appointment or election; fewer than 15 percent were under forty, while only 21 percent were over sixty. Pitirim A. Sorokin (1925), working with a sample of mostly pre-twentieth-century rulers, also discovered that the late fifties appear to be the peak age for attaining high office in democratic countries. One reason for this is that in most cases the presidential nomination is the culmination of a long political career. That career normally requires that certain lower-level offices be held, offices that frequently have their own age minimums. According to the Constitution, a politician cannot be sworn in as a member of the House of Representatives until he or she is twenty-five or as a member of the Senate until age thirty; the age requirement for the presidency, as noted above, is five years higher. Even though the actual peak ages for winning election to these offices are about twenty years later than the constitutional limits allow (see also Oleszek 1969), these offices form a ladder to the presidency such that presidents who climb to the top will often be of the same mature age. Presidential candidates who try to skip some rungs of this ladder, such as the war heroes Grant and Eisenhower and the crusading outsiders Wilson and Carter, certainly must still look comparable in maturity and experience with opponents who have ascended by the more usual path.

It is interesting to record the transformation that has occurred in the state governorships over the years, for the governorship is now considered one of the chief rungs on the ladder to the White House (see Simonton 1985b). In colonial days, when the governorship of an American colony was the highest position available to a colonial, the peak age fell in the 65–69 bracket, a very mature interval rivaled only by that of Supreme Court justices (65–74). Yet ever since George Washington labored to establish that the president of the United States holds the nation's most prestigious and powerful office, state governorships have become more likely to be a stepping stone, so that the optimal age for serving as a state governor now falls into the 43–49 age period.

This downward shift in the age of governors is even more dramatic when we consider that it goes directly against another trend that Lehman has amply documented: from the time that our nation was founded the usual age for entering the various federal offices, whether elective or appointive, has increased dramatically (see also Oleszek 1969). The increase is about a decade or more. In 1825 most members of the House of Representatives fell in the 35–39 age range (mean forty-three years), but a hundred years later this range became 55–59 (mean fifty-three years). Between 1825 and 1925, senators moved from the 45–49 age range (mean forty-seven years) to the 60–64 age range (mean fifty-seven years). Comparable age shifts are seen for speakers in the House of Representatives (about a thirty-year increase), cabinet members (almost fifteen years), heads of federal bureaus and services (about twenty years), Supreme Court justices (about a decade), and ambassadors (about twenty-five years). Our nation, when young, truly had more youthful leaders. More important, because some of these governmental offices can be viewed as routes to the presidency, it is reasonable to infer that the optimal age for becoming president may have shifted upward as well. Thus, the fact that Eisenhower and Reagan were both twentieth-century presidents who in less than thirty years twice broke the record for age at election—a record held by W. Harrison for over a century—may indicate a trend following that of the lower offices. As indicated earlier, the age at which future presidents attain their first public and first national offices has also increased over the years (Simonton 1985b).

The ever-increasing maturity of presidential candidates may

not be synonymous with enhanced performance in the White House. One scholar has suggested that the greatest presidents were in their early fifties on inauguration day, whereas those who were older than sixty-five proved to be inferior chief executives (Murphy 1984). Although direct evidence on this point is equivocal (Simonton 1981c, 1986c), data exist that imply that the optimal age for effectiveness as a leader is rather lower than the most advantageous age for winning elections (Simonton 1984b, chap. 6). Just as the early forties appear to be the peak age for creativity (Simonton 1984a), so it seems that the same interval marks the best age for success as a leader, whether political or military (Simonton 1980, 1984c). It is conceivable that the preference of the American voter for older presidents militates against presidential performance after inauguration day. This potential antagonism may represent yet another example where the various criteria of presidential success need not have consistent predictors. Certainly, what makes an excellent vote-getter may contrast dramatically with what guarantees accomplished leadership in office (see Aldrich 1980).

Height. When we meet people for the first time, two of the things we are most likely to notice about them (besides their sex) are their age and their height. On a couple of occasions in this book I show that taller presidents may indeed have an edge over shorter ones, but right now I would like only to point to some indirect evidence that height may be pertinent to election success (compare Rosenstone 1983, p. 42). In a study of voting behavior in the 1969 New York City mayoral election (Berkowitz, Nebel, and Reitman 1971), full advantage was taken of the fact that the two leading candidates, John Lindsay and Mario Procaccino, were a noticeable nine inches apart in height. A survey revealed that the people were prone, on the average, to vote for candidates near their own height. However, since this height-to-height loyalty held differentially across voters of different heights, the overall advantage went to the taller candidate; shorter voters were about evenly divided in their preferences, whereas taller voters preferred the taller candidate by more than three to one. This empirical result may help explain why in the twentieth century the taller of the two majority-party presidential candidates has been more likely to win the election. One of the exceptions to this rule, when Carter defeated Ford in 1976, is interesting, for during the televised debates Carter reportedly wore shoes with built-up heels to compensate for his three-inch disadvantage. Nixon could more easily have accomplished this adjustment in the 1960 presidential debates, because he was only an inch shorter than Kennedy.

Why should height be germane at all? There are two explanations. First, people may find taller politicians more attractive, perceive them as more dominant, or by some other means judge them to be more impressive personalities. Second, taller politicians may actually possess superior personality characteristics, judged from the standpoint of the political world. Having had years of experience literally towering over peers, tall people may be more used to dominating people, to commanding respect. The tallest president, Lincoln (six feet four inches), was elected captain of his company during the Black Hawk War; he was selected to be floor leader for the Whigs in the Illinois legislature at the age of twenty-seven, and was a serious contender for the position of speaker just two years later. Thus he was used to exploiting his commanding presence. Lyndon Johnson would probably not have been able, as Senate majority whip and leader, to accost his colleagues with his brutal "Johnson treatment"—backslapping, rugged hugging, punching, and shin kicking—had he not been six feet three inches tall. It is difficult to imagine the most diminutive president, Madison, who was only five feet four inches tall and weighed but one hundred pounds, bullying the members of the Constitutional Convention that way.

I wish I could enumerate more personal characteristics besides age and height that may contribute to election success. Certainly it is easy to imagine other factors, such as education, occupation, and political experience. As noted above, one problem with investigating this question is that the biographical information about the losers of presidential elections is often somewhat sketchy. Another difficulty has to do with the complexity of the research techniques that would permit a large number of personal attributes to be examined simultaneously. A multivariate statistical design that has been used to predict which of two generals is most likely to win on the battlefield might be applied, mutatis mutandis, to predicting which presidential candidate will be victorious (Simonton 1980; see Rosenstone 1983). So there is reason to hope that in future years the inventory of predictive traits may enlarge. However, we should also acknowledge the possibility that individual characteristics are largely irrelevant to success in the November election, the irrelevance being the logical consequence of the merciless winnowing that occurs during the nomination process. As Aldrich (1980) has suggested, a very special personality type may be required for a politician to choose to run and to run successfully for the nomination, homogenizing the pool from which the president is finally drawn. In addition, what individual differences remain may be rendered irrelevant by the overwhelming impact of purely situational variables.

Campaign Rhetoric

An interesting transformation apparently occurs every four years. A politician running for the nation's highest office travels the country giving campaign speeches that promise much, offer simple solutions to complex problems, and in many other ways seem to make the issues quite clear. Candidates who prefer to present the issues using the full panoply of scholarly elaboration, as Adlai Stevenson did against Eisenhower, are seldom successful. But once the American public has, in effect, elected the more simple-minded candidate, a metamorphosis takes place. Simplistic rhetoric is replaced by sophisticated presidential policy statements. Simple promises are out and complex compromises are in. To be sure, as John F. Kennedy admitted in a 1962 television interview on CBS, "It's much easier to make the speeches than to finally make the judgments." Even so, this shift can be extremely disillusioning to voters who expect a product to be as advertised, and not a little cynicism is born when someone sees their favorite politician change from a man of firm convictions to a mystifying excuse maker. But I am speaking only of subjective impressions that many people voice regarding the American political process. Does such a shift from simplicity to complexity really happen? If it does, why?

Philip Tetlock (1981b) presented two alternative hypotheses

for why such changes occur. In the first hypothesis, candidates and presidents may be engaged in straightforward impression management. During the election campaigns the candidates may quite deliberately present the issues in very simple ways in order to broaden their appeal to large groups of people. But after assuming office, the president must often confront the problem of justifying sometimes very unpopular decisions to constituencies that have grown a bit skeptical. The goal both before and after the election is impression management; it is one matter, however, to promise the future, quite another to rationalize the past and present. Naturally, the impression management hypothesis does not cast a favorable light upon our presidential politicians; instead, it assumes them to be sly Machiavellians who manipulate appearances according to the demands of the immediate situation.

The second hypothesis, that of cognitive adjustment, is much less cynical. Perhaps presidential candidates truly are as ignorant as they may sound, their simple-minded campaign ideas representing the state of the art of their own expertise. What they deliver to the American public is not insincere, manipulative rhetoric, but straight-from-the-heart naiveté. The successful candidate is in for a rude awakening, for the business of running a nation is a complicated one indeed. As the new president becomes increasingly aware of the high-level policy issues, he must adjust his cognitive apparatus to a higher plane of sophistication. The result is that his thinking becomes gradually more complex. While the impression management hypothesis faults the American public for being gullible when manipulative politicians promise to deliver the moon, the cognitive adjustment hypothesis tends to blame the voters for electing inexperienced evangelists who require considerable on-the-job training.

To determine which hypothesis best fits the facts, Tetlock collected records of pre- and postelection statements by twentieth-century American presidents from McKinley to Ford. This documentary material was then scored for integrative complexity, a content analytical measure that gauges how many dimensions are differentiated in the process of decision making and the extent to which these differentiations are integrated in a coherent fashion (see Schroder, Driver, and Streufert 1967). Speeches with low integrative complexity tend to treat issues in a simplistic, dichotomous manner, whereas those with high integrative complexity make numerous fine distinctions which are then coordinated into a sophisticated overall perspective. Two trained scorers objectively coded the documentary materials, with a reasonably high level of agreement ($r = .86$).

Careful analysis of the integrative complexity scores lent virtually unequivocal support to the impression management hypothesis. For the ten presidents who were elected directly to the office (rather than succeeding via the vice-presidency), the shift in integrative complexity from preelection to postelection policy statements was swift and complete. Within the first month the complexity level was attained that would be sustained in the next couple of years. In other words, all the change occurred immediately after inauguration, there being no linear upward trend during the course of the presidential administration. This sharp flip-flop contradicts the cognitive adjustment hypothesis insofar as it is improbable that a president could learn so fast how to handle policy issues at a high level of sophistication. Support for the impression management hypothesis comes from another quarter. Those presidents in the sample who ran for reelection would have had to revert to old-style campaign rhetoric if their motivation was always impression management. In contrast, the cognitive adjustment hypothesis would not lead us to believe that a president unlearns over three years of political experience once he is nominated for another term. When Tetlock compared the policy statements in the next-to-last year of the terms with those of the last year, he found a significant drop in integrative complexity in the latter. The almost scholarly enumeration of extenuating circumstances and considerations again gives way to plain political salesmanship.

Though the evidence for the impression management hypothesis is still tentative, it remains a plausible interpretation of the contrast between pre- and postelection rhetoric. Presidential candidates, even presidents, do appear to be cultivating an image with the American people, a task that requires a different strategy when the goal is to win an election rather than to govern a nation.

Although this explanation may seem terribly pessimistic, it does have a silver lining. Many knowledgeable voters have been frightened by some of the campaign statements made by more extremist presidential candidates, Ronald Reagan offering perhaps the most recent case in point. Therefore, it might be comforting to think that the candidates themselves may not really believe in what they are saying. Sometimes we do not want a president to carry out his campaign pledges.

These conclusions pertain solely to the more gross aspects of campaign rhetoric. Campaign rhetoric may sharply differ from presidential policy statements, but we would equally expect such rhetoric to vary from campaigner to campaigner, from one campaign to another, and even from the starting gun to the final stretch of a single campaign. If the candidates are engaged in impression management, then they should show sensitivity to the kind of rhetoric that best complies with the constantly varying situational demands (see Miller and Stiles 1986). For example, Darrell West (1980) has obtained evidence that audience reactions to speeches during the 1980 presidential campaign were used as feedback by the campaigner to monitor public receptiveness to specific appeals. In addition, the crowd's response, expressed by applause, cheers, boos, and laughter, apparently rewarded candidates more for nonpolicy than for policy appeals. Audiences would rather hear about general goals and even personal qualities or party appeals than about policy issues, which can readily lapse into dry and incomprehensible technical or historical disquisitions. Thus one reason that campaign rhetoric lacks sophistication is that presidential candidates, who are almost invariably experienced campaigners, have learned, perhaps the hard way, that the crowd does not respond very favorably to integrative complexity.

According to a recent study by James Campbell (1983), experienced campaigners may adjust their campaign rhetoric in yet another way. Sometimes candidates take unequivocal stands on an issue, while other times acrobatic fence-sitting is required. The latter practice often causes intense frustration to voter and journalist alike, especially when no one can pin down the evasive candidate to one side or another of some great debate of the time.

Instead, audiences and interviewers are treated to masterly hedging that leaves even the most attentive in the dark. Martin Van Buren, known as the "Little Magician" for his cunning in politics, was one of the most distinguished practitioners of evasion, yet recent times are not lacking in exemplars. This gravitation toward equivocation may at times make voters wary of the middle-of-the-road candidate (see Rosen and Einhorn 1972). Even if some presidential candidates may be more evasive than others, it is also true that some issues provoke more scrambling for cover than others. Campbell in fact sought the reasons that some issues elicit such ambiguous rhetoric from a politician, whereas other issues are honored by a more forthright response.

Three possible causes were examined. First, ambiguity may depend on how salient the issue is during a given campaign. Some questions are quite conspicuously central subjects of debate; others are much more secondary. Of course, the salient issues vary from one election year to another. Urban unrest was a major point of contention in the 1968 battle between Nixon and Humphrey, but only a peripheral one in the Carter–Ford battle of 1976. The second possible cause is opinion dispersion, that is, the degree to which the American public lacks a widely accepted consensus, even to the extent of utter polarization. For instance, national health insurance was a divisive issue in the 1976 Carter-Ford campaign, with an exceptional dispersion of opinion, yet there was very little disagreement about inflation in the 1972 Nixon–McGovern campaign. The third possible determinant is the candidate's own proximity to the median opinion of the middle-of-the-road American voter. Are a particular candidate's views mainstream or extremist?

Taking advantage of survey data, Campbell scrutinized the stands taken on twenty-six issues by the two major-party candidates in the four presidential elections from 1968 to 1980. A regression analysis indicated that a candidate's issue ambiguity—as gauged by how much survey respondents differed as to the candidate's true position—was a positive function of opinion dispersion ($\beta = .39$) and a negative function of issue proximity ($\beta = -.31$). That is, a candidate's rhetoric dipped into the obscure and indecipherable when the public was highly polarized on a particular issue and when the candidate's own position was far removed from that of the typical voter. Here we have another reason that candidates may be quite outspoken when it comes to such "issues" as national well-being (for who would disagree with such an abstract goal?), yet waffle when someone in the audience inquires about their stand on abortion, school prayer, busing, or other controversial topics. Those candidates whose beliefs depart considerably from the norm (if a "norm" can even be said to exist for the more polarized positions) would dissimulate all the more. On the issues of the moment, naturally, we might expect that skillful politicians would work their way, however subtly, closer to the median opinion, and this is what Campbell actually discovered. Even though issue salience exerted no direct effect on a candidate's ambiguity, it did have a significant indirect effect via issue proximity. That is, as issues become more salient, candidates advocated positions more proximate to the average voter's views. Once this shrewd slide toward the middle was accomplished the candidates could take up more forthright stands. Herbert Hoover's advice that "the first requisites of a President of the United States are intellectual honesty and sincerity" may be correct for the incumbent, but not for the presidential candidate.

Campaign Strategies

The political rhetoric a presidential candidate employs is part of a general strategy about how to best spend limited resources, including both time and money, in order to be elected. Let me mention a few empirical studies that illustrate some of the strategic considerations that presidential candidates and their campaign managers must face (see also Kessel 1980).

West (1983) conducted a study of the travel allocations made by candidates in the 1980 presidential campaign. His purpose was to show that candidates plan their oratorical and ceremonial activities in order to reach certain constituencies which will form part of a winning coalition. West carefully scrutinized the itineraries of the major candidates during both the nominating process and the general election. In particular, he counted the number of campaign events—such as receptions, rallies, and fund raisers—that could be linked to various specific constituencies (for instance, a speech before a local chamber of commerce). During the nomination process, the several candidates adopted distinctive constituency allocations. Thus, Anderson and Brown, both of whom were pledged to establishing new political coalitions outside the mainstream, emphasized audiences of college students more than any of the other candidates, Democratic or Republican. More traditional candidates sought out more typical constituencies. On the Republican side, for example, Crane and Dole stressed business organizations, whereas Baker and Reagan concentrated on Republican groups. Reagan's allocations were especially striking. Reagan evidently gave up trying to reach certain constituencies—visits to blacks, environmentalists, energy groups, and the unemployed were noticeably absent from his schedule. He directed his coalition-building strategy toward such groups as religious fundamentalists, Italians, Hispanics, Poles, and unions—constituencies normally not so actively courted by Republicans during the nomination process. It is clear that candidates vary greatly in the degree of specificity of the coalition-building strategies. Some candidates, such as Connally and Brown, focused on general audiences and virtually ignored most special constituencies. Others, notably Dole, spent most of their time with such specialized audiences. Almost three-quarters of Dole's time was so assigned, including many campaign events with such groups as farmers, veterans, and the handicapped.

When the nomination process is complete and the convention nominees aim their efforts toward the general election, the constituency allocations shift accordingly. For the most part, the candidates pursue broader schedules, though each major-party candidate still directs efforts toward the typical constituencies that compose the usual party coalition. However, if the opponent's party coalition has certain vulnerable spots, a candidate may try to make inroads into selected constituencies. Thus, Reagan courted the Catholic, ethnic, union, and Jewish voters, who had become less firmly tied to the Democratic party led by Carter. Curiously, there is reason to believe that Carter himself took certain groups for granted, in particular blacks and women's organizations, evidently thinking that these constituencies could not be lured from the Democratic fold.

It is evident from the foregoing inquiry that presidential candidates are acting as rational decision makers when formulating campaign strategies. That is, an aspirant must carefully allocate limited resources so that the probability of election success is maximized. This assumption of rationality is often explicit in research on campaign strategies both before and after the convention (see, for example, Aldrich 1980). A respectable and mathematically sophisticated literature has grown up around the question of the extent to which presidential candidates concentrate their resources on the states with the biggest blocks of electoral votes. Brams and Davis (1974) have argued, for instance, that campaign resources are allocated according to the $\frac{3}{2}$'s rule, that is, in direct proportion to the $\frac{3}{2}$ power of the electoral votes of each state. Empirical research lends support to this rule (for instance, Brams and Davis 1974; Owen 1975), at least if we take it as a rough approximation (compare Colantoni, Levesque, and Ordeshook 1975) and if we assume that it applies to instrumental resources—candidate appearances and advertising expenses—more than ornamental resources—state-level organizational personnel and funds (Bartels 1985b). The electoral college is in part responsible for this emphasis, for electoral votes from each state are assigned on a winner-take-all basis, which makes it more likely that the more populous states will become swing states in close elections. The incentive to distribute campaign resources disproportionately to the larger states renders the general election somewhat less democratic than the authors of the Constitution may have envisioned. The vote of a citizen in New York or California is more actively courted than that of a citizen in Wyoming or Arkansas (see also Rabinowitz and MacDonald 1986).

A related consideration in forming a rational campaign strategy is more specifically tied to a single state: How necessary is it to spend precious time and money in the candidate's native state? Does the hometown boy invariably carry his state in the general election no matter how few resources he expends there? We have seen that regional exposure has a critical influence on winning primaries; does a similar but more specific effect hold in the general election? This question is addressed by Lewis-Beck and Rice (1983). They begin by pointing out that since 1884 around

58 percent of the presidential candidates have hailed from the half-dozen most populous states in the Union. Hence, not only are the votes of citizens residing in big states assigned more weight, but these already fortunate citizens are more likely to have the opportunity to vote for one of their own. The convention delegates, in making such nominations, are clearly operating on the assumption that the hometown advantage will swing a huge block of electoral votes into the desired column in November. Yet there appear to be many instances where a presidential candidate failed to carry his home state, including Grover Cleveland in 1888 (New York) and George McGovern in 1972 (South Dakota). In fact, of the forty-two major-party candidates since 1884, just 23 percent received the majority of the popular vote in their home states. This poor showing for the localism effect suggests that presidential candidates from large states may not enjoy that big an edge after all.

Yet Lewis-Beck and Rice indicate that these raw statistics do not fairly assess the impact of the home-state advantage. Two considerations must be introduced into any precise measure. In the first place, the candidate's performance must be judged in the context of how well previous presidential candidates of the same party have tended to poll in the state. Obviously, a native-son Democrat running in a predominantly Republican state may exhibit a home-state advantage if he does better than Democratic candidates usually run in that state. In the second place, the candidate's showing in his home state must be gauged against his success in the nation as a whole; if a candidate does better at home than in other states he clearly reaps some advantages from being the hometown boy. When these two factors are used to evaluate the effects of localism, the result is edifying. In the case of McGovern, for instance, his loss in his native state appears in a totally different light once provision is made for South Dakotans' preference for Republican presidential candidates and for McGovern's rather poor performance in the United States as a whole (he carried only Massachusetts and the District of Columbia). Taking the previous five presidential elections to establish the appropriate base line at both state and national levels, Lewis-Beck and Rice calculated an adjusted home-state advantage score for McGovern of 14 percentage points, a substantial effect. Carter's advantage in Georgia during the 1976 election was higher still, a full 18.4 percentage points. More generally, analysis of forty-two major-party candidates from 1884 to 1960 (excluding the 1904, 1920, 1940, and 1944 races, in which the two leading candidates came from the same state), the average home-state advantage is about four percentage points. This asset is large enough, of course, to tip the balance in a doubtful state. Nixon's advantage of 3.6 points, for example, was enough to capture the crucial state of California in the 1968 election. Without California's forty electoral votes the election might have been tossed into the Democrat-controlled House of Representatives, and Humphrey might have been the thirty-seventh president of the United States.

Lewis-Beck and Rice did not stop at estimating the magnitude of the home-state effect, but went on to examine some factors that may moderate its influence. One possible moderating variable is time. It is possible that American politics have become increasingly nationalized; thus favoritism toward native sons may have declined proportionately. However, analysis of the data reveals no such negative secular trend. If anything, the home-state advantage variable has increased somewhat, though not to a statistically significant extent. This result parallels what I indicated earlier in this chapter, namely, that state governors have assumed a larger role in providing candidates. In any case, Lewis-Beck and Rice isolated three factors that did indeed moderate the effect of being a native son. First, presidential incumbency tends to dampen the effect. A president running for reelection is usually in such a strong position that the challenger's home-state advantage is substantially lessened. Second, because Democratic candidates are more likely than Republican candidates to get out the vote from normally inactive groups—Democrats are less likely to go to the polls than Republicans and consequently it is possible to mobilize a larger Democratic turnout—Democratic candidates should benefit more from political localism. A nonissue like being a hometown boy is just the sort of asset likely to motivate people to go to the polls who would otherwise remain at home. And in fact, the home-state edge is more powerful for Democrats than for Republicans.

Third, the population of the state relative to the total American population is an influential factor. Presidential candidates from smaller states are probably closer to the people back home than are candidates from large states, especially those with large, heterogeneous cities and strong regional divisions. The loyalty of a South Dakotan voter to a fellow South Dakotan who made good is on average higher than that of a Californian voter to a Californian candidate. The fact that small states send only a handful of senators and representatives to Congress while large states send whole congregations means that the voters in the small states are more likely to be familiar with the political leaders in their states. Thus, the size of the home-state advantage decreases as the population increases. For example, a candidate from a state with one percent of the population (such as Arkansas) will have a home-state advantage almost nine percentage points higher than a candidate from a state with ten percent of the population (such as California). This effect is about twice as large as the impact of either presidential incumbency or Democratic affiliation.

The overwhelming importance of relative population ironically undermines some of its relevance as a criterion for selecting a presidential candidate with optimal chances of victory in the general election. A candidate from a small state is more likely to carry it, but also to earn fewer electoral votes in the process; a big state's favorite son can muster a larger block of electoral votes, yet the probability that he will win it is far slimmer. Therefore, a candidate from one of the largest states cannot take his state for granted, and must plan a campaign strategy that allots an appreciable number of campaign events to the home turf.

The limited resources available to a presidential candidate are consumed mostly by efforts to exploit the mass media. The republic is now far too large for most voters to be seen directly, even in large campaign rallies, and thus candidates must rely heavily on advertisements and endorsements in newspapers and on television. Whistle-stop campaigns are useful only insofar as they become media events, portraying the candidate as a man of the people. This necessity raises the broader issue of the degree to which the media actually make a difference in national elections

Let me just briefly indicate two of the many ways that the media may leave an imprint in November.

First, it is quite evident that the media can be influential. In the case of newspapers, for example, the reporting of the results of political polls can affect voter preferences regarding both candidates and issues (Atkin 1969). That newspapers may be improving their reporting of public opinion polls might even accentuate this impact (see Salwen 1985). Furthermore, newspapers can affect the outcome of an election more directly than television, by taking editorial stands on candidates. For instance, Erikson (1976) has demonstrated that in counties dominated by a single newspaper, a candidate's success in the voting booth is indeed enhanced by newspaper endorsements. Specifically, for 223 northern counties in the 1964 presidential election, Democratic endorsements added five percentage points to the Democratic gain over the 1960 election. Even if the television networks do not enjoy such extensive influence, they can influence how viewers perceive the candidates using more subtle means (see, for instance, Iyengar, Kinder, Peters, and Krosnick 1984), a point we will return to in chapter 3.

Second, different kinds of media vary appreciably in how effectively they communicate the pertinent facts of a campaign, facts essential for evaluating the candidates. In particular, a recent inquiry by Joseph Wagner (1983) found that newspapers, in contrast to television, are informative as well as influential. The primary source of political information had an impact on how the voters perceived the candidates in the 1976 presidential race: newspaper readers were more capable than television watchers of discriminating between the candidates. Only in a newspaper, in both front-page stories and editorials, can one find the kind of factual reporting and in-depth analyses required for a full appreciation of how the various presidential candidates stand on the key issues of the day. Moreover, this media difference cannot be blamed on the characteristics of the readers or viewers, for the contrast holds even after statistical control for education, class, and interest in public affairs (see Kessel 1980, chap. 7). What renders this media effect especially unfortunate is that Wagner obtained evidence that television nightly news watchers are less likely to turn out at the polls on election day than newspaper readers. If the contrasts between candidates are lessened, the reason for voting is vitiated as well. Given that the American people have become more dependent on television than on newspapers over the years, the homogenizing impact of the nightly news might be responsible for more than a little political apathy.

Although Wagner's study does not lead us into any immediate recommendations about how a candidate might most effectively exploit the mass media, it may give us insight into why a certain campaign strategy is so popular among candidates today—namely, the emphasis on image and symbols rather than on issues and commitments (see Shyles 1984b). If television dominates the process of political communication, and if television is weakest at conveying finely differentiated political positions, candidates can (and must) invest all their energies in image-building without substance, symbolic gestures without practical consequence. It is far easier to duck the controversial questions when the focus is on appearance and presence. While newspapers treat politicians within the larger context of current events with deliberation and detail, the television news casts politicians almost as another variety of entertainment. Given such reduction, it should come as no surprise that, as noted earlier, voters often place more weight on personal qualities than on issue positions; in a very real sense the voting public, numbed by audio-visuals rather than educated by print, may not know any better.

The above studies represent a fair sampling of the principal empirical approaches to understanding what campaign strategies contribute to election success. In some respects, however, this work is not very helpful, for it can normally be assumed that the two leading contenders in the general election will pretty much employ the same strategies, with predictable adjustments for any divergences in constituencies. Take the $\frac{3}{2}$'s rule as a case in point. Even if we assume that both candidates operate according to this rule, and disproportionately devote resources to the more populous states, their strategies do not then differ, and thus we cannot use this principle to account for why some candidates are more successful than others. To be sure, some candidates might be more adept at distributing resources than others; for the most part, however, the primary process has probably weeded out all but the most effective campaigners (Aldrich 1980), reducing the expected variance in political acumen. Even if the nominating convention selects a candidate from a populous state in order to capitalize on the home-state advantage, the rival candidate will often be selected from a comparably populous state; if that does not completely neutralize the asset, then the precariousness of the home-state advantage in large states will finish the job. All in all, though certain strategies are optimal for election success, other individual and situational factors decide which candidate will be victorious. One critical influence may be how well the individual characteristics of the candidate match the general political situation, or zeitgeist.

Zeitgeist

From 1928 to 1948 Norman Thomas was six times the unsuccessful Socialist Party candidate for president. His unhappy experience illustrates the plight of minority-party candidates: even though Thomas lived to see many of the reforms he advocated become incorporated into mainstream American politics, he never was elected. Thomas might be said to have been ahead of his time. We can hypothesize, therefore, that a presidential candidate who is out of step with the spirit of the times, or the prevailing zeitgeist, can look forward to minimal success at the polls. It is likely that one criterion employed by the voting public to select the best candidate is the extent to which he fits in with the current concerns and infatuations of the nation. In the next sections, I will discuss the impact of economic conditions on authoritarianism, and the relation of political crises to the leader's birth order. I will conclude with a brief account of a complex approach to gauging a candidate's relation to the political zeitgeist, namely, spatial theory.

Authoritarianism. For the most part, the American public has not been fond of truly authoritarian leaders. Our democracy is self-protective and looks askance at any leadership style that smacks of dictatorship. "Imperial presidency" is a pejorative term. Nonetheless, there are times when Americans are more tolerant, even appreciative, of an autocratic style in the nation's highest office. During the Great Depression, Franklin Roosevelt was granted powers never before enjoyed by a president of the United States. To be sure, when his powers are compared with those of his contemporaries, such as Stalin, Hitler, or Mussolini—even with those of Governor Huey Long of Louisiana—FDR appears by far the least autocratic. Yet the fact remains that the American public permitted some movement in the direction of more authoritarian rule. Is there something about economic hard times that renders an authoritarian presidency far more probable?

Although there has been no research that directly addresses this question, there have been some studies with suggestive implications. Sales (1972) examined the rates of conversion to authoritarian versus nonauthoritarian churches as a function of economic conditions. An authoritarian church is one that demands absolute obedience, whereas a nonauthoritarian church permits its members more latitude in both belief and behavior. Sales studied the conversion rates for these two church types both for the United States as a whole from 1920 to 1939 and for the city of Seattle during the 1960s. Per capita disposable income was used to indicate economic gains and losses for the United States data, and unemployment statistics were used in a similar way for the Seattle data. Consistent with hypothesis, for both data sets, economic good times brought about increased conversion to nonauthoritarian churches, whereas economic bad times saw increased conversion to authoritarian churches. It may be no accident, therefore, that the declining American economy in the late 1970s and early 1980s was concomitant with a rise in the political influence of authoritarian (fundamentalist) religious groups and the self-proclaimed Moral Majority.

The original research on the authoritarian personality found that authoritarians, besides wishing to subordinate themselves to a strong leader, also tend to be highly superstitious, viewing the world as subject to mysterious forces and influences (Adorno et al. 1950). An investigation by Padgett and Jorgenson (1982) indicated that this orientation, too, may be symptomatic of declining material conditions. Looking at Germany between the two world wars, they found that economic depression was strongly associated with the popularity of astrology and mysticism, as judged by book sales. The same economic conditions, of course, were equally responsible for the rise of Adolf Hitler. When a people's standard of living declines or becomes insecure, the masses seem to retreat to the shelter of authoritarian leadership and irrational ideas.

One more study is germane to this issue, and this one brings us back to the United States. Jorgenson (1975) used content analysis to measure the amount of authoritarianism in the television programs shown to the American public between 1950 and 1974. He also gauged the amount of economic hardship during the same years (using both unemployment and inflation statistics as well as Gallup poll assessments of consumer confidence in the economy). The two sets of variables were significantly correlated: economic prosperity was negatively related to televised authoritarianism. Naturally, this and the previous two studies tell us only how people change their leisure-time and weekend activities, not how they vote. Nonetheless, it seems probable that those members of the public who join authoritarian churches, read literature of the more superstitious type, and watch more authoritarian television programs might also prefer to vote for a strong, directive leader to whom they can relinquish responsibility for solving their own financial ills.

Birth Order and Crises. The above illustration suggests that being the right person is less important than being the right person for the time—that individual factors may interact with situational factors in determining the probability of electoral success. A politician who is authoritarian in orientation may be victorious during a depression or recession, and defeated in a time of material prosperity. Louis Stewart (1977) has proposed a similar individual-situational interaction effect, this time involving the interplay between a presidential candidate's birth order and the political zeitgeist behind the election. According to Stewart's Adlerian theory, there are four major types of political conditions. First, the nation may be experiencing a total breakdown of social institutions, such as happened to so many Western nations during the

Great Depression. During such periods the only child has the advantage, for the only child can more readily dissociate himself from personal relationships to identify with society as a whole. Second, the nation may be involved, whether as perpetrator or as victim, in imperialistic expansion and confrontation, such as the two world wars. This condition gives the most opportunities to the first-borns—those who have had plenty of experience playing boss and practicing authority on their younger siblings. Third, the emphasis of the national zeitgeist may be on retrenchment and realignment of domestic and foreign commitments. The 1950s offers a good example of this political milieu in both the United States and Europe, when alliances were being structured abroad and new political orientations were being built at home. Under these circumstances, Stewart argues, the middle child is more likely to come forth. Having had abundant opportunity to bargain and negotiate, and to reconcile differences, between older and younger siblings, the middle child seems more able to do the same at the higher level of domestic and foreign policy. Finally, the political system may break down into rebellion and revolt, as happened during the American Civil War. It is then that the last-born child emerges in positions of leadership, a child who has acquired the requisite hostility to authority and privilege. Curiously, though Abraham Lincoln was a second-born child and first-born son, Jefferson Davis, the president of the Confederacy, was the youngest of ten children, and the fifth-born son.

The assumption behind Stewart's theory is that birth order affects the kinds of experiences encountered during early development, and that these experiences influence the personality style and interpersonal skills that emerge. The appropriateness of a particular style for a leader's greatest effectiveness depends on the requirements of the political environment—the kinds of interpersonal capacities that are needed. Fortunately, Stewart did not leave matters to armchair speculation but actually subjected his theory to empirical tests using two samples, United States presidents and British prime ministers. In the former case, of greater interest to us here, Stewart examined the elections between 1789 and 1960. Though first-borns have a sizable edge in getting elected, it is also true that times of crisis were much more likely to see the election of first-born sons, whereas calmer times were more likely to see younger sons elected. (I computed the correlation coefficient of .38 from his chi-square test.) John Adams, Madison, and Polk are examples of presidents in the first category, Jackson, Taylor, and Pierce of those in the second. Moreover, six of the seven wars that the United States engaged in had a first-born son as the commander-in-chief. The lone exception, McKinley, a third son and seventh child, is interesting insofar as he was pushed quite reluctantly into the Spanish-American War. Just as fascinating, perhaps, is Stewart's discovery that the leading presidential contenders are often of the same birth order—almost as if all the nominating conventions were settling on similar responses to the national mood. In the 1860 election, for example, the three primary presidential candidates—Lincoln, Douglas, and Breckinridge—were only sons.

The data Stewart collected on the British prime ministers corroborates his thesis just as well. Research done by others on totally different samples lends further endorsement to his ideas. For example, one investigation of twentieth-century famous personalities found that politicians were more likely to be middle children, and very unlikely to be only children (Goertzel, Goertzel, and Goertzel 1978). Since most of these politicians attained fame in the post-World War II era—when the political zeitgeist favored reorganization and consolidation of foreign and domestic priorities—we can call this preponderance consistent with what Stewart would expect. Another inquiry into pre-twentieth-century eminent persons revealed that revolutionaries are more likely to be later-born sons (Walberg, Rasher, and Parkerson 1980). A theory of revolution proposed by Matossian and Schafer (1977) predicts that revolutionaries will come from large families, something which is almost required if revolutionaries are to have a high probability of being later-born, even last-born, sons. Finally, an examination of Chief Justices of the Supreme Court noted that first-borns presided during times in which the Court notably expanded its power or pursued a novel course, whereas the Court was more likely to be passive and occupied with consolidating prior gains whenever a middle-born child presided (Weber 1984).

This is not to say that Stewart's theory can be accepted as empirically proven. But the evidence on its behalf is so provocative that the theory should receive serious consideration in future empirical research. Stewart may have succeeded in isolating an individual-situational interaction effect that transcends the peculiarities of any one political institution or historical period.

Spatial Theory. To argue that the successful presidential candidate is the one who best fits with the political zeitgeist is to claim that election success is at least partly the consequence of a politician advocating positions that most closely approximate the attitudes held by the vast majority of the electorate. Teddy Roosevelt may have claimed that "the first duty of a leader is to lead," but he asserted with equal force that "the most successful politician is he who says what everybody is thinking most often and in the loudest voice." Spatial theory provides a formal approach to studying this beneficial compatibility between the candidate and the voters. Though complex in its full mathematical formulation, the gist of spatial analysis is both simple and intuitively compelling. Presumably the positions adopted by American voters on diverse issues can be arranged along one or more dimensions. The commonplace concept of a political spectrum running from liberal to conservative is a prime example; over the past few decades, in fact, ideological placement has become more crucial than party affiliation in the determination of voter preferences (Rabinowitz, Gurian, and MacDonald 1984; Rollenhagen 1984; compare Kessel 1980, chap. 9). However, two or more dimensions may be involved, yielding a space or volume on which political attitudes are projected. It is assumed as well that voters place both themselves and presidential candidates in this coordinate system, and that each voter casts his or her ballot for that candidate whose position lies most proximate to the voter. A corollary of spatial theory is that registered voters may not vote when they are not afforded a clear choice in candidates. If two candidates fall into the same area on the map of political issues, it makes no difference who wins the general election, and thus it may be in the voter's interest to attend to more urgent obligations.

As reasonable as spatial theory sounds, a recent test of the theory yielded mixed results. Poole and Rosenthal (1984) scrutinized the four presidential elections from 1968 to 1980. In two-candidate races, such as that between Ford and Carter in 1976, the evidence supports the hypothesis of sincere, spatial voting. That is, people vote their true preference, independent of strategic considerations. Though one- , two- , and three-dimensional spaces were examined, the principal contrast between candidates involved the standard difference between liberals and conservatives. This liberal/conservative dimension more or less corresponds to the traditional division between the Republican and Democratic parties, but the historical allegiance of southern conservatives to the Democrats complicates the picture for all elections prior to 1980, requiring a second dimension to adequately define the spatial configuration. These conservative southern Democrats have from time to time provided the impetus for third-party candidacies, the most recent being that of George Wallace in the 1968 presidential election. Third-party candidates in the American political system can immensely confuse matters, especially if sincere voting is replaced by strategic voting. Voters may cast a ballot for a given candidate not because they prefer that candidate but rather for some other reason, such as the desire to register a protest vote or to throw the decision into the House of Representatives for lack of a winner in the electoral college.

Poole and Rosenthal demonstrated that even in three-candidate elections voters support the candidate nearest to them on the spectrum. The main difference is that support for the third-party candidate often drops precipitously beyond a certain voter-candidate distance, where the candidate's lesser viability detracts from any ideological loyalty. Hence, in 1968, those voters whose attitudes were most proximate to those of Wallace voted for him, but voters further away were deterred by the impracticability of his candidacy and opted instead for Nixon or Humphrey. For the most part, therefore, that candidate who is most remote from the position maintained by the most voters can expect the fewest votes.

On the other hand, spatial theory fails to explain voter turnout. Poole and Rosenthal discovered that, contrary to prediction, voters are granted distinct choices on election day, and, accordingly, voter apathy cannot be blamed on having to choose between political twins. The remarkable thing, in fact, is that the presidential candidates tend to diverge more on key political questions than the voters do; the vast majority of the public is middle-of-the-road. The researchers suggested that politicians are pulled away from the center by special-interest and activist groups who provide endorsements, campaign contributions, and teams of zealots willing to go from door to door on their behalf. The impact of these support groups is likely felt most strongly during the primaries and party caucuses when the general public has relatively little influence. In a sense, there really is a silent majority whose inertia permits, by default, more vocal extremists to tug the candidates away from moderate positions. Conservatives are dragged more to the right, liberals to the left. It is perhaps fortunate that issue-driven activists are not utter ideologues devoid of practical acumen; there is evidence that party extremists will often concede the need to nominate an electable candidate (Abramowitz and Stone 1984; Stone and Abramowitz 1980). Consequently, even if the presidential candidates are polarized by idealistic support groups, the candidates are probably not as extreme as these groups. Occasionally, ideological purity does supersede political reality, with the result that the party is smothered in a landslide defeat. This happened when the Republicans nominated Goldwater in 1964 and when the Democrats nominated McGovern in 1972. Nonetheless, in most elections the compromise between appeasing extremists and anticipating the more moderate will of the people produces a pair of viable but barely distinguishable candidates.

Spatial theory may not do a very good job of explaining why potential voters stay home, but it is fair to the theory to point out that voter turnout has proved quite resistant to theoretical explication of any kind. For example, rational voter models, which posit that voting behavior is governed by self-interest, suggest that people are more likely to vote when they have a chance to cast a decisive ballot, a vote that decides the election. Therefore, close presidential elections should inspire larger rates of voting than lopsided contests, yet such is not the case (Foster 1984). This relation is absent in presidential primaries as well (Norrander and Smith 1985). Even conventional wisdom about what dissuades voters evidently lacks strong empirical justification. In particular, early projections of election outcomes by the television networks may not substantially suppress voter turnout, even in those states located in the Mountain and Pacific time zones. This negligible effect held in the extreme case of the 1980 election, when network projections of Reagan's victory were followed shortly by Carter's concession speech while the polls were still open in the western states (Carter 1984). Though the networks' early call probably affected the outcome of a dozen congressional races, the impact was strongest for the better-educated and higher-status voters, who are more alert to news events, and the influence was in any case too small to alter the outcome of the presidential election (Carpini 1984). In sum, while people may tend to select candidates who will represent their beliefs, the actual decision whether or not to vote may have a less rational motivation.

Although I announced in chapter 1 my intention of concentrating on political leadership rather than voter behavior, it will prove worthwhile to mention just a few considerations that may render voter presidential preference far more complicated than spatial theory thus far allows. For one thing, voters favor candidates not merely on the basis of compatible political attitudes but also according to personality similarities. Birds of a feather flock together in the political domain as well as in the everyday world of personal attraction (see, for example, Winter 1985). Yet this similarity-attraction relationship may vary from voter to voter according to each voter's own self-meaningfulness (Leitner 1983). Those voters with high self-meaningfulness have well-articulated conceptions of their own personalities and tend to prefer those candidates with similar dispositions, this personal preference carrying over to evaluations of both foreign and economic policies. To illustrate, those voters who saw themselves as being highly compassionate and who perceived Carter as more compassionate than Reagan would be more disposed to support Carter's policies and ultimately to vote for Carter (see Gelineau and Merenda 1978). In contrast, voters with low self-meaningfulness, who have weakly differentiated self-descriptions, are less affected by the degree of personality similarity between themselves and the candidates.

A related complication stems from the fact that voters do not perceive their preferred candidates all that accurately (Brent and Granberg 1982; see also Page and Jones 1979). Rather, people tend to assimilate the candidate of choice, perceiving more agreement on the fundamental issues than is true in reality. This forced proximity is enhanced when voters become very involved in the issues of the presidential campaign. In 1980 Carter's supporters exaggerated their agreement with Carter and Reagan supporters did the same with Reagan (Brent and Granberg 1982). In any event, it is obvious that the American public is not fully objective in its determination of presidential preferences. Subjective, perhaps even emotional, evaluations of the candidates may confound if not actually take precedence over objective and more rational assessments of policy compatibilities (see also Abelson, Kinder, Peters, and Fiske 1982; Glass 1985; Markus and Converse 1979).

This subjectivity manifests itself in another manner: voters do not realistically estimate the probable outcome of the presidential election. Granberg and Brent (1983) have shown, in a study of presidential elections from 1952 to 1980, that voters tend to expect their preferred candidate to win (see Bartels 1985a). This preference-expectation link is conspicuous, for people are four times as likely to believe their candidate of choice will win as they are to expect defeat. This bias is most potent for those voters who are poorly informed but deeply involved in the presidential election (see Abramowitz and Stone 1984). People are more likely to bend their expectations to comply with their preferences than the other way around. So it is more a matter of wishful thinking than of joining the bandwagon. In 1980, voters who supported Reagan expected him to win, but few became his supporters just because they anticipated his success in the polls. This relation leads us to a curious paradox. If voters expect their preferred candidate to win, why do they even feel it is necessary to cast a ballot? We are sent back to the voter-turnout problem. Why do people bother to vote?

A recent experimental inquiry into the "voter's illusion" offers a hint of an answer (Quattrone and Tversky 1984). Voting behavior may be considered diagnostic of the election outcome. The typical voter may believe that if all voters of like mind vote, then the candidate of his choice will enter the White House. If the voter proceeds to cast a ballot, it is diagnostic of the tendency of voters of similar persuasion to cast corroborative votes. By comparison, a voter who declines to vote may be likely to infer that others with kindred attitudes will not vote either, and the preferred candidate will correspondingly lose. Voters may take the trouble to vote to reassure themselves that their political kindred will do the same—although one person's vote cannot compel the votes of others. The voter's illusion may help explain why spatial theory and rational voter models cannot predict voter turnout. Instead of reacting to self-interest, voters may be reinforcing a comfortable worldview. The causal effects are more in the mind of the voter than in the election returns, yet they are no less potent. This superstitious self-deception may also account for the negligible influence of early projections on voter turnout. Voters may battle for a lost cause in the voting booth primarily to console themselves with the belief that their preferred candidate did not lose for want of commitment from supporters.

Enough has been said about the American voter to affirm the following: the presidential candidate whose attitudes coincide most closely with that of the public has the greater probability of success in the voting booth; yet the public's final choice of a favorite candidate, as well as the decision to vote, are swayed by considerations that lie beyond the confines of spatial theory. For a presidential prospect to have reasonable hopes, an attitudinal match with the people is no doubt desirable, but the voters also have other criteria in mind, including the correspondence between the candidate's personal attributes (such as his authoritarianism and birth order) and the larger political context (such as an economic depression or international crisis).

REELECTION

Only three presidents—Polk, Buchanan, and Hayes—decided categorically not to seek a second term in office. Many others sought but were denied nomination for another term (Tyler, Fillmore, Pierce, A. Johnson, and Arthur) or were defeated when they actually ran in the general election (J. Adams, J. Q. Adams, Van Buren, Cleveland, B. Harrison, Taft, Hoover, Ford, and Carter). Only a baker's dozen were reelected (Washington, Jefferson, Madison, Monroe, Jackson, Lincoln, Grant, McKinley, Wilson, F. D. Roosevelt, Eisenhower, Nixon, and Reagan), and another four were elected president after first entering the White House via vice-presidential succession (T. Roosevelt, Coolidge, Truman, and L. B. Johnson). The remaining five presidents (W. Harrison, Taylor, Garfield, Harding, and Kennedy) died before their first term had been completed. Reelection to the presidency is thus not guaranteed by any means, and it can be definitely viewed as one criterion for judging a president's success in office. Indeed, if we are going to rely on the voters to assess presidential leadership, then reelection offers a test far superior to nomination and first-time victory in the general election. Only in the case of reelection is the public most immediately engaged in what has been labeled retrospective voting (Fiorina 1981; Miller and Wattenberg 1985), deciding whether the incumbent should be returned to office on the basis of the performance of his first administration.

Many of the variables discussed in the last section are germane to understanding an incumbent's reelection prospects. For instance, there still must be a tight fit between the president's individual characteristics, such as personality and attitudes, and the political zeitgeist. An initially popular incumbent can fail to keep up with the times and thus suffer defeat, as Herbert Hoover did. On the other hand, some of the factors listed earlier are less pertinent to reelection. For example, the optimal campaign rhetoric and strategy may remain fairly unaltered, and certain personal traits, including age, may not change sufficiently in four years to figure in the reelection equation. Here I survey some individual and situational variables that may raise or lower the odds of being elected to another term.

Individual Assets

The search for personal characteristics that allow a first-term incumbent to remain in the White House has been none too successful (see Rosenstone 1983). The few attributes that have been isolated can be grouped under two headings: biographical and personality variables.

Biographical Predictors. An exploratory inquiry discovered three biographical items that are related to an incumbent's reelection odds (Simonton 1981b). First, former college professors, such as Taft, are less capable of obtaining a second term in office, though Wilson proves that exceptions to this broad tendency exist. Second, tall incumbents are slightly less likely to be rejected by the voters when seeking another four years. To take some extreme cases, of the six tallest presidents only Arthur was denied a second term, whereas of the six shortest presidents only Madison and McKinley were reelected. This association further supports the earlier discussion of the political asset of unusual height. Third, incumbents who were middle children are less likely to be defeated. If it is true that middle children more readily adopt conciliatory policies, this may explain why they may be reelected, for fewer potential supporters will have been alienated. Also, the political conditions most favorable to the success of first-borns and last-borns, international crises and civil unrest or revolution, are far less frequent than those that favor middle children in leadership positions.

A second investigation added three more items to the above list (Simonton 1986c). First, Democratic incumbents, as representatives of the more popular party throughout most of American history, have better chances of being returned to office (Simonton 1981c). The best example is F. D. Roosevelt, who served over a dozen years as the head of state. Second, incumbents whose fathers were also well-known politicians are at a disadvantage when pursuing another term (see also Simonton 1981c). For example, J. Q. Adams' father was John Adams, the second president. John Tyler's father, also John Tyler, had served as governor of Virginia, and Franklin Pierce's father, Benjamin Pierce, had been a two-term constitutional executive of New Hampshire. Maybe politicians from such backgrounds participate in politics partly because of the connections established by their parents. As a consequence, a leader could be of lower general quality and still enter the nation's highest office.

The third finding is that incumbents have a much higher probability of being nominated for a second term if they had been considered presidential material long before their first inauguration, even long prior to running for the office in the primaries. Although at first blush it may seem unlikely, the incumbent may not have been viewed as a viable and available candidate before the nominating convention. In some instances, the incumbent was a dark horse little known to the American public; in other instances the incumbent entered through vice-presidential succession, upon the death or resignation of his predecessor (Simonton 1981c). Polk is considered the first dark-horse candidate for the presidency: he was a virtual nonentity until, at the 1844 Democratic national convention in Baltimore, his name was entered as a compromise candidate after the seventh ballot, receiving the nomination two ballots later. The most recent example is Carter, who was initially greeted on the campaign trail with "Jimmy who?" Chester Arthur was a compromise vice-presidential candidate whose sole prior political experience had been as collector of the Port of New York, from which position he was fired by President Hayes; he exemplifies the accidental president who (unlike Lyndon Johnson in 1963) had never before been considered to possess presidential ability. Ford is the most recent example of such an accidental president. Whether he is a dark-horse entry or an obscure successor, it is improbable that a little-known chief executive can establish, in four years or less, a constituency broad enough to secure the nomination. Thus, Tyler, Fillmore, A. Johnson, and Arthur, accidental presidents all, were denied renomination, a fate endured as well by Pierce, the second dark-horse candidate. Polk may constitute the exception that demonstrates the rule, for he denied his party the opportunity to spurn him by announcing from the start that he would be a one-term president. Carter and Ford may be true exceptions; both, however, were renominated only in the face of extensive discontent, and neither survived the general election. Therefore, for an incumbent to have a reasonable chance of spending another four years in the Oval Office, he must have been in the public eye as a presidential prospect years before his first inauguration day.

Personality Predictors. The supply of biographical factors potentially contributing to reelection success is not only scanty, but relatively unimportant besides: only about 10 percent of the variance in reelection chances can be explicated by each of these individual assets. Before we infer that personal attributes play a minor role in reelection, however, we should consider the possibility that certain personality types have better chances of being returned to office. Previously, we saw that conceptual complexity might contribute to a candidate's election chances; the same factor should participate in reelection (see Suedfeld and Rank 1976). A president's achievement drive is even more pertinent, however. Running for office, even from the White House Rose Garden, is hard work, and accordingly it is probable that an incumbent must have the will to do it. A stronger than average achievement motive is empirically associated with the number of election victories that a politician attains during his prepresidential career, an association that may carry over when the politician seeks reelection as president (Simonton 1986e). Another potentially relevant trait is Machiavellianism, for the tendency to be sly, deceitful, unscrupulous, evasive, and shrewd is linked with serving many years in national elective offices (Simonton 1986e). The impression management so vital to electoral victory requires both skill and the willingness to be manipulative.

Finally, a president's intellectual brilliance may have a part to play as well. While in theory people may admire the Platonic philosopher-king who is sophisticated, insightful, inventive, curious, intelligent, and even wise, in practice the masses settle for appreciably less intellect. Indeed, a recent formal model indicates that the function between intelligence and leadership may follow an inverted-U curve (Simonton 1985a). In other words, while leaders may be somewhat brighter than followers, a wide gap in intellect can work against the full exercise of leadership. This adverse consequence is especially prominent in democratic systems. Accordingly, it comes as no surprise that the intellectual brilliance of a president is *negatively* correlated with the proportion of the popular vote that he received on election day. Woodrow Wilson offers an exquisite case in point. The only chief executive with a Ph.D. (in political science, no less), Wilson can certainly be counted among the most intelligent presidents. Yet in the 1912 election only two out of five voters cast their ballots for him. Even in 1916, when running as an incumbent, he received less than half of the popular vote, making him the sole president in history to serve two consecutive terms with a minority of the votes cast in both elections.

Although reelected presidents can be distinguished from one-term chief executives on several individual characteristics, these traits have questionable value as predictors. Besides the fact that the correlations are uniformly low, one can accurately predict election outcomes without recourse to individual variables (Lewis-Beck and Rice 1984; Rosenstone 1983). What is mandatory for the precise prediction is a description of the circumstances under which the incumbent is obliged to run for reelection.

Situational Assets

The American voter is quite favorably disposed toward the incumbent. From the founding of our country to 1984, only nine incumbents lost in the general election. Because one of these losers, Cleveland, won a majority of the popular vote despite defeat in the electoral college and was eventually reelected to a second (nonconsecutive) term, eight may be a truer count. In any case, only about one out of five incumbents renominated by their party was denied another four years. The incumbency advantage, in fact, can be traded for between a 6 and 10 percent vote edge in the polling booth, and even an incumbent vice president acquires a lead of 4 percent (Rosenstone 1983). Why do incumbents have this asset?

To properly address this question we first must recognize that not all incumbents are even renominated. As noted before, Tyler, Fillmore, Pierce, A. Johnson, and Arthur all were refused renomination, a slap in the face that has not happened to a twentieth-century incumbent (albeit Ford and Carter did not enjoy a strong hold on their respective nominating conventions). All but one of the incumbents so spurned by their party were accidental presidents. Because chief executives who enter the office via vice-presidential succession tend to perform less well in office (as I will show in chapter 4), it may be justified for delegates to look for a new leader. And even though Pierce was not an accidental president, his dark-horse entrance into the White House had an effect quite comparable. For example, accidental presidents tend to have a large proportion of their regular vetoes overturned in Congress; Pierce is one of only two presidents (the other being A. Johnson) who witnessed the majority of their vetoes overridden (Simonton 1985b). We accordingly can surmise that an incumbent will be renominated only when the party leadership believes that the administration's record will not be a severe handicap in the election (see Fiorina 1981; Miller and Wattenberg 1985). Another illustration is the finding that an incumbent's renomination chances are a positive function of the sheer volume of legislation that he signed—as recorded in *United States Statutes at Large* (1845–1982)—during his first term in office (Simonton 1986c). Bill-signing ceremonies in the White House give the incumbent the appearance of accomplishment even if the bills were not introduced or sponsored by his administration. In any event, one reason why incumbents do so well is simply that only the effective chief executives are renominated in the first place. And given that most astute politicians from the opposing party will understand the handwriting on the wall, strong candidates for reelection usually face weak challengers.

Another critical predictor of an incumbent's renomination prospects, in accord with the above conclusion, is the extent to which the president's party controls the House of Representatives (Simonton 1986c). The lower house, whose members all go up for reelection every two years, is clearly the most responsive to public opinion about an incumbent's performance. Discontent with the president is correspondingly translated into the probability that representatives of his party will lose seats in the House. The delegates to the national conventions will therefore come under acute pressure to oust an incumbent whose presence in the White House only harms the electoral success of the party in congressional elections (see Campbell 1985). An incumbent whose party is poorly represented in the House has a low probability of winning reelection should he be renominated notwithstanding the warning signs (Rosenstone 1983; Simonton 1986c; see also Simonton 1981c). This dependence on party control in the House helps explain why the odds of reelection are, on the average, slightly more favorable for Democratic incumbents. The Democratic party tends to have greater representation in the House on inauguration day, and the party control exhibited at the beginning of a presidential term is highly predictive of the degree of party control that will survive the midterm congressional elections (Simonton 1986c), even if the incumbent party normally forfeits some seats (see Campbell 1985). However, the edge that Democratic candidates have generally enjoyed may be diminishing as Americans progressively detach themselves from party loyalties (see Ladd 1985; Rollenhagen 1984).

It must be emphasized that the incumbent does not always have much leverage. We can even speculate that this asset has been declining. In the nineteenth century fewer than 17 percent of the presidents were defeated, whereas in the present century this proportion has increased to 33 percent, or one-third, including two in a row, Ford and Carter. Perhaps with the advent of the mass media, especially television, the incumbent no longer enjoys a monopoly of news coverage. If the challenger projects a good image to the camera, as Carter did in 1976 and as Reagan did even better in 1980, the incumbent may be unable fully to exploit the asset of holding news conferences on the White House lawn (see Stovall 1984). Scholars have conjectured, too, that the presidential coattails have shrunk over the years. Although a convincing case has yet to be made for this historical trend (Born 1984), shortened coattails imply a diminished incumbent's edge: his reelection chances at least in part depend on sweeping crowds of like-minded senators and representatives into Congress. Finally, it is conceivable that an incumbent president encounters the same disadvantage experienced by other office holders desiring reelection. For instance, Hibbing and Brandes (1983) have demonstrated that the likelihood of an incumbent senator being reelected is inversely proportional to the population of the state he or she serves. Because senatorial incumbents from smaller states have more homogeneous constituencies, it is far easier for them to satisfy a majority of the voters back home. In contrast, senators running for reelection in large states are confronted with preeminently heterogeneous constituencies—ethnic diversity, class divisions, regional hostilities, and rural-urban conflicts abound. Since a president's constituency is more diversified than that of a big-state senator, an incumbent president is more vulnerable to this population effect. The presidential incumbent must please or appease ten times as many voters as the senatorial hopeful from the nation's most populous state. And the heterogeneity of those voters has been steadily increasing.

Whether or not incumbency credit is waning, an incumbent president is by no means sure of a second term. Incumbency necessarily must be coupled with popularity. Victor Hugo may have been right when he protested, "Popularity? It's glory's small change," yet in the political arena popularity is the sine qua non. Lee Sigelman (1979) demonstrated that a president's approval rating in the last preelection poll predicts whether the incumbent will serve another four years. Sigelman took the results of the Gallup poll for the seven presidential elections between 1940 and 1976 in which an incumbent ran for reelection, and derived an equation that predicts the president's percentage share of the popular vote. Since the correlation between popularity and vote share is .74, over half of the variance in the voting outcome can be predicted on the basis of the preceding Gallup poll. If only one quarter of the voters surveyed approve of the president, the incumbent can expect only 45 percent of the popular vote. A president's approval rating must climb to 41 percent to capture half of the popular vote, while an approval rating of 65 percent in the polls converts to 58 percent of the vote. To be sure, the popular vote is imperfectly translated into votes in the electoral college, yet it is most unlikely that a president with merely 45 percent of the popular vote will receive a majority of the electoral votes.

In an update and extension of the above study, Brody and Sigelman (1983) devised a prediction equation that accounts for 84 percent of the variance in the vote share of the incumbent party on the basis of the incumbent's approval rating. According to this equation, not only will an unpopular president fail to earn reelection, but even his successor on the ticket will pay for his low score with the populace. Vice President Hubert H. Humphrey's loss in 1968 was partly caused by voter discontent with the Johnson administration, whereas Martin Van Buren, another incumbent vice president, was elected in 1836 as the hand-picked successor to the popular Andrew Jackson. Events such as these illustrate how electoral defeat may be more a matter of being at the wrong place at the wrong time than of being the wrong person.

Given the impact of popularity on the reelection prospects of both the incumbent and the incumbent party, the obvious question is what determines the incumbent's approval rating. Because the whole of chapter 3 is devoted to this subject, a detailed response is out of place here. Instead, it will suffice to state the two situational factors that may make the most direct contribution to an incumbent's reelection opportunities.

The first is war. Voters in the 1864 election accepted Lincoln's advice not to "swap horses while crossing the stream." Actually, the public was then following a precedent established much earlier in American history. Jefferson was returned to office in the midst of the Tripolitan War, as was Madison shortly after the outbreak of the War of 1812. This practice was, of course, continued in the twentieth century when FDR was elected to a fourth term. In general, the likelihood of reelection increases if the incumbent is leading the nation in war (Simonton 1986c). Incumbents themselves may be aware of this connection, for there is evidence that presidents up for reelection in wartime make more visible uses of military force during an election year (Stoll 1984). Fortunately, there is no empirical basis for worrying that peacetime incumbents might rattle the saber to enhance their electoral support. The voting public does not want incumbents to provoke military conflicts. Sometimes, as in 1916, the public has returned an incumbent who kept the troops at home. Moreover, serving as a wartime president will not aid the incumbent if the people feel that he has mismanaged the war; for every 10 percent of the electorate opposed to the conflict, the incumbent's party drops almost 2 percent in the polls (Rosenstone 1983). Both Truman and LBJ gave up points with the public for having presided over unpopular wars. In the latter case, the dissatisfaction—as revealed by Eugene McCarthy's surprising showing in the 1968 New Hampshire primary—sufficed to dissuade Johnson from seeking another term, although he could have done so under the Twenty-second Amendment.

Second, but more consistently influential, is the economy (see Monroe 1979). American voters respond to economic hardship by turning against the party in power (see, for example, Abramowitz 1985; Bloom and Price 1975; Campbell 1985; Fiorina 1981; Kiewiet 1983; Kinder and Kiewiet 1979; Lewis-Beck 1985; Lewis-Beck and Rice 1984). For one thing, downturns in the material well-being of the average citizen put everyone in a throw-the-rascals-out mood that shows up in the ensuing election results for the House of Representatives. By one early estimate, the incumbent administration forfeits about 5 percent of the congressional vote for every 10 percent decline in real per capita personal income (Kramer 1971). Given that the outlook for presidential reelection rests heavily on the amount of support the incumbent has in the lower house, the clear implication is that the hopeful incumbent must avoid economic hard times at all costs. This indirect consequence is strengthened by a more direct effect, namely, that the correlation between voter preference and personal finances is higher for presidential than congressional elections; the president is, rightly or wrongly, held accountable for dire economic conditions even more than Congress (Kiewiet 1983; Lewis-Beck 1985).

Edward R. Tufte has proposed, in his provocative *Political Control of the Economy* (1978), that the administration desirous of self-preservation deliberately, and rather cynically, juggles the economic state of the nation to make matters as auspicious as possible for the general election. The president has access to numerous powers and techniques that enable him to augment a voter's disposable income at just the right moment. The upshot is a "political business cycle" in which prosperity is suspiciously synchronized with election years, followed by retrenchment if not by recession. Despite the extensive documentation Tufte provides, I think it is fair to say that the jury is still out on this connection (see, for example, Brown and Stein 1982; Browning 1985; Chappell and Keech 1985; MacRae 1981; Wallace and Warner 1984). Perhaps the only election outcome to have been decisively fixed by a well-timed economic stimulation was the

1948 upset victory of Truman over Dewey (Rosenstone 1983). Between 1946 and 1949, real disposable income per capita fell in every year but 1948, when a remarkable spurt took place, just sufficient to swing the election. Of course, the dearth of examples of successful manipulation does not mean that incumbents do not try anyway. Nixon probably had no need to manipulate the economy to beat McGovern in 1972, but he apparently attempted to do so—via monetary and fiscal policies and wage-price controls—for reasons having more to do with his personality than with urgent political realities (Keller and May 1984).

Whatever the final word on this issue, it remains true that a healthy, thriving economy is an absolute prerequisite for an incumbent's reelection. This necessity is sometimes overlooked by political analysts. As an example, experts and laypersons alike were quick to infer a dramatic shift to the right from Reagan's impressive landslide victory over Carter in 1980. Yet, as Douglas Hibbs (1982b) pointed out, Carter's downfall can be almost entirely ascribed to the poor economic performance of his administration (see also Miller and Wattenberg 1985). For the first time since Roosevelt vanquished Hoover in 1932, real per capita disposable income had dropped in an election year, by 3 percent (Rosenstone 1983). Consequently, the mandate Reagan received was more for economic than for ideological change. Then again, the Reagan administration profited a great deal by blurring this distinction in order to enact its conservative agenda. Happily for the American right wing, the economy was strong enough in 1984, whether due to Reaganomics or not, to assure another overwhelming defeat for the Democratic opposition. Nevertheless, the election of 1984 no more endorsed Reagan's brand of American old-time individualism than the 1932 election discredited Hoover's somewhat similar grand vision. Herein lies an article of wisdom, I think; we must be extremely cautious in drawing inferences from landslide victories, dramatic though they are. Not everything the loser stands for is repudiated, nor is everything the winner advocates endorsed. The mandates received from the people may be far more circumscribed than the victors are accustomed to believe.

To sum up, such situational factors as the manner of political succession, the state of war or peace, and the condition of the economy all appear to affect the chances that an incumbent will be honored with a second term in office, these factors operating in part through their impact on presidential popularity.

CONCLUSION

A sizable amount of literature has been reviewed on the origins of presidential election success, both as a first-time candidate and as an incumbent. By one standard these research efforts have proven fruitful: social scientists can now predict the outcome of U.S. presidential elections with an imposing degree of precision. This capacity is conclusively demonstrated in Steven J. Rosenstone's *Forecasting Presidential Elections* (1983) (see also Lewis-Beck and Rice 1984). Rosenstone carefully specified a complex prediction equation that incorporated the most crucial antecedent variables discussed throughout this chapter. Included are the concordance of the candidate with the prevailing public opinion on the salient issues of the day (especially racial and social welfare policies); the incumbent party's management of the economy and war; whether the candidate is an incumbent president or vice president; home-state and regional loyalties; and secular political trends indicated by changes in the balance of power on Capitol Hill. The parameters of this equation were estimated using data from the elections between 1948 and 1972, and the predictions were then tested for accuracy.

At the statewide level, the equation explains 93 percent of the variance and correctly picks who will carry the state 91 percent of the time. On the national level, the electoral college error is 6.2 percent, or thirty-three electoral votes, and the winner is correctly anticipated in every year except 1960, when the equation forecasts a toss-up. That year Kennedy defeated Nixon by the narrowest popular vote margin in U.S. history. Rosenstone further validated his model by testing it against data not used in estimating the parameters, the 1976 and 1980 election results. Once more, the equation predicts the victor with considerable precision, often performing better than the journalists and pollsters who make a business of election forecasts. As a final illustration of the model's utility, Rosenstone used it to simulate alternative election outcomes. For example, Hubert H. Humphrey really had no opportunity to become president; he would have lost to Nixon in 1972 and to Ford in 1976. Likewise, LBJ's crushing victory in 1964 cannot be blamed on the Republican convention having been captured by Goldwater extremists, for the more moderate Rockefeller would have lost by almost as much. And the Democrats had no hope in 1980; if the delegates had renounced their sitting president and nominated Edward Kennedy, Reagan's margin of victory would have been all the more awesome. Finally, Rosenstone showed that if racial issues had been as important in 1960 as they became in 1968, or if the disposable income at the close of the Eisenhower administration had been just one percent higher, Nixon would have been inaugurated as the thirty-fifth, not the thirty-seventh, president.

Rosenstone's (1983) model represents only a beginning, as its creator would be the first to admit. Many more predictors might be constructively inserted, and the model does not accommodate third-party candidacies with any elegance. Furthermore, as a model designed to predict the general election results, it does not tell us who will actually be nominated (compare Aldrich 1980). Only if the voters in the primaries and caucuses could be persuaded to use Rosenstone's equation to select the most promising aspirant could it have predictive value months in advance. The most critical deficiency is that the model does not inform us how to predict the predictors. We cannot anticipate which issues will become prominent in the future, and therefore we cannot determine with any confidence which candidate will best comply with the political zeitgeist some years hence. Nor can we possess secure expectations concerning the repercussions of various economic policies. Accordingly, even if we can foresee who will become the next president, we are completely at a loss when betting on the new incumbent's reelection chances four years later. We must wait until the midterm congressional elections to obtain the first hints of the incumbent's prospects, and many other predictors will not be known until the final stretch. Of course, it would be asking far too much to demand that a model support such long-range forecasts. The required model would entail not just a theory of voter choice behavior, but also comprehensive and precise theories of how economic, ideological, social, and political systems change over time (see Coleman 1985; Elder and Holmes 1985).

Yet because prediction is not the same thing as theoretical explanation, we should inquire how the empirical research reviewed in this chapter enlarges our understanding of presidential success. Specifically, we must return to the principal substantive interest of this book: What do the predictors of election success tell us about the differential significance of individual and situation? The bulk of the literature seems to suggest that the personal traits of a presidential candidate carry rather less weight than the context of a political campaign for the presidency. Rosenstone's (1983) forecast equations are able to adequately anticipate the victor without resorting to personality traits, physical characteristics, or other individual variables. The attributes of the candidates only enter the formulae as individual-situational interaction effects, such as the degree of compatibility between candidates' and the public's attitudes on the political issues of the day. Even if we look beyond Rosenstone's analysis, such leader variables as birth order and authoritarianism likewise function not as main effects, but merely in interaction with political and economic circumstances. And although certain individual factors, such as height, exhibit reliable zero-order correlations with the apparent ability to win votes, these factors seldom survive multivariate statistical analyses, implying that such variables may, at best, have but indirect and weak effects in the voting booth. Therefore, the evidence appears to proclaim that the situation overrides the individual in the determination of election victory. Perhaps, as suggested earlier, politicians of presidential caliber are so highly selected that variation in personality is severely truncated, the residual variance being easily swamped by utterly unedited fluctuations in the political and economic milieu.

Nonetheless, if one is willing to speculate, one may still argue that individual variables play an important role, obscured but not obliterated by the situational variables. For example, if the voters' personal evaluations of the candidates distort how they perceive the candidates' positions on the issues, then these global assessments may be swayed by more intuitive, even emotional, considerations that permit some input from individual traits, such as height, intelligence, and authoritarianism (see Abelson, Kinder, Peters, and Fiske 1982; Brent and Granberg 1982; Markus and Converse 1979; Page and Jones 1979). Furthermore, it is impossible to predict presidential election success accurately without incorporating in some way the incumbent's popularity, whether gauged by approval ratings in the polls or by midterm congressional elections (Lewis-Beck and Rice 1984; Rosenstone 1983). When the incumbent is running for reelection, such popularity may serve to some extent as a proxy variable for underlying personal traits. The incumbent may project a charming, likable personality, or may possess definite leadership skills that contribute to a high performance rating by the American public. As a consequence, if we can isolate personality traits that make an incumbent more popular or that enhance executive effectiveness, the impact of individual factors will have been identified. In contrast, if it turns out that popularity is not dependent on the incumbent's personal traits, whether directly or via their implications for performance, we once again will be obliged to say that circumstance is more crucial than character in election success.

◆ 3 ◆
POPULARITY IN THE POLLS

Since 1941 the Gallup Poll has presented the same query to its nearly periodic samples of the American public: "Do you approve or disapprove of the way the incumbent is handling his job as president?" The responses to this question can be said to constitute a gauge of presidential popularity, one of several potential indicators of presidential success. Indeed, as we saw in the preceding chapter, the incumbent's approval rating is a good predictor of his chances of getting reelected. Since the administration of Harry Truman, this poll has been taken about once a month, generating an impressive body of data on perceived presidential performance. It consequently becomes natural to ask what factors determine the president's popularity in a given month. The first behavioral scientist to address this question systematically was John Mueller (1970). Mueller analyzed the 292 survey points between the beginning of the Truman administration in April 1945 and the end of the Johnson administration in January 1969. Though Mueller's inferences have at times been challenged by fellow political scientists (such as Kernell 1978), his work represents the starting point of any discussion of the president's approval rating (see also his 1973 book which incorporates seven additional data points).

Mueller began by noting that the percentage of people who

support the president fluctuates greatly. Truman, ironically enough, was both the most popular president, with a whopping 85 percent approval rate upon succeeding to the presidency after the death of Roosevelt, and the least popular president, falling to 30 percent in late 1951 and early 1952. President Eisenhower's popularity rating, which changed less than that of most presidents, nonetheless fluctuated from 79 to 49 percent, a respectable range. For the most part, the majority of the American public tends to approve of the chief executive, the average over the twenty-four-year period being 58 percent. Though the disapproval rating of the president does not follow the approval rating perfectly, the relationship is quite close, the correlation being conspicuously negative ($r = -.98$). The lower the approval rating, the higher the disapproval rating, and vice versa. The percentage of those surveyed with no opinion tends to stay close to 14 percent.

Such is the measure. What are its predictors? The factors that Mueller studied can be grouped into two broad categories, those intranational and those international in origin.

INTRANATIONAL INFLUENCES

Much of a president's popularity in the polls has to do with how matters are going at home. There are two principal domestic forces. The first has to do with the president's ability to make crucial policy decisions without disenchanting the people who elected him; the second concerns the state of the economy.

Alienating Adherents

When Mueller (1970) first scrutinized the popularity of presidents from Truman through Johnson, one conclusion seemed obvious: presidents begin their terms with high levels of popularity, but they gradually lose that support as their terms progress. Only if reelected will they recoup some of that loss. In other words, the popularity of a president over a single term apparently decays with time, a political reality recognized as long ago as 1796 when Thomas Jefferson observed, "No man will ever bring out of the Presidency the reputation which carries him into it." Mueller chose to explain this phenomenon in terms of the coalition of minorities that forms in reaction to the president's policies that aim to please or appease the majority. Each action the president takes, no matter how popular with most Americans, alienates a minority with strongly held opinions on the issues involved. An adamant minority is alienated here, another there; eventually the proportion of disaffected voters can become uncomfortably large. The potential exists for the organization of a coalition out of these alienated minorities, and the opposition to the president becomes thereby more vociferous and effective. His popularity rating suffers accordingly. Some critics may dislike the president's handling of the economy, others his vigor in promoting civil rights, still others his cabinet and Supreme Court appointments, but all of these critics concur that the chief executive's performance is not up to par. Of course, when the president begins to campaign for reelection he will be able to retrieve matters somewhat. Promises can be substituted for achievements, the future offered as compensation for the past. The president consequently can start his second term with a resurgence of popularity—assuming that the coalition of antagonists does not prevent his reelection.

To test this hypothesis empirically, Mueller defined the coalition of minorities variable as the length of time (in years) since the incumbent was inaugurated (in the first term) or reelected (in the second term). As expected, this variable exhibits a strong negative relationship with presidential popularity ($r = -.48$). When the variable is placed in a multiple regression equation with several other variables as statistical controls, the following generalization results: popularity in the polls averages around 69 percent at the beginning of the term and then drops about 6 percentage points each year. The precise rate of decline depends on the president. In the case of Eisenhower, the coalition of minorities variable was more or less irrelevant to his popularity—he was a "nice guy" immune to the antagonisms of everyday politics.

The coalition of minorities variable is expressed as a linear predictor; each year brings the same decline in popularity no matter whether the interval is from the first year to the second or from the third year to the fourth. Mueller admits that this is an oversimplification, but he claims that he tried other operations, including short-term honeymoon and logarithmic effects, and found no appreciable improvement over the linear form. Stimson (1976) has taken issue with this conclusion, however. Rather than a linear relationship, Stimson observes a curvilinear, quadratic relationship: the decline is rather quick at the beginning (and almost linear) but then bottoms out. The result is very much like the decay curve for radioactive emission. Stimson has shown that this curvilinear form fits all polled presidencies except Kennedy's. The last exception probably exists because Kennedy was assassinated before the popularity decline could level off. The quadratic equation explains over 87 percent of the variance in popularity over time. Not content with altering the mathematical form of the prediction equation, Stimson offered a psychological explanation as well to replace Mueller's political interpretation. The American public greets each newly elected president with high expectations inflated by naive credence in the campaign promises and idealism of the candidates. Yet when the president gets down to the reality of running a nation, disillusionment settles in among the voters, and a more cynical attitude develops. Fairly quickly, the American people realize that he is just like all the others.

Samuel Kernell (1978), however, doubts whether time can serve as an explanatory variable. After all, Kernell argues, time itself has no true substantive significance but is merely a proxy variable. In particular, he proposes that fluctuations in popularity respond directly to contemporary conditions and events. A president does not simply become less popular; rather, things happen over the course of his administration to undermine his popularity. What operates to smooth out this adverse reaction to discrete events and chronic conditions is the fact that presidential standing in the polls is autoregressive. That is, a president's approval rating in one month is largely a function of his rating in the previous month, producing a sluggish movement in popularity. This inertia may stem from numerous sources. For one thing, the reporting of the results of past polls may affect how future survey respondents perceive the incumbent (see Atkin 1969), creating a certain consistency from poll to poll. In addition, a person's support for the president is affected by his or her personal attributes, such as level of education, mental flexibility, and abstract evaluation of the American government (Kernell, Sperlich, and Wildavsky 1975), as well as the degree to which an individual can identify a president's personality as representing his ideal self (Thomas, Sigelman, and Baas 1984). For instance, worse-educated and less flexible persons are prone to be less critical in their evaluation of presidential performance. Given that these characteristics cannot fluctuate very rapidly in the population from month to month, or even year to year, presidential popularity necessarily enjoys a certain resistance to change.

This is not to say that Kernell rejected time altogether, for he did subscribe to the idea of a honeymoon effect. At the beginning of each term the chief executive is allowed a spell of freedom from vehement criticism—a "give the guy a fair chance" suspension of judgment. Kernell devised an early term variable which is equal to six at the start of the term and drops one unit per month until it equals zero after six months in office. Besides this variable, Kernell measured a large number of actual events and conditions, most of which will be described in later sections of this chapter. A multiple regression analysis indicated that the early term variable accounts for a respectable proportion of the popularity drop (the zero-order correlations for the various presidencies taken separately ranged from .20 to .67), the concrete events accounting for much of the remainder. Most significantly, once the effect of the inaugural honeymoon and the specific concrete events are removed, time, as defined by Mueller's coalition of minorities variable, no longer predicts anything. Thus the impact of decay over time has been reduced to the drop in the first six months of a term (an idea closer to Stimson's findings), the rest of any popularity loss being attributable to specific events and the president's response to those events. Kernell's reanalysis of the popularity data presents the American presidency and public in a more favorable light. The atrophy of public support is not inexorable inasmuch as most of any decline depends on how the president deals with particular issues and decisions.

As noted by Sigelman and Knight (1983), one difficulty in wholeheartedly accepting Kernell's negligible role for time is that his "argument does not explain why popularity almost always *declines* over time" (311). It is an unlikely coincidence that all external events work to damage a president's standing with the voters. In fact, the deterioration occurs independently of other events, both foreign and domestic (Norpoth 1984). In an attempt to provide a substantive basis for the virtually inevitable decline in popularity, Sigelman and Knight returned to an examination of Stimson's expectation/disillusion theory. They first tested Stimson's hypothesis by closely studying attitudes toward President Carter. Consistent with prediction, the steep decline in Carter's popularity did indeed take place alongside sharp declines in expectations about what the new president would be able to accomplish. Furthermore, those who expressed the highest expectations of what he would achieve tended to evaluate Carter the most positively. These basic findings were recently replicated using Reagan as the test case (Sigelman and Knight 1985a). Although not all predictions derived from the expectation/disillusionment hypothesis were borne out by the data, Sigelman and Knight at least show that Stimson's interpretation deserves further consideration in empirical research.

More indirect support for the Stimson hypothesis comes from another quarter. A similarity exists between the way a president loses popular support and the contrast between pre- and postelection rhetoric discussed in chapter 2. Because the simplistic rhetoric of the preelection campaign probably raises the hopes of the American electorate, the sudden switch to complicated presidential excuse-making after inauguration day might be partly responsible for the disillusionment that sets in after the honeymoon. It is significant that both the shift in integrative complexity in the speeches and the drop in popularity are rapid. Furthermore, the return of simple-minded campaign rhetoric when the incumbent runs for reelection may help rejuvenate the popularity ratings of the president who is returned to office. It would be interesting to calculate directly the correlation between the complexity of a president's speeches and his popularity in the polls.

Economic Slump

One of the specific conditions that may affect a president's popularity is the state of the national economy. As pointed out in the preceding chapter, economic hard times influence both voting behavior and party identification (Bloom and Price 1975). That effect, moreover, is often asymmetrical, economic decline exerting a negative influence while economic growth has very little impact. Mueller (1970) looked for a similar asymmetry in the consequences of economic conditions for the president's approval rating in the polls. His indicator of economic prosperity was the unemployment rate, where only upward changes were counted, not downward ones. Specifically, the unemployment rate at the time the incumbent's term began was subtracted from the rate at the time of the poll to yield an economic slump score, though this score was set at zero if the change was positive rather than negative. Placing this variable within a multiple regression equation, Mueller found that popularity fell by three percentage points for every percentage point rise in unemployment. A deteriorating economy does adversely affect a president's popularity. Unfortunately, as Hibbs (1974) pointed out, Mueller failed to take into account the autoregressive nature of presidential popularity, and this may contaminate the result. When Hibbs reanalyzed Mueller's data making the necessary statistical alterations, the support for the economic slump variable was very weak indeed.

The problem may reside with Mueller's selection of unemployment rates as the key economic indicator. In contrast, when Kenski (1977) examined the impact of economic conditions on presidential popularity from Eisenhower through Nixon, he used, besides unemployment statistics, measures of inflation, in terms of both the general price index and the food price index. Unemployment is an economic condition that does not affect everybody the same way; only the unemployed themselves are directly affected. Inflation, in contrast, concerns almost everyone. Price indexes were much better predictors of popularity than employment rates, and general prices were more influential than food prices. Kenski also showed that six-month moving averages were more effective predictors than monthly rates of change for general inflation. The amount of variance explained for food prices increased from 9 to 38 percent, that for general prices from 35 to 57 percent, when six-month comparisons were used instead of monthly rate changes. The American public apparently is more concerned with how conditions change in the long haul, and momentary ups and downs are viewed as transient changes with few implications regarding the real state of the economy. All in all, the best predictor of presidential popularity, according to Kenski's research, is the six-month change in general inflation. It should be noted that Kenski did not inspect the possibility that the effect of the economy might be asymmetric. Inflation and deflation were treated equally, as were unemployment increases and decreases.

Kenski's study scrutinized the impact of economic indicators with a bivariate format; thus other potential influences were not entered as statistical controls. This deficiency was rectified by Kernell (1978), who inspected the effects of the unemployment rate, the monthly consumer price index, and total personal income within a multivariate framework. Personal income turned out to perform weakly as a predictor when subjected to statistical controls, and was consequently dropped. The change in the unemployment rate also proved to be of little relevance for predicting presidential popularity. That left inflation, gauged by consumer prices, as the only economic indicator that might predict the approval ratings. For almost all presidents, the change in consumer prices over six months is negatively associated with popularity. In particular, a one percentage point increase in prices may lower popularity by anything from one percentage point (for Eisenhower) to over four percentage points (for Johnson).

Other researchers have provided further evidence for the decisive role of inflation. MacKuen (1983) scrutinized the 1963–1980 period and discovered that the immediate impact of unemployment on popularity is much larger than that of inflation, yet its impact is of extremely short duration. In contrast, the effect of inflation, while initially less striking, displays far more persistence; hence, inflation emerged as the most important factor over the long haul (see Norpoth 1984). Monroe (1978) applied a distributed lag model to Gallup data from 1950 to 1974 and calculated that a one percentage point increase in the annual inflation rate translated into a decrease of 3.75 points in presidential popularity (compare Hibbs 1982d). He also demonstrated, however, that military expenditures leave a favorable imprint on the chief executive's approval ratings after a lag of thirteen to twenty-two months. Each annual increase of one billion dollars results in a one percentage point popularity increase. Clearly, it costs the American taxpayer when a president tries to shore up a sagging approval rating by purchasing military hardware.

It is not apparent why defense spending has this consequence. One possibility is that such expenditures, involving contracts to local defense industries, boost the economy, lowering unemployment and raising disposable income. In the preceding chapter we observed how some scholars insist that the president can almost buy reelection in this manner. Yet no direct evidence exists for this interpretation, and some data indirectly oppose it. We know, for example, that local federal spending does not affect an incumbent's chances of reelection to the House of Representatives (Feldman and Jondrow 1984). If bringing in government money is irrelevant to a local politician's election success, the president may earn no popularity points for defense spending either. An alternative interpretation is that military expenditures have a symbolic value that allows the president to project an image of power and strength. In the next section we will discuss the rally-around-the-flag effect, in which a president gains support during times of international crisis. Perhaps the purchase of weapons exemplifies the same effect, particularly since the president often justifies appropriations for military systems with a patriotic appeal to national security. Thus Ronald Reagan rallied votes for the controversial MX missile by invoking the Soviet menace. The greatest difficulty with this second explanation is that it fails to account for the long delay between military spending and the increase in popularity.

Indeed, even if it is manifest that the president's approval rating tends to follow economic indicators, the theoretical significance of this correspondence is far from established (Monroe 1984). One fact that intrudes upon any interpretation is that the various economic statistics affect the presidents differently depending on their political affiliations. Kenski (1977) showed that unemployment was only disadvantageous for Republican presidents whom the voting public often see as being "soft" on jobs. Moreover, it is not precise to speak of the American people as a single homogeneous bloc. The Republican and Democratic parties attract different constituencies, each with distinctive economic priorities. Traditionally, Republicans are more concerned with inflation and evaluate presidents of either party primarily on that basis, whereas employment is the Democrats' criterion of presidential success. Because inflation and unemployment are often inversely related (MacRae 1981), Republican and Democratic chief executives perforce have divergent economic agendas. The Republican president may lower inflation by sacrificing employment, while the Democratic president may increase employment by pursuing government policies, such as deficit spending, that spur inflation.

Kernell and Hibbs (1981) have developed this discrepancy in party economic priorities into a critical threshold model of presidential popularity. In simple terms, this model examines how much a president has to gain or lose in support by making tradeoffs between inflation and unemployment, given that the economic priorities of a president's core constituency conflict with those of the opposition's constituency. Though the mathematical and empirical analysis is too complex to review here, the implications are simple and provocative: Democratic presidents are at a definite disadvantage. A Democrat who fights unemployment and thereby stimulates inflation loses more support than a Republican who puts a clamp on the price index by increasing unemployment. Inflation carries more weight than unemployment (Hibbs 1979); accordingly, a Republican chief executive's agenda is more conducive to earning a high approval rating. Reagan's popularity going into the 1984 election can be ascribed to his success in dampening inflation without tremendously expanding the ranks of the jobless.

Another implication of this analysis concerns the changes that take place over time in the degree to which the incumbent is deemed responsible for current economic ills. When a president first enters office, he will hardly be taken to task for economic conditions inherited from his predecessor. Indeed, dissatisfaction with the previous president may create a hopeful expectation on the part of the populace that *this* chief executive will answer everyone's prayers. Thus, even when the nation suffers from double-digit inflation and excessive unemployment, the new incumbent will suffer no corresponding loss in popularity. The public's unpleasant memories of the past administration steadily fade, however, and it becomes increasingly difficult to blame the previous incumbent. The present administration is held more and more accountable for the material welfare of the nation; by the second term in office, the incumbent is on his own, for the baseline for comparison becomes his administration's past performance (Hibbs 1982a). When Reagan was first sworn in he could easily point to the terrible economic mess inherited from Jimmy Carter; during his second term memories of stagflation under the Democrats have dimmed, obliging Reaganomics to stand or fall on its merits. Hibbs has elaborated this fundamental idea into a sophisticated dynamic model that does an excellent job of predicting the fluctuations in popularity (Hibbs 1982a, 1982b; see also Hibbs 1982c; Keech 1982). A provocative implication of this model is that, as long as the economy affords some justification for complaints, the honeymoon effect that attends the president's first year in office is bound to occur. Because the American economy has almost always been infected with some disease—whether inflation, recession, unemployment, or stagflation—the Hibbs model explains why popularity usually declines over the course of the president's administration.

Although our interest is more in the president than in the public, it is worthwhile to consider briefly why the state of the economy affects the president's approval rating. As Donald Kinder (1981) pointed out, two rival explanations are most likely (see Kinder and Kiewiet 1979). The pocketbook citizen hypothesis maintains that economic hard times spell personal hardships, and consequently the president is held responsible for directly experienced economic difficulties. The sociotropic citizen hypothesis maintains that the state of the national economy is a clue to the president's capacity to cope effectively with economic problems, for many citizens see the capacity to solve such problems as an essential attribute of the ideal president (see Kinder et al. 1980). In the first hypothesis, the citizen operates out of pure self-interest, whereas in the second hypothesis, the citizen evaluates the president out of a concern for the welfare of the nation as a whole. After detailed analysis of the fluctuations in popularity in the Nixon, Ford, and Carter presidencies, Kinder concluded that the judgments of survey respondents are affected more by sociotropic than by pocketbook considerations. What happens to fellow Americans matters more than the specific economic deprivations that a survey respondent might suffer. Hence, people tend to be less self-centered than is often supposed. To be sure, just because Americans judge a president by the national repercussions of his economic policies does not guarantee that those consequences will be correctly assessed. And it is unfair to grade a president according to economic ups and downs that may have little connection with specific presidential decisions. Even so, it is comforting to learn that a particular citizen's assessment of presidential performance does not hinge exclusively on his or her personal material welfare.

The state of the economy appears to determine, up to a point, the support the president receives from the American public. Economic conditions that affect virtually everybody, such as inflation, exert more influence than those that affect relatively few, such as unemployment. It bears repeating that these studies are based on polls taken from Truman's presidency on. Conceivably, therefore, the results might not apply to all presidents. I particularly question the conclusion that inflation is a far more potent factor than is unemployment. This may be true in the postwar era, when inflation has gotten out of hand more often than unemployment, and when we have more safeguards against unemployment than we do against price increases. But this has not always been the case. Certainly Hoover's tremendous loss of approval cannot be ascribed to inflation. The unprecedented human suffering caused by mass unemployment—dramatized by the construction of Hoovervilles and the march of the Bonus Army on Washington—was the primary cause of his landslide defeat in the 1932 election. A similar conclusion might be said to hold for other unfortunate depression presidents, from Van Buren on. Still, we know that the economy in some way has some pertinence for predicting presidential popularity. Few things matter more to the average American than a comfortable life style; rightly or wrongly, the president is held accountable for any difficulties that prevent the attainment of the expected standard of living.

INTERNATIONAL INFLUENCES

Given that the president often has more power over foreign policy than over national affairs, it comes as no surprise that his approval rating depends in large part on what is happening in the world. In fact, when it comes to highly dramatic, symbolic acts, the president's behavior in foreign affairs is more closely linked to his popularity than his behavior in domestic matters (MacKuen 1983; see also Norpoth 1984). Two classes of foreign affairs events turn out to be particularly crucial for presidential popularity—international crises and military conflicts.

Rally around the Flag

The monthly fluctuations in a president's approval rating can sometimes pull some odd tricks. The popularity of John F. Kennedy actually increased after the Bay of Pigs fiasco, one of the biggest blunders ever made by a modern American president. There seems to be a tendency for the American people to rally around the president in times of international crisis, with little concern for the rightness or wrongness of the president's position, at least for a while. This idea is as old as world history; leaders have often provoked conflict with neighbors to consolidate support at home (Kick 1983). Secretary of State Seward was rash enough to suggest to President Lincoln that a war be started with Great Britain in order to keep the Southern states in the Union.

Mueller (1970) was again the first to verify the importance of this rally-around-the-flag effect. He began with a list of thirty-four distinct rally points—events that were specific, dramatic, and sharply focused. There were six distinct categories of events. First were specific military interventions, such as the sending of United States troops to the Dominican Republic under L. B. Johnson. Second were major military developments in conflicts already going on, such as the Inchon landing in the Korean War. Third came such major diplomatic developments as the announcement of the Truman Doctrine. Fourth were major technological innovations like the Soviet launching of Sputnik I. Fifth were the meetings between the president and the Soviet leader, as when Eisenhower spoke with Khrushchev at Camp David. As the sixth category, Mueller chose the start of each presidential term. This class of rally points, naturally, is debatable insofar as international crises are being lumped together with a president's inauguration. Mueller defined the rally variable as the time (in years) since the last rally point. Not only did this variable exhibit a significant correlation with popularity from Truman to Johnson, but the rally-around-the-flag effect survived a multivariate analysis. On the average, popularity declines about six percentage points for each year after the rally point. It is worth mentioning that Mueller originally tried to separate "good" from "bad" international events, but found that the public reaction to both was the same, as the Bay of Pigs episode illustrates. A study of monarchs discovered a parallel effect: the fame of a king or a queen was influenced by the sheer number of historical events that occurred during the reign, events with favorable outcomes having about the same positive consequence as those with unfavorable outcomes (Simonton 1984d). Perhaps the crucial requirement is that something be happening.

Kernell (1978), while endorsing the general notion of a rally effect, disagreed with Mueller's definitions, especially the inclusion of the president's inaugural among the rally points. When he dropped this rite of passage from the definition, and counted only international crises, the impact of the rally event was less than originally claimed. Much of the rally-around-the-flag effect assessed by Mueller resulted from the early term effect. Nonetheless, the purer measure still correlated significantly with the approval rating. When a rally point happens, such as a military confrontation, diplomatic maneuver, or summit conference, a 5 to 7 percentage point improvement appears within the first month (see also Hibbs 1982a). Hence it is safe to conclude that many of the upswings in presidential popularity may be attributed to the presence of these rally points. The effect is short-lived, particularly if the crisis passes from an acute to a chronic stage. President Carter at first received a considerable boost in support when Iranian militants took over the United States embassy in Teheran, yet his popularity declined as the hostage situation continued.

War

According to the Constitution, the president is the nation's commander-in-chief. None of the events that have been shown to affect presidential popularity have a closer connection to a president's explicitly mandated powers than war. The Constitution does not say that the president is responsible for unemployment or inflation, but it does make the president the sole person in charge of military affairs. Here, the checks and balances among the three branches of the federal government mostly disappear; even the congressional power to declare war and to appropriate funds places few constraints on the chief executive, especially today. Historically, wars have not always been popular with the American public. A significant proportion of New Englanders were opposed to "Mr. Madison's" War of 1812, and many Northerners had misgivings about the Mexican-American War of 1845 (Henry David Thoreau even went to jail rather than pay a tax that would help pay for it). On the other hand, some wars, such as the Spanish-American War and the Second World War, were supported with intense nationalistic vigor. Thus we are led to consider the consequences of war on American public opinion about the president's performance. Does a war cause another form of the rally-around-the-flag effect? Or will a long war drag down a nation's spirits and undermine patience with the president's policies?

As we might expect by now, the two primary figures in this area of research are Mueller (1970) and Kernell (1978). Mueller inspected the repercussions of war by defining a dummy variable that equaled one when the United States was involved in a war and zero when the United States was at peace. Because Mueller considered presidents from Truman to Johnson, he essentially dealt with the Korean War and the Vietnam War. The overall correlation between war and popularity was quite negative ($r = -.66$). When this dummy variable was examined within a multivariate design, the Korean War was found to have had a negative effect on Truman's popularity—about an 18 percentage point drop—while the Vietnam War had no appreciable implications for Johnson's approval ratings. Mueller attempted to interpret this striking contrast by asserting that the two presidents had different relationships with their respective military entanglements. Truman was never able to make the Korean War a fully bipartisan effort, and therefore it became "Truman's War," with consequences damaging to his reputation. Johnson, in contrast, was able to enlist a broad-based support for the Vietnam War; accordingly, it never became closely identified with him. The Gulf of Tonkin Resolution, for example, gave Johnson's policies a congressional endorsement that was denied Truman. Such, at least, was Mueller's contention.

This interpretation is surprising, but the empirical result on which it is based is even more so; Johnson himself once admitted that he probably lost some twenty percentage points in the polls because of the Vietnam War. The difficulty may result from Mueller's definition of variables, as Kernell (1978) pointed out. A zero-one dummy variable does not capture all that we mean by war. Those of us who remember watching news programs about the first living-room war, for instance, were certainly not struck as much by the fact that a war was "on" as by the raw statistics of casualty figures and the seemingly interminable bombing of North Vietnam. Kernell employed United States casualty figures for both the Korean and Vietnam Wars, and the number of bombing missions for the latter war. These indicators were negatively associated with presidential popularity for both wars. Casualty figures correlated −.68 with popularity during the Korean War and −.78 with popularity during the Vietnam War. Bombing missions in the latter war correlated about −.84 with the president's approval rating. Mueller was thus quite unjustified in concluding that the Vietnam War had no effect on Johnson's popularity. Indeed, the net effect of this controversial war was a loss of about 3 percentage points per month. The adverse impact was cumulative, so that by the third quarter of 1968 LBJ's Gallup approval rating had dropped by as much as a dozen percentage points (Hibbs 1982a).

These results should be accepted with some reservations. It

would be ill-advised to infer that all wars harm presidential popularity. Roosevelt would not have been elected to an unprecedented fourth term had World War II hurt his reputation in the way that the Korean War damaged Truman's or the Vietnam War undermined Johnson's. (Both Truman and Johnson chose not to run for a second full term.) The Korean and Vietnam Wars were a breed apart from all other wars fought by the United States. These were the first wars in which the United States could not be said to have been directly attacked or affronted by the enemy power (although the provocations in the Spanish-American and Mexican-American Wars were largely if not entirely contrived by the United States). Nothing equivalent to a Pearl Harbor brought the United States into the two Asian wars. These two wars were peace-keeping "police actions." Another difference is that, unlike all previous wars except the War of 1812—after which Americans could only boast weakly, "Not one inch of territory ceded or lost!"—these two wars were not really won. The Korean War was fought to a standstill, and its limited objectives proved to be a constant irritation to militaristic Americans, like those who supported General MacArthur after his dismissal. The Vietnam War never seemed to make much headway either; escalation often only kept us in the same place we were in a year before. And, of course, the propped-up regime in South Vietnam collapsed shortly after the American withdrawal. Both of these unpopular wars were unsuccessful international police actions in which the American self-interest was not immediately obvious and which, as a consequence, did not receive the full commitment of United States military forces required for victory. Given these differences, it appears dangerous to generalize. What we would need (though not want) is another war of the world war variety to fully appreciate how the president's service as the commander-in-chief contributes to his public image as an effective chief executive.

CONCLUSION

It is useful now to summarize what we have learned about the factors behind presidential popularity. As far as the passage of time is concerned, a president's approval rating seems to be a partial consequence of an early term effect. A honeymoon occurs at the onset of a presidential term in which the president receives high, and usually his highest, ratings. Economic conditions also have a part to play, inflation having more effect than unemployment. International crises of a military, diplomatic, or technological nature tend to rally people around the flag, producing a unity of public opinion which directly benefits the president's standing in the polls. Finally, war has been shown to adversely affect presidential popularity, at least in the instance of two highly unpopular wars. All of these effects are smoothed over somewhat by the autoregressive nature of presidential popularity; a president's rating one month is very close to his rating of the previous month.

These are the principal factors, but not the only ones. Mueller (1970), for example, observed that major labor strikes can lower a president's approval rating by a bit less than three percentage points. Furthermore, Kernell (1978) demonstrated that the Watergate scandal substantially hurt Nixon's popularity ($r = -.89$). The loss has been estimated at around 10 percentage points (Hibbs 1982a; see also Norpoth 1984). In general, when all the predictors are put together in a single equation, something close to 90 percent of the variance in popularity can be explained. That figure is very good indeed, yet not good enough to prevent some big mistakes in the poll-by-poll predictions. Mueller's final equation, for instance, appreciably underestimates the exceptionally high popularity that Truman enjoyed at the beginning of his first term. Even though the death of Roosevelt and the succession of Truman to the presidency were duly recorded as a rally point, the trauma associated with the death of a long-tenured president and successful war leader may have had an unparalleled impact.

I must note that the literature on presidential popularity has become large and complex in the dozen or so years since Mueller's efforts, and many issues remain to be settled. For example, we still do not know precisely why the incumbent's approval rating tends to decline with time, nor do researchers in this area agree on how far back the survey respondents think when passing judgment on the president's performance. Nevertheless, enough findings have been firmly established to permit us to address the question of whether the ups and downs in presidential popularity are intrinsically fair indicators of the president's true performance. These approval ratings, in a just world, would be a response to actions within the president's control and responsibility. Sometimes the public's assessments do not follow this fundamental doctrine of fairness, however. The data at times echo Iago's claim that "reputation is an idle and most false imposition; oft got without merit, and lost without deserving." This is most apparent when the president is held to blame for economic bad times. In perhaps no other realm of national affairs are a president's hands more tied than in the state of the economy. Unemployment, inflation, and labor unrest are not subject to the president's direct control. Roosevelt's New Deal legislation had relatively little consequence for the Great Depression, and it required a major war to pull America out of its biggest economic slump. The drastic economic downturns that struck both Van Buren and Hoover near the beginning of their terms were not their fault but the fault of their predecessors, Jackson and Coolidge—if anyone can be held responsible at all. In the domain of foreign affairs, the president's popularity seems equally subject to the whims of events over which he can exercise little control. Not all the events that create fine rally-around-the-flag effects are initiated or even provoked by the president's policy decisions. The president serves more or less as a figurehead to receive blame for bad times and take credit for good.

The news discrepancy theory of opinion change advanced by Brody and Page (1975) falls in line with this argument. The theory holds that good news enhances presidential popularity, while bad news detracts from a president's approval rating. The American people are presumed to read the newspaper headlines or watch the key events depicted on the television evening news programs and then judge whether things are getting better or worse. This theory was tested on data for the Johnson and Nixon administrations by content analyzing the most significant news stories; strong endorsement was obtained. News that stemmed directly from presidential action carried about the same weight as news that arose from agents beyond the president's control. The chief executive thus often receives credit or blame that is not properly his due. The news discrepancy theory also implies that the president is assessed primarily on recent events rather than on the state of national affairs during the whole course of his administration. Presidential popularity varies because the American people have short memories.

MacKuen (1983) estimated that the president's standing with the people in a given month depends most heavily on what has been happening in the previous few months. The president cannot rest for long on even the most justly earned laurels. Carter's achievement in the Camp David accords meant nothing as the Iranian hostage crisis dragged on, and Nixon's famed China trip was forgotten by the time the Watergate scandal peaked. This short memory span of the average American renders the chief executive all the weaker in the quest for public appreciation and acclaim. The adverse consequence of recent news is aggravated when the media choose to place the bad news in the headlines and relegate the good to the back pages. One experimental simulation of television evening news demonstrated that by emphasizing some national problems while ignoring others, the media can help decide the standards by which the incumbent is evaluated (Iyengar et al. 1984). This effect is especially prominent for the more naive news watchers.

To be sure, we can go overboard in this affirmation of presidential impotence. MacKuen (1983) showed that the people's amnesia for recent history can be exploited by any shrewd politician. All that is required is to stage dramatic acts that can inspire an upsurge in popular support. Public opinion is easily swayed by acts highly symbolic of presidential authority, especially if these demonstrations occur in the sphere of foreign affairs. By wrapping himself in the flag with highly visible gestures, the president can prove that he is still in charge, thereby ameliorating any bad news that has soured public feeling toward him. Moreover, some presidents manage to maintain a public image that rises above the vicissitudes of current events. The popularity of President Eisenhower, for example, was strikingly immune to the usual capricious pushes and pulls that plagued other administrations in the polls (Mueller 1970). Eisenhower was evidently viewed as the one chief executive who rose above politics. Maybe this is the way the American public normally treats war heroes, for Grant, despite scandals in every corner of his administration, preserved his popularity to the point that he was seriously considered for a precedent-breaking third term.

Furthermore, we must recognize that some presidents are demonstrably responsible for certain actions that reflect upon their popularity. Johnson himself decided to bomb Vietnam, and Carter virtually invited the Iranian takeover of the American Embassy by allowing the former Shah to come to the United States for medical treatment. Nevertheless, a president cannot always anticipate how these events will turn out in the end, and the impact is often the opposite of what is anticipated. Kennedy certainly expected that a successful invasion of Cuba would raise his standing in the eyes of the American people, while an unsuccessful one would damage his reputation. And yet, as noted earlier, the disaster in the Bay of Pigs provided a rally-around-the-flag booster shot to his popularity. Thus, even in those rare instances where a president has control over events, he may not be completely able to manipulate their consequences.

We do not fully understand precisely why the public holds the incumbent personally responsible for events independent of his control. Such personalization has been ascribed to a number of psychological tendencies, including cognitive simplification (it is easier to consider a single cause than a myriad of complex and often subtle causes) and defensive attribution (it is comforting to a citizen's ego to blame the incumbent for personal financial failures), but much research needs to be done before these attributional predilections are fully understood (see, for example, Sigelman and Knight 1985b; Tyler 1982). Nevertheless, one inference is certain: to some extent, the president is a victim of external events and their repercussions on public opinion. What Lincoln once said of the presidency in general can be applied specifically to presidential popularity: "I claim not to have controlled events, but confess plainly that events have controlled me." Although the public assumes otherwise, situation appears to dominate individual characteristics in the determination of presidential popularity. Respondents to opinion polls, though explicitly asked to evaluate how the incumbent is "handling his job as president," are deflected by extrinsic events that have little bearing on actual presidential performance.

Even so, it still may be possible to salvage an interpretation that offers more latitude for the influence of individual variables. To some extent the incumbent may deserve the approval ratings he receives. The role of individual factors can be expanded if we acknowledge two facts. In the first place, when dummy variables are inserted into the equations to account for the different popularity of the various presidents from Truman on, these variables account for a considerable proportion of the variance, often more than the other substantive predictors. For instance, when Mueller (1973) assigned dummy variables for Eisenhower, Kennedy, and Johnson (Truman getting the intercept) to an equation already containing variables that registered the impact of time, rally events, and economic conditions, the amount of variance explained was almost tripled. Hence, knowing who the incumbent is enhances our predictive advantage more than the other, largely situational, variables. This result leaves room for individual effects, for the more popular incumbents may do things that maintain their popularity. Eisenhower may have surpassed Truman in the polls because of intrinsic differences in the styles of leadership they each displayed in the Oval Office.

The second fact that should enter our calculations is that many of the supposed situational influences on approval ratings may nonetheless contain some component that reflects the personal attributes of the incumbent. Certain presidents may actually be more adept at building a consensus on policy, engaging the nation in international affairs, managing the economy, directing war, or avoiding scandal. Even if it is rather difficult to interpret the predictors as having an entirely personal foundation, some portion of the scores the incumbent receives in the polls may truly be a consequence of objective performance in the White House. Accordingly, if we can show that certain personal traits contribute directly to presidential performance, then we might be able to show that contrasts among incumbents in approval ratings are partially rooted in the qualities of particular presidents. Rooting popularity in individual performance would equally provide a personal basis for election success, given the tight link between opinion polls and voting behavior noted in chapter 2.

◆ 4 ◆
ADMINISTRATION PERFORMANCE

From the preceding chapters it has become obvious that an incumbent president is only returned to office if he is popular, and that in an ideal state of affairs, his popularity on election day should be contingent on how well he performed in his first term. Consequently, a more direct way of assessing presidential success may be to shift focus from election success and popularity in the polls to actual administration performance. This question of presidential accomplishment also makes the required connection between the narrow issue of presidential popularity discussed in chapter 3 and the broader issue of presidential greatness treated in chapter 5. There are innumerable approaches to assessing how adequately a president has executed his responsibilities (see, for example, Bailey 1966, chap. 20); fortunately, my initial decision to confine attention to empirical inquiries dramatically reduces the quantity of material to be considered.

I commence with an examination of specific criteria by which a chief executive's achievements may be evaluated—his foreign and domestic policies. The chapter ends with a series of empirical studies, some highly speculative, of the all-around leadership style that a president may bring into the office, a style that sets the tone of his administration. One leadership attribute, flexibility, will receive special attention, both as an important effect and as an individual factor that interacts with the prevailing political situation.

FOREIGN POLICY

American participation in international affairs can be defined by two distinct states or conditions. There is the state of peace, during which the United States is involved in diplomacy, especially in the negotiation of treaties and executive agreements. Treaties define America's obligations to allies, delineate the rights and privileges America enjoys with respect to other powers, and in other ways clarify the position of the United States in the international system. When this system breaks down, however, and the established world order cannot be enforced by pieces of paper or verbal exchanges, the United States may find itself entrapped in the second state, war. "War is nothing more than the continuation of politics by other means," as Karl von Clausewitz expressed it, and the severing of diplomatic communications is often the first step toward war. The military conflict that ensues creates a new world structure, defined once again by treaties, and the cycle of peacetime diplomacy and wartime destruction continues. Hence, sometimes the president is concerned with employing the diplomatic process to preserve the peace, at other times with deploying military power to reestablish that peace.

Diplomacy

The formulation of American foreign policy, insofar as it is embedded in treaties that specify United States commitments and alliances, results from a give-and-take between the presidency and the Senate. In the next two sections I will show that neither governmental body is ruled completely by rational considerations, but that personalities have a tendency to interfere. Because American diplomacy is an often highly personal product of individual human beings, its success is not always assured. Subjectivity may sometimes override the responsible considerations of objectivity.

Dominance and Extroversion. American foreign policy usually originates in a collaboration between the president and one or more advisers, including, most notably, the secretary of state. The president and his advisers must formulate a conception of the proper relations among independent nations. In making this formulation, the policy makers may model their conceptions of international relations on their own views of interpersonal relations. Persons who are outgoing in their social interactions may prefer a similar outgoing role for the United States in world affairs. Likewise, those who like to dominate others in their personal lives may recommend the same sort of behavior for the United States. This notion has been called interpersonal generalization theory, and has been subjected to a valuable empirical test by Lloyd S. Etheredge (1978a, 1978b).

Etheredge studied the makers of American foreign policy from 1898 to 1968, a significant period in which the United States emerged from its isolationism to the status of a world power and peacekeeper. The president and his advisers usually agree with one another on policy questions, not surprisingly given that the president picks his own policy advisers. Moreover, a policy issue often concerns areas where the national interest is overwhelmingly self-evident (for example, when natural resource lifelines are threatened) or where a strong precedent has already been established (such as the Monroe Doctrine). Policy questions on which all policy makers concur, Etheredge assumes, tell us very little about how personality affects policy, for situational demands seem then to override individual dispositions. Therefore, Etheredge concentrated on sixty-two cases of disagreement on a foreign policy issue. In forty-nine of these cases the debate concerned the use of force to achieve foreign policy goals, as in the conflict between President Wilson and Secretary of State Bryan over the proper response to German submarine warfare. The remaining thirteen cases concerned inclusionary issues, that is, debates about the most suitable relationship between the United States and the Soviet Union and Soviet bloc. An example is the debate between President Harding and Secretary of State Hughes over whether to recognize and increase trade with the Soviet Union (something that was not actually done until Franklin Roosevelt's administration). Presumably, when two or more policy formulators are at odds on a question of fundamental importance, as in these sixty-two instances, their personality biases are more likely to surface.

Etheredge's next step was to scrutinize the personality characteristics of the thirty-six presidents, secretaries of state, and selected advisers involved in foreign policy-making by consulting biographies and autobiographies, insiders' accounts, and other sources. Two personality dimensions were assessed, namely, general dominance over subordinates and extroversion. To maximize objectivity in these assessments, relevant passages were excerpted with clues to identity deleted. Etheredge and two others scored this anonymous information on 10-point scales. There was a high degree of consensus on the personality dimensions. For dominance the correlations among the three judges ranged from .83 to .91, and for extroversion from .83 to .93. As a check, Etheredge correlated the scores that eleven presidents received on the dimensions with the scores they earned on power and achievement motivations assessed by Donley and Winter (1970). For example, dominance correlated .54 with the need for power and .77 with the need for achievement. Hence, Etheredge's measures appear to be reliable.

Given the two classes of intraelite policy disagreements and the two personality descriptions, Etheredge was free to state two hypotheses. First, in debates on force-related issues, those who score high in dominance will be more likely to advocate the threat or use of military force, and less likely to support efforts toward disarmament and arbitration agreements. Second, with regard to the more specific question of policy toward the Soviet Union and the Soviet bloc, those with high extroversion scores will advocate inclusive or cooperative policies, such as more trade, summit conferences, negotiations, and the like. The data analysis endorsed both hypotheses. In over 75 percent of the cases the direction of disagreement could be predicted from the policy makers' orientations in interpersonal relations. Dominant types had a higher probability of recommending the use or threat of force, while extroverted types had a higher probability of advocating more inclusionary policies toward the Soviet Union and its allies. Thus, the less dominant Bryan resigned rather than sign a threatening note to the German Kaiser written by Wilson, and the more extroverted Eisenhower advocated a more conciliatory stand toward the Soviet Union than Dulles on the Open Skies inspection plan, the Atoms for Peace initiative, and the value of summit conferences.

Having confirmed interpersonal generalization theory, Etheredge made it the basis of a useful two-way typology of orientations to international affairs. The two dimensions are the personality dispositions in preferred interpersonal relations—dominance and extroversion. Along the first dimension, the policy makers can be classed as either high-dominance types, who seek to reshape the political system, or low-dominance types, who strive merely to persevere. Along the second dimension, policy makers can be categorized as either introverts or extroverts. Four distinct combinations emerge.

Bloc-excluding leaders are high-dominance introverts who seek to reshape the world order by forming exclusive blocs that restrain potentially disruptive forces. President Wilson and Secretary of State Dulles are examples. *Maintainers* are low-dominance introverts, such as President Coolidge and Secretary of State Rusk, dedicated to little more than passively preserving the status quo. Calvin Coolidge was so uninvolved in international affairs that he nowhere broaches the subject of foreign policy in his autobiography. *Conciliators* are also low-dominance, but they are extroverted as well, involved with international affairs without the will power to carry any consistent foreign policy into effect. According to Etheredge, McKinley, Taft, Harding, Truman, and Eisenhower were all conciliators, as were Secretaries of State Bryan and John Hay. The final type consists of the high-dominance extroverts who go out and actively reshape the international political system; these are the *world-integrating leaders*, including Lyndon Johnson, both Roosevelts, and Kennedy. They work hard at setting up world organizations in order to build bridges between international factions; they seek to lead at the global level rather than simply to contain sinister forces; and they are willing to advocate change in order to attain a more integrated world system of nations.

Etheredge argues that the striking contrast is not between high-dominance and low-dominance leaders, but rather between the extroverts and the introverts—between the bloc leaders and maintainers on the one hand and the world leaders and conciliators on the other. The introverts are more disposed to search for a world system that functions by impersonal mechanisms, with abstract institutions, laws, and moral principles. The extroverts are more interested in the direct involvement of world leaders in discussion and negotiation. To illustrate this contrast, Etheredge offers the difference between President Wilson, who saw the League of Nations as a promulgator of rules and sanctions against transgressors, and Secretary Stettinius, who viewed the United Nations as a gathering place where world diplomats could engage in give and take.

The lesson to be learned from Etheredge's interpersonal generalization theory is that the president and his advisers, when they conceive American foreign policy, may not be always guided by rational, objective considerations. Rather, it may happen all too often that the large, complex, and dangerous world of nations is judged in terms of the far smaller and simpler realm of interpersonal relations. Hostilities and insecurities that drive a president's social interactions may also contaminate his foreign policies. That this may at times produce disastrous results is evident enough from history. President Wilson destroyed his health in the process of trying to sell his League of Nations to the American people. By failing to approach his selling job rationally, by turning it into a personal crusade on which he staked his whole being, he effectively prevented the United States from entering the League under the rather modest reservations imposed by the Senate. Without the United States, the success of the League was far from assured.

It may not prove comforting to argue that the president's orientation toward interpersonal relations, and hence toward international affairs, may only be representative of the people who elected him to office. The three interaction effects discussed in chapter 2—between authoritarianism and economic conditions, between birth order and the political zeitgeist, and between the candidates' policies and the voters' preferred stands on the issues—all suggest the incumbent may be the most proper spokesman for his people. The degree of dominance and extroversion manifested by the president may correspond to what the public seeks at that particular moment in history. For instance, the international scene may be so riddled with recurrent crises and war that the voters want a strong helmsman in the White House to guide the ship of state through the troubled waters. However, even if this possibility renders foreign policy more democratic, in the sense of being responsive to the people's will, it does not assure that the decision makers will pursue the correct course. To some extent, the design of foreign policy must be independent of such subjective influences, and the chance that irrational inputs may be shared by millions of Americans does not make them any more objective, nor does it guarantee that the resulting decisions will be any more successful. This precaution also applies to the next factor, isolationism, as well as to the variables that affect the odds against the nation entering a war.

Isolationism. The Versailles treaty, which provided for the League of Nations, was rejected by a United States Senate that was experiencing a resurgence of old-time American isolationism. Senator Henry Cabot Lodge and his allies did not wish to see the United States involved in foreign entanglements, and they were willing to suffer vitriolic abuse from President Wilson in order to foil Wilson's project. The issue of isolationism versus internationalism has arisen on numerous occasions throughout the history of the United States. In fact, the question first arose under the first American presidencies, when the French Revolution and the wars it provoked threatened to embroil the United States in general European affairs. (Instead, we entered into the more limited wars with France under J. Adams and with England under Madison.) The debate about isolationism continues to this day. Much of this debate takes place in the Senate, the institution that is required, by constitutional decree, to proffer its advice and consent on foreign policy to the president. The Senate approves treaties and nominees for ambassadorships and for secretary of state; thus it can monitor the direction of executive policies in world affairs. Accordingly, factors that influence the degree of isolationism in the Senate have direct relevance for our comprehension of presidential policy formulation. This relevance is augmented by the fact that the Senate is a major source of presidential candidates, and hence of presidents (Aldrich 1980; Peabody, Ornstein, and Rohde 1976). Truman, Kennedy, L. B. Johnson, and Nixon are four recent examples of former senators who entered the White House.

Philip Tetlock (1981a) wanted to uncover the connection between personality and isolationism in the United States Senate. He focused on the speeches delivered in the Eighty-second Congress (1951–1952), a Congress that saw an appreciable amount of debate over the place that the United States should take in international affairs. The North Atlantic Treaty Organization had just been established, the United States was fighting in Korea, the Nationalist government of Chiang Kai-shek was huddled defensively on Formosa, and Robert A. Taft, son of President Taft, had begun the first session of the Eighty-second Congress with an attack on President Truman's foreign policy. This attack launched a three-month debate about American international commitments, especially sending United States troops to Europe.

Tetlock chose thirty-five senators who were articulate on questions of foreign policy, of whom eleven could be clearly classified as isolationists, eight as ambivalent isolationists, and sixteen as nonisolationists (according to their votes on such issues as security pacts, foreign aid, and sending troops abroad). Included among the isolationists were Senators Dirkson and McCarthy, among the ambivalent isolationists, Taft and Brewster, and among the nonisolationists, Humphrey, Fulbright, Connally, Kefauver, and Sparkman. The speeches of the thirty-five senators were coded for two content analytical variables. First, the speeches were scored for integrative complexity on a seven-point scale using the same scoring procedure used for assessing campaign rhetoric in the study discussed in chapter 2. This scale takes into consideration both the degree of differentiation (the number of dimensions or aspects of a problem that are taken into account in making a decision) and the degree of integration (the development of elaborate connections among differentiated ideas). A senator who scores high in integrative complexity is a complex, sophisticated thinker; a senator who scores low tends to treat foreign policy questions in a dichotomous manner, there being only the bad (defeatist) positions and the good (patriotic) positions, with no gray area between. This scoring was done by several coders with a respectable consensus (mean interrater agreement: $r = .87$).

The second coding scheme used evaluative assertion analysis, an objective method for gauging how a speaker feels toward specified attitude objects. Tetlock was particularly interested in assessing how the senators felt toward in-groups and out-groups, especially the United States and the Soviet Union. This assessment was done on another seven-point scale ranging from -3 for a very negative attitude to $+3$ for a very positive attitude. The judgments of two independent coders correlated around .90, and so this scoring was highly reliable.

As he had expected, Tetlock found that isolationists differed from nonisolationists on both content analytical dimensions. First, the isolationists made considerably simpler policy statements, whereas the nonisolationists evidently took into consideration many perspectives and criteria and connected them in complex ways. Second, the isolationists exhibited much more positive attitudes than the nonisolationists toward the in-group (particularly the United States and the free world) and much more negative attitudes toward the out-group (particularly the Soviet Union and its allies). The ambivalent isolationists tended to fall between the isolationists and the nonisolationists on these two dimensions. Hence, there seems to be justification for concluding that isolationists rely heavily on simplistic, dichotomous thought processes accompanied by strikingly polarized attitudes.

Tetlock is the first to admit that an alternative interpretation may be reasonable. Since most of the isolationists were Republicans expressing a minority viewpoint in the face of a Democratic majority in Congress and a Democratic president (Truman), the assessed differences may represent merely a rhetorical strategy employed by an out-of-power minority to make itself heard (and thus more like campaign rhetoric than policy discussion, directed at the American voters rather than at colleagues in the Senate chamber). Tetlock suggested a couple of ways in which future research might determine which interpretation is most correct. For example, one can check whether minority-party members in Congress usually assume more simplistic, polarized positions than majority-party members on various issues. In a more recent paper, to be discussed later, Tetlock showed that there was some tendency for this to happen, though more conservative senators (who tend to be isolationists) overall still fall behind their more liberal colleagues in integrative complexity (Tetlock, Hannum, and Micheletti 1984). Also, in light of Etheredge's (1978a, 1978b) demonstration that two other personality dimensions are germane to foreign policy formulation, Tetlock's (1981a) addition of a third dimension, that of integrative complexity, may be granted tentative acceptance pending further inquiry.

War

At first glance, whether or not an American president becomes a wartime commander-in-chief seems in large part determined by situational forces (Simonton 1981c; see also Simonton 1986e). For one thing, the number of military interventions a president engages the nation in is a positive function of presidential order ($\beta = .48$). That is, more recent presidents, especially the twentieth-century ones, were far more likely than earlier presidents to employ American troops abroad to achieve foreign policy goals. From Woodrow Wilson's intervention in Mexico to Ronald Reagan's in Grenada, such acts have now become part of the president's bag of tricks in the execution of foreign policy. That this trend reflects a change in America's place in world politics rather than any shift in executive disposition toward military power is revealed in the fact that there is no corresponding decline in presidential pacifism from Washington through Reagan (Simonton 1986e). Another situational influence on military intervention is the duration of the president's administration ($\beta = .40$). Not only are the longer-tenured chief executives more prone to military intervention ($r = .46$), but they are also more likely to have Congress declare war ($r = .61$) and to lead the nation through more years of war ($r = .61$). Of course, the causal connections among these variables are not all that clear. The longer a president dwells in the White House, the more opportunity he has to become a wartime president, just by the laws of chance (see Houweling and Kuné 1984). On the other hand, as noted in the preceding chapter, a wartime president may be more confident of being reelected, and thereby attain a longer tenure in office (Simonton 1986c). Abraham Lincoln was re-elected in 1864 by voters who were persuaded not to change horses in midstream, and the same was true of F. D. Roosevelt eighty years later. Naturally, this is not invariably the case. Some presidents, most notably Wilson, have been reelected for keeping the United States out of war; Americans on the whole prefer that the incumbent not get the country involved in unnecessary wars (Kinder et al. 1980). Hence, the problem of untangling the connection between war and administration duration is a complex one indeed.

This task would be easier if we could isolate some individual variables that might help us predict who will become a wartime chief executive. Below, I review research on two characteristics of the president that may contribute to his becoming an active commander-in-chief. I start with the personal motivations that may color how he perceives and responds to international affairs, and then conclude with the information-processing capacities that may prevent an international crisis from escalating into a military conflict.

Power Motivation. The American public, in more cynical moods, often conceives of politicians in general, and presidents in particular, as driven by an excessive hunger for power. Thus, in one study, over three-quarters of the respondents specified that the ideal chief executive should not be "power-hungry" (Kinder et al. 1980). Candidates frequently have very different motives for seeking the presidency, and some of these motives, such as a need for achievement or a sense of public duty, may have very little to do with personal power (see Aldrich 1980, chap. 2). As a consequence, those who are elected may vary immensely in their power requirements. And this variation may have crucial repercussions for foreign policy. We have already witnessed how dominance, extroversion, and intellectual complexity may affect positions taken on foreign policy issues. If dominance makes a president more inclined to advocate the use of force, might not the closely related personality trait of power motivation make a president more prone to actually use force? Will a power-hungry president be more likely to enter the United States into a military conflict?

David G. Winter, in *The Power Motive* (1973), offers the beginning of an answer to these important questions. He and one of his students (Donley and Winter 1970) obtained the inaugural addresses of the dozen presidents between T. Roosevelt and Nixon, that is, all of the twentieth-century presidents at the time of the study (largely using Israel 1965). Using techniques adapted from the Thematic Apperception Test of Henry Murray (1938), these speeches were scored for two types of motive imagery, the need for power and the need for achievement. The two presidents highest in power motivation were Kennedy and T. Roosevelt, the lowest, Taft and Hoover. Nixon and Johnson had the highest scores in achievement motivation, Taft and Coolidge the lowest. Taft, in fact, scored lowest on both needs. It is of interest that scores on these two very distinct motivations were highly correlated with one another ($r = .71$), unlike the scores of most average citizens. Evidently presidents fall into two, not four categories, the "strong" presidents who seek both power and achievement, and the "weak" presidents who desire neither.

The next question is whether these motivation scores have anything to do with a president's entering the United States into a war. Half of the presidents studied, including Taft, Coolidge, and Eisenhower, were peacetime presidents, who did not start any military conflicts. The other half, including Wilson, F. D. Roosevelt, and Kennedy, were wartime presidents, who engaged American troops in combat. The correlation between power motivation and war entry is sizable ($r = .40$), that between achievement motivation and war entry negligible ($r = .02$). Having strong power needs accordingly seems to be associated with a proclivity for employing military force to the point of bloodshed. The power motivation scores of the peacetime and wartime presidents do not even overlap, with one exception. Theodore Roosevelt, the second highest scorer in power motivation, failed to engage the United States in a military conflict. This is not to say that he was a peace-loving or spineless chief executive, for, despite the fact that he got the Nobel Peace Prize, he was clearly one of our more belligerent presidents. The way he took the Panama Canal region from Columbia, and sent the Great White Fleet around the world as a show of force, as well as his many other actions both before (as assistant secretary of the Navy and as leader of the Rough Riders) and after his presidency, such as his support of early participation in World War I, all suggest that he deserved his high score in power motivation. That the United States did not enter a war under his administration probably says more about the nature of international affairs during those eight years than about Roosevelt's personal disposition.

The power motive has implications for administration events that are closely related to war as well. Winter shows, for instance, that power needs are positively correlated with the gaining of territory ($r = .74$), whereas the achievement needs are negatively associated with such acquisition ($r = -.65$). Theodore Roosevelt acquired the Canal Zone, Wilson the Virgin Islands, and Truman the Pacific Trust Territories and Okinawa. Wendt and Light (1976) have studied the inaugural addresses of the fifteen presidents since Hayes and have found some interesting facts that fill out the picture of the power-seeking chief executive. Again, power motivation was strongly associated with the achievement motivation ($r = .74$), but Democratic presidents were also shown to be more power-motivated than Republican presidents ($r = .67$). (This party contrast may be partly responsible for the impression voiced by some political commentators that Democratic presidents are more likely than Republican presidents to get the United States involved in foreign wars.) Finally, those presidents who are more likely to apply the presidential veto to legislation—a potential indicator of a president's use of power on the home front—have a higher probability of engaging the United States in military conflicts.

There emerges a profile of a power-motivated president who, while active and strong, may be a bit dangerous besides. This conclusion is even more evident in a follow-up study published by Winter and Stewart in 1977. Two elaborations were introduced. First, another motivation, the need for affiliation, was added to the power and achievement motives. This motive is virtually uncorrelated with the other two and thus represents a whole new assessment of presidential personality. Of the thirteen presidents from T. Roosevelt to Ford, Ford exhibited the highest score on affiliation motivation, Taft the lowest. Second, these three personality measures were correlated not only with entry of the United States into war under a president's administration, but also with any agreements that were reached on arms limitation—an event which is likely to be an inverse indicator of a warlike disposition.

In estimating the impact of these three motives, Winter and Stewart calculated the (second order) partial correlations wherein each effect was determined after statistically controlling for the other two motives. In the case of war entry, once more only power motivation emerged as a significant positive predictor ($r = .62$). The achievement and affiliation motives actually exhibited slightly negative relationships, though not statistically significant ones. The outcome for arms limitation agreements was even more striking. The need for achievement was positively correlated, although only to a marginal extent, with such concords ($r = .44$). The need for affiliation displayed an impressive positive association; thus, those presidents who most strongly desire friendship, social approval, and positive social interactions are most inclined to work out less hostile military relations with America's rivals ($r = .80$). If the affiliation drive can be linked with extroversion, then the pattern is quite in keeping with what Etheredge (1978a) found to be the foreign policy goals of extroverted presidents and presidential advisers. Yet any propensity for arms limitation is undermined should the president have a high drive toward power, for the power motivation is negatively connected with such agreements ($r = -.63$).

Once again the power motive emerges as a primary influence on American foreign policy, especially on those policies that may destabilize the international system, such as an unwillingness to agree on the reduction of weapons. In this era, when the nuclear holocaust is held over our heads in the name of deterrence, and when effective reduction in strategic nuclear arms is needed, the American people should perhaps look for presidential candidates whose affiliation needs surpass their need for power. The fulfillment of a president's personal power fixations is potentially far too lethal for the rest of us on this planet.

Integrative Complexity. The complexity of a politician's information processing has already been shown to be associated with foreign policy attitudes. In an earlier chapter we saw as well how this individual-level variable may be germane to election success. Not surprisingly, a psychological factor that is so pervasive in influence has been shown to have relevance for war, too. At risk of sounding a little simplistic, war very frequently results when international crises get out of control (see Midlarsky 1984). Suddenly two or more world leaders are confronted with a complex conflict in which innumerable issues are at stake—national security, national honor, personal prestige and ambition, and many more. To resolve the conflict without resorting to hostilities requires exceptional agility of thought. The opposing leaders must be able to imagine the opponents' points of view and simultaneously examine a host of scenarios and contingencies. Avenues for retreat and for saving face must often be left open for both parties, something that is not likely to happen if each antagonist develops a rigid, egocentric, and self-righteous attitude.

Peter Suedfeld and his associates have tried to demonstrate how integrative complexity might serve as a useful factor for predicting the outbreak of war. Though their focus was not restricted to the American presidency, two of their studies regarded military conflicts that directly or indirectly involved the United States. The first inquiry, by Suedfeld and Tetlock (1977), closely scrutinized the diplomatic communications exchanged during two types of international crises, those that led to war (in 1914 and 1950) and those that were resolved without bloodshed (in 1911, 1948, and 1962). Three of these crises—the 1950 Korean conflict, the 1948 Berlin blockade, and the 1962 Cuban missile crisis—directly involved the United States and thereby obliged the president to make some critical policy decisions. The communications were scored for integrative complexity. The results indicated that when the diplomatic exchanges displayed very low levels of communicative complexity, the international crisis was more likely to result in an outbreak of war. Even more important, when the preliminary phase of a crisis was compared with the climax phase, a peacefully settled conflict was more likely to show an increase in complexity of intercourse, whereas a conflict that precipitated war usually witnessed a decrease in complexity. In the case of the Cuban missile crisis, for instance, both the United States (represented by President Kennedy and Secretary of State Rusk) and the Soviet Union (represented by Prime Minister Khrushchev, Minister for Foreign Affairs Gromyko, and Soviet Ambassador to the United Nations Zorin) raised the complexity of their communications, thereby preventing a possible nuclear holocaust.

The second study, by Suedfeld, Tetlock, and Ramirez (1977), inspected, using the same methodology, the United Nations speeches presented from 1947 to 1976 by the leading participants in the Middle East conflict. The speeches were made by the representatives of the Arab countries (Egypt and Syria), the Soviet Union, Israel, and the United States. Speeches made in months preceding the onset of war (in 1948, 1956, 1967, and 1973) were characterized by an appreciable reduction in the complexity of information processing. Even the United States, which was only indirectly engaged in these conflicts, exhibited a drop in complexity with an outbreak of war. However, the United States also had the highest overall complexity levels of the participating parties.

An inherent ambiguity plagues both of these studies, the same ambiguity that infects almost all correlation studies: we cannot infer with absolute confidence in which direction the causal arrow points. I have been speaking as though a president's failure to find a peaceful resolution of an international crisis may be due to some rigidity of his thought processes. If he becomes more simple-minded rather than more complex and flexible, not all alternatives are weighed and overtures from the opposing side may be misinterpreted, resulting in war. Yet can we not reverse this course of events? When a crisis starts to head down the path to military hostilities, the leaders may become more confined in their thinking because of the much heavier burdens of stress. Indeed, we might even argue that as a war-destined crisis reaches its climax, the increased simplicity of the diplomatic communications is an example more of deliberate propaganda maneuvers than of anything substantial. The leaders may decide to give up on reconciliation and to begin mobilizing the home front with patriotic exhortations. The audience may not be foreign but domestic when the language changes from sophisticated communication to jingoistic rhetoric. Although right now we cannot vouchsafe any generalization, one fact should be taken into consideration: there is some evidence that even persons uninvolved in the political decision-making process will nonetheless evince less integrative complexity in communications composed under crisis and wartime conditions (Porter and Suedfeld 1981; Suedfeld 1980). Hence, it is possible that information-processing simplicity is a reaction to, not a cause of, a crisis rolling inexorably toward violence.

Acute stress is not the only condition that might degrade the decision-making deliberations of the president and his advisers. Irving Janis (1972) has described what he called the groupthink phenomenon, which has much the same consequence. Groupthink occurs when members of a group are more strongly motivated to maintain group cohesion than to give a critical analysis to the problem facing the group. To avoid generating disharmony, the group members do not express unpopular opinions or doubts, and consequently the group is led to an uncritical solution to the problem at hand. Janis gave as an example the decision to support the Bay of Pigs incursion at the beginning of the Kennedy administration.

Though Janis himself did not base his conclusions on any quantitative analysis of pertinent documents, Tetlock (1979) has tested some of Janis' inferences empirically. Tetlock specifically analyzed the public statements of key decision makers in five United States foreign policy crises. Three of these crises supposedly exemplified the groupthink phenomenon, namely, the invasion of North Korea, the Bay of Pigs incursion, and the Vietnam War escalation. The other two decision situations, the Marshall Plan and the Cuban missile crisis, were not subject to groupthink. As in the study of senatorial isolationism mentioned earlier, the public statements were coded for integrative complexity and an evaluative assertion analysis was employed to determine attitudes toward in-groups and out-groups. Decision makers caught in groupthink made more positive references toward the in-group (though not necessarily more negative references toward the out-group) and, significantly, were far less complex in their perceptions of policy issues than their non-groupthink counterparts. So there is some relatively hard evidence for the conclusion that groupthink conditions may cause a simplistic, and hence unsuccessful, approach to decision-making.

Despite the theoretical ambiguity inherent in the above studies of integrative complexity, their potential practical or predictive value cannot be denied. Whether simplicity of information processing is an agent or a mere symptom, we can still use this construct to monitor the policy statements of the president and his advisers. If, in a crisis situation, these policy makers become too one-dimensional in their thinking, too all-or-none and undifferentiated, we may be witnessing the early warning signs of catastrophe. Perhaps these signs can inspire countermeasures that might prevent the decision-making processes from terminating in war.

DOMESTIC POLICY

According to the Constitution, the president has at his disposal a variety of devices for affecting the internal condition of the nation. Two of these tools stand out far above the rest: the power to propose, sign, and veto legislation and the power to make appointments to high federal office. Consequently, when a president's success in the domestic sphere is evaluated, it is frequently judged in terms of his legislative and appointive accomplishments.

Laws

The authors of the Constitution did not originally envisage the president in the role of primary lawmaker. Instead, the president's principal responsibility was to execute faithfully the laws passed by Congress. The only direct authority the president has to propose legislation is the charge that he periodically deliver a State of the Union address that contains his recommendations. Hence, some occupants of the White House, the so-called Whig

Presidents, have adopted rather passive stances in the legislative domain. Nonetheless, the first president established the precedent that the chief executive may actively propose bills and even push bills through Congress. George Washington had no choice, for he had to advise Congress on the statutes he deemed necessary to set up a central government that could put into effect the more abstract guidelines of the Constitution. Subsequent presidents with a more activist bent have pursued this precedent with gusto. These enthusiastic lawmakers enter office with a program that they wish put into place by the legislative branch, and at once. The most prominent example, perhaps, is Franklin Roosevelt, who forced the New Deal through Congress in an epoch-making hundred days.

The president with an urgent legislative program in mind uses both a carrot and a stick to prod a recalcitrant Congress. He can specify what bills he would most like to have appear on his desk for his signature. He may do anything from presenting the rough outlines of a legislative idea to submitting, via his congressional supporters, actual drafts of bills for consideration on Capitol Hill. In this case the issue of presidential success is reduced to the question of whether he can summon the congressional votes for his proposals. Congresses often have plans of their own, however, plans that run counter to what the incumbent views as optimal policy. In these instances, a president may have no recourse but to use the veto power. Once a bill is sent back to Congress, the executive and legislative branches of government enter a confrontation. If the veto is sustained, the president's will has been respected; if it is overridden, the House and Senate have emerged victorious.

Congressional Votes. We cannot challenge the significant place that a president's legislative accomplishments have in the ultimate evaluation of an administration. Many of the most important presidents are closely identified with the programs that they pushed through Congress. Besides FDR's New Deal, we have Wilson's New Freedom and Lyndon Johnson's Great Society. Further, as we noted in chapter 2, the number of bills a president signs in his first term in office is related to his chances for renomination and hence reelection. Some theorists have argued that a president's legislative acumen may constitute a key indicator of political creativity, a presumed asset (for example, Alker 1981). Nevertheless, it has proven hard to single out those presidential attributes and political circumstances that would tell us when to expect notable legislative achievements. And what we do know often turns out to be less than surprising. For example, it has been established that the more recent a president is, the more legislation will be passed during his administration, and that the longer his tenure in office, the larger the mass of bills as well (for example, Simonton 1981c). But these statistical tendencies are not really very informative about how a president manages to become a distinguished lawgiver. Even if two presidents are near-contemporaries and reside at the executive mansion an identical number of days, they may differ dramatically in their legislative success.

One possible reason is readily apparent: popular presidents may be able to translate their favorable standing with the people into votes for executive-sponsored programs in Congress. We know that presidents are opinion leaders. Page and Shapiro (1984) found, for instance, that presidential pronouncements appearing in the national press (the *New York Times*) had a powerful impact on public opinion recorded in Harris and Gallup surveys. Indeed, the president's influence is virtually unrivaled. Spokespersons for special-interest groups, for the opposition party, and even for the administration have a negligible impact on the policy preferences of the American people. Only editorials in major papers may be said to rival the president's impact (and even here the incumbent can bully editors into compliance with administration designs, according to Senter, Reynolds, and Gruenenfelder 1986). Nevertheless, this tremendous power is only enjoyed by popular chief executives. Presidents with inferior approval ratings in the opinion polls have either no influence at all or a harmful influence. Unpopular presidents are sometimes better off keeping silent about their personal causes. President Nixon, whose approval rating had sunk to one-third in the latter part of 1973, may have hurt the prospects for certain administration energy proposals; public support for his energy policies declined with each repetition of his endorsements. The ideal president is deemed knowledgeable (Kinder et al. 1980), and thus his opinions should carry weight; yet an incumbent who loses the respect of the nation may correspondingly suffer in apparent expertise.

If popular presidents lead the opinions of the American public, then certainly the people's representatives in Washington should follow as well. Letters from constituents may advise a member of Congress that a vote for the president's programs is the order of the day. There always exists pressure on national legislators to support their president, and this pressure is no doubt more potent when the president is simultaneously popular and vocal in his policy preferences. In modern times, moreover, members of Congress can read the opinion polls and thereby find out more directly which way the wind blows.

This argument notwithstanding, the empirical evidence suggests that the president cannot always exchange popularity in the polls for votes in Congress. Bond and Fleisher (1984) scrutinized roll-call votes for bills on which the president had expressed a position, introducing various control variables, separating House and Senate votes and the type of vote (such as foreign versus domestic policy, key versus nonkey votes), and gauging the presidential influence several ways (such as wins versus losses and percent support overall). Although the president's popularity was often correlated with his legislative score, the correlations were very modest: usually less than five percent of the variance in presidential performance could be predicted on the basis of a president's approval rating (see also Zeidenstein 1985). In some cases the association was actually negative; if a key bill is on the House floor, the more popular incumbent receives less support from representatives of the opposition party. Of the six presidents examined in this study, from Eisenhower to Carter, only Lyndon Johnson displayed a consistently large correlation between popularity and victory in roll-call votes. Yet even LBJ experienced a negative correlation in the case of Republican members of the lower house; the more popular he was, the less support he could expect from the House opposition. At the time of this writing, Reagan's legislative box score has declined to one of the lowest levels since Eisenhower's administration—while his standing with the public remains exceptionally high (Hook 1986).

Naturally, several factors might work to minimize the connection between popularity and legislative influence. Bond and Fleisher (1984) pointed out, as an example, that the constituencies behind the legislators are far more specific than the national constituency supposedly represented by the president and tapped by the opinion surveys. Because senators must seek reelection from their states' citizens and House members must seek reelection from constituents in even more narrow congressional districts, the incentives may just not be there to go along with the president's wishes on most bills. Even when the chief executive has correctly identified a legislative solution to a national problem, what is good for the nation as a whole may not be so beneficial for particular states or districts. This conflict between national and local interests probably is one reason that the president's support in Congress is not uniform among its members, even within his own party. In the Senate, for instance, floor leaders and whips exhibit higher levels of support for the president than the rank and file in the same party (Hayes et al. 1984). We might say that these legislative leaders have two constituencies, one at home and another in the party organization over which the executive putatively presides. The rank-and-file members have less cause for sacrificing the interests of home constituencies for the sake of party, and presidential, loyalty.

Rivers and Rose (1985) point to another complication. Some presidents choose to send large legislative packages to Capitol Hill, whereas others are far less ambitious in the programs they request to be made into law. By the nature of things, those who submit bigger programs will experience lower success rates than those with lower aspirations. Yet the bolder presidents may get a larger number of bills through Congress despite a lower overall batting average. When Rivers and Rose held the size of the president's legislative program constant, a one percent increase in presidential popularity increased the president's legislative approval rate by about one percent. Complicating matters further, the size of the program put forward by the incumbent for congressional consideration is partly a function of how successful the president was in the previous legislative year. If Congress shoots down a large percentage of proposals, the president scales down his legislative plans, whereas an exceptional ratio of wins to losses emboldens the president to launch a program of greater scope in the following year. By reducing his legislative expectations, the president will be rewarded with a higher percentage of victories, which then may encourage him once again to be more vociferous in his legislative recommendations. A feedback loop thus links program size and success rate.

The insecure relation between a president's popularity and his effect on legislation is one of the few to withstand scientific tests. As critical as the legislative criterion may be, we are still a long distance from obtaining a full list of well-established antecedents. A prime obstacle in isolating predictors is probably the difficulty in defining what precisely is to be predicted in the first place (Edwards 1985). It is easy to announce our broad intentions—to determine the president's success in getting his programs through Congress—but most definitions of this fundamental concept are too glib. A president may lend his support to a bill that would have passed without his endorsement, for example. Indeed, it may behoove the president to do so in order to get credit where credit is not due. Even when a bill was actually introduced into Congress by the president it is often nearly impossible to accurately gauge his success. Usually legislative committees add their amendments and modifications, further alterations are made on the Senate or House floor, and additional changes may materialize when the Senate-House conference committee irons out any discrepancies in the two versions of the bill. How much can an administration bill be watered down before it ceases to represent a victory for the president? In an appropriation bill, what percentage change from the president's initial request still counts as an executive win? Solutions to these puzzles are not made easier when a president behaves as a shrewd negotiator and publicly fights for more than he wants to nudge the final compromise closer to what he privately seeks.

Additional complexities in this measurement issue are revealed in a paper by Hammond and Fraser (1984). These investigators sought a base line for weighing the president's performance in House and Senate roll calls. They defined that base line in terms of what could be expected according to chance alone (see Hammond and Fraser 1983). Just by luck, the president will get some hits and some misses. A true presidential lawmaker is one who consistently beats the odds. This definition does not immediately settle the question, for Hammond and Fraser were able to derive three different models for a chance base line with which to compare presidents. Though the derivation of each is somewhat involved, model 1 essentially posits that each member of Congress in effect decides to vote for or against a bill by flipping a coin; model 2 inserts the stipulation that these coin-tossers are split into two party factions, one represented by the sitting president; model 3 permits the existence of loose coalitions that can cut across nominal party divisions. Applications of these distinct base lines to recent presidents do not yield the same outcomes, so these inconsistencies prove how vulnerable any evaluation of presidential legislative performance is. Only model 1 implies that practically all presidents do better than expectation. Still, an approximately stable ranking emerges from all three models, which Hammond and Fraser maintain should oblige some revisions in the accepted wisdom about the adequacy of certain past presidents as legislators. In particular, the authors show that when tested against a reasonable comparative base line, Eisenhower, Kennedy, Nixon, and Carter frequently outperform expectation, thus belying their historical reputations. On the other side, Lyndon Johnson may have a somewhat exaggerated image as a phenomenal legislator. While his success in the House is noteworthy, his effectiveness in the Senate is much less admirable. According to all three models Carter's effectiveness in the Senate throughout his four years ranks above Johnson's in the Senate of the Ninetieth Congress.

In a footnote, Hammond and Fraser mention a valuable fact: when the presidency and Congress are controlled by the same party, the chief executive's success rates exceed the chance base line (under model 2), whereas when these two branches are controlled by different parties, the president's legislative effectiveness falls far below expectations. Although the correlation was not given, it is easy to calculate the phi coefficient from the published table, and it amounts to an impressive .50. That means that around a quarter of the variation in a president's effectiveness can be explained by whether his party dominates the two chambers. Expressed in more concrete terms, Rivers and Rose (1985) have calculated that if the representation of the president's party in Congress grows by one percent, his approval rate will expand by two percent. The magnitude of this effect surpasses that of the presidential popularity factor and thus goes a long way toward explaining why it is so hard to locate individual attributes that predict who will become a master lawmaker in the White House. Much hinges on whether a president can command a party majority in both houses. This situational factor will reappear in the forthcoming discussion of the presidential veto.

Presidential Vetoes. Even though the word *veto* is not even mentioned in the Constitution, the president's power to send bills back to Congress is explicitly granted. Yet early presidents were somewhat slow to exploit this gift. In the early phases of the office the veto was felt to be justified only when an act appeared to be unconstitutional. Andrew Jackson firmly established the prerogative of rejecting legislation that, though falling within constitutional restrictions, went against the grain of executive philosophy or ideology. By the twentieth century the executive veto had become a potent tool for shaping legislation. The mere threat of its use could persuade an unruly Congress to alter bills to more closely conform to presidential policy. FDR was very aware of this asset, even to the point of asking his advisers for a bill to veto in order to keep Congress mindful of his power. The veto power can also be a valuable indicator of the relationship between the executive and legislative branches. When the two are in a cooperative, even collaborative, mood, the veto is seldom seen. Yet when the mood sours, not only will the presidential veto be used against one bill after another, but, the two houses may retort with a two-thirds override. Though Washington was the first president to exploit the veto power, Madison was the first who saw a congressional override attempt, and Tyler was the first to see one of his vetoes canceled by Congress. In just four years Pierce exceeded all of his predecessors in the use of the veto; over half of the bills he vetoed were made law anyway by a two-thirds majority in both houses. Andrew Johnson's working relationship was even worse, for he vetoed over twice as many bills as Pierce and 71 percent of his regular vetoes were overturned. Thus one criterion of presidential success is whether matters deteriorate so much that a fight breaks out between president and Congress, the former armed with the veto, the latter with the power to override.

The most direct approach to investigating a president's propensity to veto bills is to examine how presidents differ in the frequency with which they use that power. Yet the most obvious way is not always the best way. One problem is that veto activity is largely dependent on how long a president serves in office; the correlation between tenure duration and total vetoes is around .62 (Simonton 1981c). Franklin Roosevelt vetoed 635 bills, a record, but he also served over a dozen years, another record. Therefore, a better line of attack is to scrutinize the president's veto behavior per unit of opportunity to employ the veto, such as per unit of time. Jong Lee (1975) introduced just such a refinement in a study of this phenomenon from Washington through Nixon. He first looked at the extent to which the tendency of the Congress to override vetoes depends on the proportion of public bills that a president vetoes. This examination yielded a useful fourfold typology of president-Congress interactions. First, there are administrations that display a cooperative pattern in which the veto is rarely used and, when used, normally sustained in Congress. Polk and McKinley with their corresponding Congresses epitomize this group. Second, there are those presidents who veto an unusual percentage of public bills only to witness an exceptional proportion of these vetoes overridden. Classic instances of this pattern of conflict are Pierce during the Thirty-fourth Congress and Andrew Johnson during the Fortieth. The third pattern, typified by Arthur in the Forty-seventh Congress and Nixon in the Ninety-first, is one of congressional authority: the chief executive seldom vetoes legislation, yet when he does the odds are very high that he will be overridden. The fourth pattern is that of presidential authority, the pattern perhaps most indicative of presidential success. Exemplified by Cleveland in the Forty-ninth, Fiftieth, and Fifty-third Congresses and by F. D. Roosevelt in the Seventy-fourth and Seventy-sixth Congresses, these chief executives veto a large proportion of bills and yet manage to keep the proportion of overturned vetoes low. Such presidents are shrewd legislators who know how to hold Congress in line without giving it many opportunities to retaliate. As Lee indicates, those presidents who have a low rate of overridden vetoes are likely to be successful in other significant domains as well: they are less likely to have a cabinet nominee rejected by the Senate and they are likely to have a higher success rate for bills they advocate before Congress.

The discussion of this typology suggests that a president's veto behavior may very much depend on the Congress he faces. The thrust of Lee's inquiry was, in fact, to determine the factors that may affect veto activity from Congress to Congress. In particular, by using a multivariate time-series analysis, with the Congress as the analytical unit, Lee was able to isolate the predictors of both the presidential propensity to veto bills and the congressional propensity to override those vetoes. Concerning the former criterion, four items allow us to anticipate who will become a "veto president." To begin with, presidents who serve when Congress is controlled by the opposition party will probably react with an abundance of vetoes, for a great number of bills placed before him will certainly reflect a contrary political ideology. Wilson is a case in point. Starting his presidential career in the cooperative mode with a Democratically controlled Congress, Wilson ended his tenure in a confrontational style when the Republicans captured control of both houses in the Sixty-sixth Congress. Another factor is whether the president received a mandate from the people in the general election. The larger his share of the electoral vote, the greater his willingness to use the veto power. Evidently, such a chief executive believes that the voters are behind him in any attempt to make an impression on legislation. A president lacking such a mandate, especially a minority president, will experience more pressure to recognize congressional authority. The third and fourth predictors of veto propensity have to do with attributes of the president that exist prior to his election. Democratic presidents are more inclined, on the average, to use the veto than are presidents of other persuasions. Fourth, and most interesting, the longer a president had himself served in Congress as a senator or representative the less disposed he is to rely on the veto power. Chief executives with ample legislative experience probably have learned ways to achieve policy goals that are more gentle than overt obstructionism.

On the opposite side of the coin is the congressional propensity to override vetoes, and here Lee (1975) identified five predictors. As described in the preceding list, Congresses controlled by the opposition party are more likely to overturn a president's vetoes. The larger a president's share of the electoral vote in the previous election, the more likely Congress is to override him. In addition, Congresses are less inclined to accept a veto after the midterm election. This loss in congressional support is over and above any loss the president's party may suffer in the midterm elections. Thus, this decline may have more to do with the popularity drops discussed in chapter 3. The final two predictors pertain to the state of the nation. If the country is plagued by economic instability, as gauged by the wholesale price index, then the president will probably see many vetoes overturned, whereas economic equilibrium brings with it more respect for the president's legislative desires. Military crisis, at least as assessed by the per capita size of the armed forces, may inhibit Congress from taking strong countermeasures against a presidential veto. Once more, these last two factors should remind us of the effects of the economy and international crises on the president's approval ratings in the polls. A legislator's decision to sustain or overturn a veto is perhaps governed by the same considerations that affect a survey respondent's decision to approve or disapprove of the incumbent's performance. In both instances political context may prove more crucial than presidential leadership per se.

Almost a decade after Lee's (1975) study came a follow-up investigation by Gary Copeland (1983). Even though Copeland added numerous improvements, including the use of the year as the analytical unit (compare Ringelstein 1985; Rohde and Simon 1985), for the most part his work corroborates that of Lee. Opposition control of Congress and a presidential electoral mandate persist as key predictors of both presidential vetoes and congressional overrides. But Copeland offers several corrections and qualifications to Lee's conclusions. In the first place, there is empirical reason to believe that presidential reliance on the veto may be partly curtailed by congressional overrides. Thus, just as a president may send bills back in order to train Congress how to behave, so may Congress send those returned bills right back with an overwhelming endorsement in order to teach the president a lesson. The veto and override are but means in a larger power struggle between two branches of the federal government. A second point made by Copeland is that Lee may have been premature to blame Democratic presidents for excessive use of the veto power. Copeland demonstrated that virtually all of that supposed proclivity can be ascribed to the veto mania of FDR and Cleveland. If these two presidents are left out of consideration, Democratic chief executives do not veto bills significantly more than Republicans. Indeed, in the period from Eisenhower to Reagan the Republicans have surpassed the Democrats, a difference attributable to the larger congressional majorities usually enjoyed by the latter (Ringelstein 1985). Moreover, not only are Democratic and Republican presidents roughly equal in veto propensity, but all presidents regardless of party appear to have about the same motives for vetoing legislation (Ringelstein 1985).

A recent study by Rohde and Simon (1985) focused on the presidents since World War II, introducing additional variables and obtaining more or less compatible results, not merely for vetoes and actual overrides but for unsuccessful congressional attempts to overturn a veto as well. For example, the proportion of seats in Congress claimed by the president's party is negatively associated with veto use and attempted overrides. Among the new variables were several that featured interesting relationships with one or more of the three touchstones of executive-legislative conflict. The higher the incumbent's standing in recent Gallup polls, the less he used the veto power, and the less likely Congress was to attempt to overturn a veto. Congressional willingness to attempt and accomplish veto overrides increased when the legislation represented a bipartisan effort, which denied the president full access to the loyalty of his own party members on Capitol Hill. The nature of the legislation had consequences, too, for Congress was more likely to let a veto stand unchallenged if the bill concerned the management of government (considered to be in the presidential sphere of responsibility) and more likely to attempt an override if the bill involved a social welfare or economic program (considered to be in the congressional sphere of responsibility). As the administration passed from year to year, moreover, the working relationship between the two branches of government tended to deteriorate: the president became more disposed to use the veto after the midterm elections, while Congress became more inclined to overturn vetoes.

Perhaps the most interesting finding in Rohde and Simon's investigation, however, was the interaction effect between the economic context and the political situation in Washington; the president was obliged to expand his use of the veto whenever the state of the economy was a major issue with the public and Congress was dominated by the opposition party. Here the chief executive had to counter legislative solutions to current economic ills that failed to comply with administration policy guidelines.

In all empirical studies of presidential vetoes, a respectable amount of variance is explained in the criterion variable, usually around half. However, one factor overlooked in all of the preceding three studies is vice-presidential succession. Accidental presidents suffer a greater likelihood of having their vetoes overturned by Congress (Simonton 1981c, 1985b). As accidental presidents from Tyler to Ford can testify, other burdens are theirs as well. Not only are they less likely to be renominated, as noted in chapter 2, but their nominees to high office are less likely to be approved by the senate.

Appointments

In addition to being instrumental in making new laws, the president must administer the laws of the land. Administration entails far more responsibilities than have been treated in empirical research. I am consequently compelled to concentrate on one particular power of the president that is germane to successful administration, namely, his power of appointment. The chief executive is expected to make sound appointments (see Kinder et al. 1980); this is, therefore, a reasonable criterion of leader success. To be sure, the president appoints a great many subsidiary officers, even if matters are not as bad as in the pre-civil service days when some presidents were practically hounded to death by hordes of office seekers. But of all these varied appointments, two kinds probably stand out: nominees for cabinet posts and nominees to the Supreme Court. These two categories of appointments differ substantially. The cabinet appointees work closely with the president in the design of government policy, and most are tied to his administration, the retention of Washington's cabinet by John Adams marking an exceptional decision for an elected successor. The Supreme Court appointees do not even belong to the executive branch, and the appointees may serve on the bench for several administrations, obliging some later presidents to live with the ideological commitments (or poor judgments) of earlier administrations. Despite this strong contrast, both types of appointments deserve discussion as two significant ways in which the president can affect domestic policies.

The Cabinet. Some presidents have been very fortunate in their cabinet selections. All of their appointees were approved by the Senate, and most served out the president's tenure, none resigning due to policy conflicts or obscure "personal reasons." Polk is a perfect example: all seven of his appointees were approved, and not one was replaced during Polk's four-year administration. Having one's appointees approved, of course, allows the president the most freedom to carry out his programs. A high cabinet turnover can interfere with executive efficiency and can make the president more vulnerable to influences from the legislative branch. But some presidents were far less lucky. They suffered a good many more cabinet resignations and may even have had to endure the rare rebuff of seeing a nominee rejected by the Senate. Though there were only six cabinet positions in Tyler's administration, he received nine resignations, and four of his nominees were denied Senate confirmation. An incumbent can also be rated according to the quality of those who serve in his cabinet. Why do some chief executives appoint more effective cabinet officials than others?

One possible cause of presidential success by the above criteria may be the incumbent's own personality, especially his motivational needs. In the case of high cabinet turnover, for example, certain presidents may drive cabinet officers away by being too demanding. Winter and Stewart (1977) related the power, achievement, and affiliation needs of twelve presidents from T. Roosevelt through Nixon to the rate of cabinet change in each president's administration. Those chief executives with the most exceptional need to achieve tended to experience more frequent turnover in cabinet officers ($r = .59$). Even more interesting, perhaps, is the finding that the power, achievement, and affiliation motives of a president may affect whom he chooses to associate with him in the cabinet. The need for power proves to be the most influential factor. Those presidents highly motivated in this regard seek out cabinet officers who are very different in age and family life (number of children), who are more likely to be lawyers, and who have previous experience in national and state legislatures. For the most part, these predilections suggest that the power-hungry chief executive wants cabinet members who will reinforce his quest for power—lawyers and experienced legislators being quite useful here—but does not care whether his appointees are similar to him in more personal characteristics. A strong achievement motivation in a president similarly inspires the selection of cabinet members who are different in age, but causes him to shy away from potential officers with legislative experience, whether federal or state. Yet the most provocative pattern may be for presidents with intense affiliation requirements. These executives, in contrast to those less sociable and approval-seeking, tend to avoid both lawyers and persons much older or much younger in age. Their apparent desire to surround themselves with contemporaries may work against the appointment of lawyers, either because legal expertise is not a criterion for nomination or because lawyers do not make quite as good chums as nonlawyers.

Whatever the interpretation, Winter and Stewart show that

those presidents who are more obsessed with satisfying basic affiliation needs than with placing experts in high executive office may have to pay a high price. High-affiliation chief executives are more likely to have scandal-ridden administrations in which a cabinet (or White House staff) member is indicted or obliged to resign for misconduct in office ($r = .68$). The classic case is Warren Harding, who placed too many old buddies in the executive branch, resulting in one of the most scandalous administrations in U.S. history. Harding himself once complained, shortly before the notorious Teapot Dome scandal began to leak out, that he could manage his enemies but not "my Goddamned friends." We might speculate that Ronald Reagan, another extroverted president with a distinct preference for placing loyalty above competence in his appointments, may further illustrate this danger (see Simonton 1986e).

Though individual factors have thus been found to predict certain aspects of cabinet appointments, a situational factor is relevant too (Simonton 1981c). Those presidents who succeed to the presidency directly through the vice-presidency have genuinely ill luck. In the first place, they have to face a great many more cabinet resignations ($\beta = .45$), perhaps an expected consequence given that the vice president turned president has to set his own policy priorities. The first vice president to so move into the White House, Tyler, actually saw every cabinet officer but one resign at once when Tyler vetoed a bill that his predecessor would have signed. More striking is how the Senate handles the cabinet appointees of the accidental president: the nominees have higher chances of being turned down ($\beta = .30$). A couple of reasons may be offered for this ugly state of affairs. First, if vice presidents are not always selected with the same high standards in mind as are presidents, they may actually do an inferior job of picking candidates. Second, because the president is seen as accidental, he may be perceived as not fully legitimate. After all, senators have been elected to office, whereas no one really elected a vice president to the presidency. It is of interest to note that Tyler had to insist doggedly that he was a full-fledged President of the United States, not a mere acting president, as the legislators on Capitol Hill were inclined to assume. Tyler was even nicknamed "His Accidency."

A more detailed analysis of this vice-presidential succession effect endorses the second explanation (Simonton 1985b). As I indicated in chapter 2, there is no evidence whatsoever that vice presidents in general differ from presidents in political experience and germane biographical traits. Accidental presidents who are reelected to office are not even different from those who fail to be reelected. Furthermore, accidental presidents who are elected to serve a second, full term in their own right are far less likely to have their nominees rejected by the Senate during their second term. An accidental president in such circumstances has received the certification lacking during his prior, unelected term in office. With the mandate of the people behind him, his appointees can receive more respect from senators. An elected president can no longer be viewed as inferior in legitimate power.

Once more, empirical research has only begun to broach this important topic. Even so, two conclusions can be put forward now, however tentatively. First, the personality of a president, especially his motivational preoccupations, may determine both how well he is able to retain his cabinet officers and what kind of officers he decides to work with. Second, situational factors, in particular having assumed power via vice-presidential succession, affect a president's ability to get his choice approved by the Senate—an effect possibly mediated by the perceived legitimacy of the person who holds the office.

The Supreme Court. Those presidents who succeed to office through the vice-presidency tend to see not only their cabinet nominees rejected by the Senate, but their Supreme Court nominees as well ($\beta = .29$) (Simonton 1981c; see also Simonton 1985b). The most striking example is Andrew Johnson. Not only did the Senate reject his appointee to the bench, but Congress voted to decrease the number of justices so that he would have no vacancies to fill during the rest of his term (the Court was brought back to its present size in the very first year of the succeeding administration, that of Grant). Hence, accidental presidents appear to be generally unsuccessful in their dealings with Congress. The Senate fails to confirm their major nominees and the Congress as a whole is more disposed toward overturning their vetoes. The relationship between the inadvertent president and the legislative branch appears to be broadly antagonistic.

Aside from the poor success of this special class of presidents, the ability to appoint Supreme Court justices often seems more a matter of accident than of design. The main correlate of how many Supreme Court justices a president appoints is how long the president's administration lasts ($r = .57$); administration duration is an even better predictor of how many nominees actually serve on the bench ($r = .69$) (Simonton 1981c). Supreme Court nominations, unlike cabinet nominations, must await the death or resignation of a previous appointee (except in those rare times when the size of the Court has been modified). As Franklin D. Roosevelt painfully learned when he attempted to stack the Supreme Court so that it would be kinder to New Deal legislation, the president cannot simply install sympathetic justices on the bench. Rather, he must wait for a current justice to leave a vacancy. This lack of control must be remembered in evaluating the success or failure of a presidency, because presidents can be unfairly assessed on the basis of their Supreme Court placements. A case in point is Carter—the only president in U.S. history who served four years without making a single appointment to the Supreme Court.

A mathematical analysis of Court vacancies from 1790 to 1980 supports this explanation (Ulmer 1982). The frequency of vacancies per unit time is adequately described by a probability model that often applies to relatively rare events, the Poisson process (see Simonton 1979). The Poisson distribution fits the observed distribution almost perfectly. Given the predictive precision of this model, it can be employed to estimate the odds that a president might serve four full years without obtaining a single vacancy to fill. The probability is .13, or better than one out of ten. Given that Carter was the thirty-eighth president, his experience really was not very unlikely after all. Indeed, in a sense it has happened before: FDR's desire to add more justices to the Court was no doubt spurred by the fact that he was unable to make any appointments during his first term. Had he not been reelected he would have been in the same boat as Carter.

The foregoing remarks should not lead us astray: the emergence of opportunities to make personnel changes in the Court is not utterly arbitrary. Justices who must wisely deliberate the constitutionality of federal, state, and local laws would presumably not remain on the bench without some weighty consideration. Each justice has a choice to confront each year. The justice may choose to stay on the bench, but in doing so risk removal by death or disability. On the other hand, the justice may decide that the time has come either to resign or to retire. Thus, justices who die in office may be said to be those who had not yet found any sound reason to opt for voluntary retirement. The task then becomes to determine what criteria enter the judgments of the justices in deciding whether the time is right to step down.

One recent inquiry scrutinized the more obvious possibilities, including characteristics of the justice (age, years on the bench, whether chief or associate justice) and attributes of the incumbent president (experience in national politics, legal experience, judicial experience), but isolated just two political context variables as the only significant contributors to the decision (Simonton 1986f). First, a Supreme Court justice was more likely to resign if he was in office after passage of the 1937 Supreme Court Retirement Act. This act made it possible for a justice to retire from the bench at full pay for life, the only stipulation being that the justice be seventy or older. Prior to this act, justices tended to persist until removed by death or disability; after the act, many justices took advantage of its generous provisions. Second, a justice was more likely to step down if the incumbent president had the same party affiliation as the president who originally had appointed the justice to the bench. Thus to some extent those who sit on the bench play partisan politics when they contemplate resignation. By manipulating the timing of retirement, a justice improves the odds that his successor will be like-minded on the principal legal controversies of the day. So Republican appointees stick it out until there is a Republican incumbent, and Democratic appointees do the same, with the peculiar consequence that when a justice does die or become disabled it is likely that the current chief executive is of the contrary political persuasion.

It is worth pointing out that these two determinants help explain the Carter phenomenon. Carter was the first president to serve exactly four years since the 1937 law was passed, and he was the first in history to do so when the majority of the Court justices had been appointed by presidents of the opposing party. Jimmy Carter was more or less the victim of bad timing.

The 1937 Retirement Act was passed as an alternative to F. D. Roosevelt's highly unpopular and politically unwise court-packing scheme. FDR had seen much of his innovative New Deal legislation ruled unconstitutional by a Court of aged Republican appointees. And he believed that the ripe ages of the justices were partly responsible for producing a Court that was markedly behind the times. FDR's plan, therefore, was to dilute the anachronistic and antagonistic Court majority with an infusion of young minds more aware of current trends. To be sure, the staunch conservatism of Roosevelt's judicial nemesis could have had two causes: either the justices represented a cohort from a bygone era that was defending old legal philosophies, or the justices had actually gotten more conservative with age. One comprehensive inquiry suggests that the second alternative is in fact correct, that aging in itself makes a Supreme Court justice more conservative in legal opinion (Schubert 1983; compare Tetlock, Bernzweig, and Gallant 1985). Consequently, the 1937 Retirement Act may be said to have arrested any trend toward increased conservatism as life expectancies increased. More important, the act may have made the Supreme Court more responsive to the president by providing incentives to resign at the most propitious moment. And presidents less often must confront justices put on the bench many administrations earlier, by predecessors who are no longer alive to view the repercussions of their selections. In FDR's case, Justice Van Devanter, a 1910 appointee of Taft and an inveterate New Deal foe, was seventy-eight when he became the first to take advantage of the act's liberal terms.

GENERAL STYLE

Up to this point we have been judging administrative performance by more or less specific criteria, usually particular acts in the domains of foreign and domestic policy. We have examined, for example, how dominance, power motivation, and integrative complexity may contribute to a president's willingness to employ force to settle problems in international affairs (see also Walker and Falkowski 1984). Yet we can attack the problem from the opposite direction, too. Rather than scrutinize specific performance criteria and ask what variables permit their prediction, we can examine how presidents might vary on certain very broad characteristics and then inquire into the performance consequences. This perspective is especially likely to unearth individual-difference variables of general application, unlike the strategy thus far employed, which tends to stress situational predictors. In any case, it is evident that performance in the White House involves more than discrete behaviors; it involves as well a general approach to the presidency, a distinctive style. Presidents' personalities have some impact on our appraisals of their administrations. For some presidents, indeed, style becomes virtually everything. Calvin Coolidge, though low in both power and achievement motivations, managed to capture the imagination of the American public in a manner quite unlike William Howard Taft, a president somewhat similar to him in personality. Anecdotes proliferated about the laconic "Silent Cal," and the American people looked fondly on his Yankee eccentricities. That he virtually slept through six years in the White House like Rip Van Winkle (and was seen by many as equally behind the times) evidently meant little to the public.

I begin by surveying some of the measurement approaches by which presidential character can be assessed. My purpose here is to present something of the range of methodologies available for tapping individual variables, techniques that may expand our empirical understanding of the personal basis of presidential success. I close by discussing at length the particular attribute of presidential dogmatism. I trace both the antecedent conditions and the performance consequences of this personality trait and demonstrate how this individual variable interacts with situational variables that describe the political context in which presidential leadership must be exercised.

Measurement Approaches

All of us tend to feel quite free to judge the personality attributes of other people, and we evaluate the character of our presidents with hardly less confidence. These judgments are almost without exception subjective and qualitative in nature, and therefore subject to bias, whether positive or negative. Can we judge a president's character in a disinterested fashion when he has just raised (or lowered) our taxes? It is imperative that we use some sort of objective, preferably quantitative, assessment device. There are many possibilities, but I would like to outline five distinct empirical methodologies.

Factor Analysis and Personality Patterns. One approach is strictly empirical and sometimes quite haphazard. Research begins by collecting massive amounts of data on behaviors, attitudes, beliefs, and the like. The correlations among these numerous variables are then calculated. A factor analysis of the correlation matrix is executed with the purpose of revealing the distinctive dimensions that can provide the basis for a personality profile. This may sound terribly abstract, so I will offer a concrete illustration.

Wendt and Muncy (1979) wished to establish the personality dimensions of the twenty-four United States vice presidents from Wheeler (under Hayes) to Mondale (under Carter). A quarter of these vice presidents later became presidents; furthermore, this study detected some interesting differences between presidents and vice presidents. In any event, the investigators scored their sample of subjects on thirteen characteristics, and computed the correlation matrix. One of the characteristics was charisma, an item that was found to correlate with traits such as talkativeness ($r = .62$), campaigning and travel ($r = .52$), liking by others ($r = .46$), feeling useful ($r = .39$), and productivity ($r = .39$). The entire correlation matrix was subjected to a factor analysis which extracted three orthogonal factors. Factor 1, "activity-charisma," consisted of talkativeness, charisma, campaigning and travel, feeling of usefulness, and treatment by president. Factor 2, "likeability, nonthreat," consisted of liking by others, flexibility, age at marriage, absence of scandal or notoriety, and absence of presidential hopes. Factor 3, "shrewd persistence, complexity," consisted of shrewdness and cunning, persistence, productivity, and campaigning and travel.

Wendt and Muncy generated factor scores for the twenty-four vice presidents on these three dimensions in order to see how they related to other variables. For example, they showed that scores on the first factor correlated positively with order in sequence (r = .42), meaning that the more recent the vice president, the higher his activity-charisma rating. Modern vice presidents are not as inclined to be inconspicuous as their predecessors were. Factor 3 was found to help discriminate which vice presidents would later have presidential aspirations. The five vice presidents who scored highest on "shrewd persistence, complexity" (T. Roosevelt, Coolidge, Truman, Nixon, and L. B. Johnson) were all independently elected to the presidency, and the five next highest (Arthur, Marshall, Barkley, Humphrey, and Rockefeller) were at one time serious contenders.

The Wendt and Muncy study amply illustrates both the vices and the virtues of a factor analytic approach. As an exploratory technique, it is excellent, and unearths many fascinating potsherds. At the same time, the approach is often too scattershot, and an uninterpretable mess is frequently left behind. Some of the thirteen characteristics are included more because they are measurable than because they have any theoretical significance (such as age at marriage). This fault is not peculiar to Wendt and Muncy; many of the pioneer developers of factor analysis could not resist factor analyzing every fact they could muster (for example, Cattell and Adelson 1951). Still, as long as factor analytic studies of presidential style are read with appropriate reservations, they can serve the valuable function of opening areas of research.

Guttman Scaling and Charisma. The trait of charisma is often thought to be of great usefulness to a president. John F. Kennedy was supposedly a charismatic leader, as was Franklin D. Roosevelt. Presidential candidates who otherwise display much promise have fallen by the wayside for lack of this quality. In the 1984 election his lack of even the slightest charisma was considered one of the worst handicaps of the Democratic candidate, Walter Mondale. But what precisely do we mean when we claim that a leader is charismatic? Most definitions skirt the issue by substituting an approximate synonym that is no more precise (see Willner 1984). What help is it, for instance, to say that a charismatic leader is one who displays extraordinary dynamism and magnetism? Do those additional terms really clarify our meaning? I do not believe so, and therefore I welcome those researchers who have struggled to make this term more exact and objective. Charles Cell (1974) is a case in point. His sample consisted of thirty-four heads of state, twenty-nine of whom were selected for their well-known charismatic powers, the other five a control group of far more bland leaders. Although only two of the leaders—F. D. Roosevelt and Kennedy—were American chief executives, Cell's study can still be instructive.

Cell defined eleven separate indicators of charisma, indicators that assessed whether or not a leader possessed a certain characteristic deemed connected with charismatic leadership. These indicators were then subjected to a Guttman scalogram analysis to determine if the indicators form a series of stepwise measures. In such a scale, the attribute lowest on the scale is that which even the least charismatic leaders possess, the attribute highest on the scale that which only the most charismatic leaders possess. The items did indeed constitute a decent Guttman scale (coefficient of scalability .73). The eleven items are listed in order, the number of leaders with the attribute given in parentheses: leader's picture posted in public or in homes (30); leader seen as uniting the country (29); leader's principles followed (27); people making sacrifices for leader (24); people asked to follow new paradigm (23); leader led country to military victory (16); leader's lack of interest in or understanding of economics (17); leader gives long speeches (15); statue of leader in capital during tenure (12); leader's reputation for sexual prowess (7); women making sacrifices for leader (4). Some leaders, like Hitler, had all eleven attributes present; others, like control group member Adenauer, had not one qualifying characteristic. The result is an 11-point scale that goes from 0 to 10. On this scale, FDR received a 6—bracketed by Castro at 7 and De Gaulle at 5—for having all the attributes except the last four most selective traits. JFK earned a 4—the same score as Jinnah, Nehru, Selassie, Cardenas, and Lenin—for exhibiting only the first five least selective traits.

Whether a reader agrees or disagrees with these charisma ratings, Cell deserves credit for trying to remove the subjectivity that permeates attributes of charisma. With some modifications, a Guttman scale might be devised to scale the charisma of all the American presidents, or at least all those in the twentieth century. Once this is done, the connection between a charismatic style of leadership and objective administrative performance can be evaluated.

Discriminant Analysis and Biographical Types. The Goertzels, first in *Cradles of Eminence* (1962) and later *Three Hundred Eminent Personalities* (1978), have gathered tremendous amounts of biographical information on distinguished twentieth-century individuals from all parts of the globe. Virtually every variety of endeavor is represented, from political, military, revolutionary, and religious leaders to scientific, philosophical, literary, and artistic creators—over twenty fields in all. The Goertzels' purpose was to isolate those circumstances in the early life of a person that may contribute to that individual's later achievement of fame or infamy. What is the effect, whether beneficial or detrimental, of birth order, parents' behaviors, socioeconomic circumstances, education, and the like on subsequent distinction? A subsidiary goal was to discover if there were important differences in early developmental experiences that might account for the choice of profession. Do the backgrounds of politicians contrast with those of military figures? Are the childhoods of scientists quite different from those of poets? The Goertzels did not examine a related issue, namely, the extent to which any given eminent personality can be taken as biographically typical of other eminent persons in the same field. For instance, was Einstein's early development typical or atypical of that of other scientists? Which American presidents had biographical backgrounds typical of politicians, and which did not?

To explore this question, a discriminant analysis was applied to the 314 famous personalities in the Goertzels' 1978 inquiry (Simonton 1986a). This multivariate technique searched among the more than fifty biographical characteristics assessed by the Goertzels in order to identify those that could help us classify each member of the sample in the correct category. There were four presidents in the sample, nine one-time presidential hopefuls, and four miscellaneous American politicians. It is instructive to inspect the primary and secondary classifications for these seventeen individuals as shown in table 4.1.

The primary classification is that with the highest probability, the secondary, the second highest; these probabilities, which range from zero to one, are given in parentheses after the corresponding classification. Notice that the majority of these American politicians were in fact rightly grouped with the politicians of

Table 4.1 Biographical Types for Recent American Politicians

Politician	Classification	
	Primary	Secondary
Presidents		
Lyndon Johnson	poet (.41)	reformer (.24)
Gerald Ford	scientist (.50)	politician (.30)
Jimmy Carter	poet (.36)	politician (.24)
Ronald Reagan	politician (.43)	athlete (.15)
Presidential hopefuls		
Shirley Chisholm	nonfiction author (.49)	reformer (.30)
Hubert Humphrey	scientist (.44)	politician (.26)
Edward Kennedy	politician (.61)	revolutionary (.10)
Robert Kennedy	politician (.62)	revolutionary (.08)
Eugene McCarthy	politician (.48)	reformer (.17)
George McGovern	politician (.34)	poet (.22)
Edmund Muskie	politician (.38)	reformer (.36)
Norman Thomas	politician (.30)	scientist (.28)
George Wallace	politician (.48)	revolutionary (.26)
Other American politicians		
Spiro Agnew	politician (.54)	athlete (.09)
William Fulbright	politician (.39)	reformer (.28)
Estes Kefauver	politician (.51)	poet (.24)
Henry Cabot Lodge	politician (.34)	artist (.25)

Note: The probability of belonging to the corresponding category is given in parentheses.

all nationalities in the Goertzels' sample. Among those who had presidential aspirations, however, two were not granted primary classification as politicians by the discriminant function. Chisholm is grouped among the nonfiction authors, though she more appropriately received a secondary classification as a reformer. Humphrey was placed with the scientists, but with a correct secondary classification. Humphrey's biographical composition is very similar to that of another former vice president, one who succeeded to the presidency, namely, Ford. Curiously, just one of the four presidents obtained a primary assignment as a politician. Both Johnson and Carter were put with the poets, though Carter's secondary assignment was with the politicians, Johnson's with the reformers. Only Reagan's early biography urged classification as a politician, with a subsidiary classification as an athlete. Reagan evinces a configuration of biographical experiences that most closely approximates that of Agnew, a former vice president.

These results summarize some of the similarities and contrasts among some notable and recent American politicians. The quantitative comparisons regard differences in biographical background attributes, yet we might speculate that these early experiences can translate into distinctive styles of leadership in the White House (Simonton 1986a). Was the approach of the two Democratic chief executives in the list more "poetic" than normal because of their greater biographical affinity with twentieth-century poets? And how much effect does the secondary classification have on the general leadership style of a president? Reagan's early life is more indicative of his becoming a politician than an actor, so in a sense he found his most appropriate activity when he become governor of California and then president of the United States. It may be of significance, too, that Reagan has an affinity with athletes. Besides his past activities as a radio sportscaster and as an actor who had a famous role as a football player, this subsidiary classification may show in the manner in which Reagan tackled his duties as chief executive. Of course, at this point this possibility cannot be proven. Even so, the outcome in table 4.1 illustrates some of the potential of applying discriminant analysis to biographical data. It may be feasible eventually to predict the leadership style that a candidate carries into the presidency.

Content Analysis and Personality. On several occasions we have seen how content analysis has been successfully applied to speeches, policy statements, and other written documents in order to assess the president on some dimension. This technique has frequently been used to scrutinize presidential inaugural addresses with the aim of discovering some of the personality differences among those who have entered the White House. For example, Evered (1983) performed a complex linguistic analysis of "modals" in the speeches of thirteen presidents from F. D. Roosevelt to Reagan in order to determine their attitudes toward the future. Truman, Reagan, and Johnson were found to be the most future-oriented presidents, Eisenhower the least. Addresses have also been content analyzed to gauge interpersonal dispositions, such as familiarity (Miller and Stiles 1986), as well as presidential values, such as the relative importance of freedom and equality (for example, Mahoney, Coogle, and Banks 1984). Yet the classic applications of content analysis to inaugural speeches all concern the presidents' motives, and all these studies were executed by David Winter and his colleagues. The first investigation of this kind was done by Donley and Winter (1970) for twentieth-century American presidents. The outcome was a measure of how these dozen chief executives varied in power and achievement motivations. As noted earlier, Winter (1973) later used these scores to show that power-driven presidents are more militaristic as well. Winter found, too, that chief executives who are high in power needs are more likely to be targets of assassination attempts ($r = .74$), a finding replicated ($r = .70$) on a larger sample of presidents examined by Wendt and Light (1976) (see also Simonton 1986e). The last two researchers have also indicated that a strong power motivation is conducive to effective press relations ($r = .62$). Finally, Winter and Stewart (1977) studied how the motivations displayed in inaugural addresses relate to the active-passive and positive-negative dimensions of Barber's (1977) influential theory of presidential character. Chief executives who are high in power drive tend to be active-positives who love being president and demonstrate that joy through a busy involvement in the responsibilities of the office. In contrast, an unusually high achievement orientation is linked with being an active-negative president whose excessive activity is devoid of true intrinsic pleasure, for it is driven by an obsession with duty and a puritanical, almost masochistic, commitment to hard work as a purgative of the soul. Winter and Stewart also looked at a third motivation, the need for affiliation. Affiliative presidents are more likely to be passive rather than active, but they compensate by exhibiting more flexibility (as measured by Maranell 1970). Such a president, in distinction from his power- or achievement-motivated colleagues, is more desirous of getting along with others than with getting a job done, an inclination in keeping with his higher likelihood of having a scandal corrupt his administration.

All in all, these content analytical studies of motives have sketched some details on the broad picture of the strong, activist president. Table 4.2 illustrates the value of this sketch. Here the original scores calculated by Winter and Stewart (1977) for the presidents from T. Roosevelt to Ford have been standardized, a

Table 4.2 Standardized Scores for 13 Presidents on Three Motivational Dispositions according to Content Analysis of Inaugural Addresses

President	Achievement	Power	Affiliation
T. Roosevelt	0.81	1.46	−0.45
Taft	−1.40	−1.59	−0.95
Wilson	−0.53	0.07	−0.77
Harding	−0.84	−0.76	−0.17
Coolidge	−1.08	−1.03	−0.68
Hoover	−0.09	−1.07	−0.46
F. D. Roosevelt	0.42	0.52	−0.82
Truman	−0.08	1.01	0.14
Eisenhower	−0.59	−0.57	0.45
Kennedy	1.07	1.50	0.75
Johnson	1.37	0.78	−0.45
Nixon	1.75	−0.04	0.70
Ford	−0.79	−0.25	2.73

Source: Standardized scores were calculated from scores in table 2.3 of Winter and Stewart (1977, 53).

transformation that permits more direct comparisons. As observed earlier in this chapter, Nixon had the highest need to achieve, Kennedy the highest need for power. Ford's score on the need for affiliation is exceptionally high. On the other side, Taft has the lowest scores on all three motivational dimensions.

There is one catch to all of this, nonetheless. Donley and Winter (1970) initiated their inquiry with the hope that by monitoring the values and motives incorporated into a president's inaugural addresses, it would be possible to predict the course of the new administration. Yet all sorts of problems plague this desired application, as Donley and Winter themselves confess. Inaugural speeches are often ghostwritten, for example, a practice that may have begun as early as George Washington's inauguration, with Madison as the hidden author. Accordingly, we have to assume that such writers are selected as ideological and psychological twins of the presidents for whom they labor. Even more important, once it becomes known that inaugural addresses are being monitored, it is easy to manipulate the content of the speech to project the desired image. In chapter 2 we saw that presidents do in fact seem to be engaged in impression management (see also Goggin 1984; Hart 1984). If a president is worried about being perceived as dangerously pugnacious—highly desirous of becoming a wartime commander-in-chief—what is to stop him from having all his speeches examined beforehand for power motivation and all offending passages extirpated? To the extent that this self-monitoring can be done, the value of content analysis as a predictive method is in jeopardy.

Standard Personality Measures. Personality researchers have devised an astronomical number of tests and inventories that assess all varieties of individual differences. Several investigators have attempted to apply or adapt these instruments to the study of historical figures (for example, Cox 1926; Hoffer 1978; Simonton 1983b, 1984d). This practice has from time to time been called historiometry (for example, Woods 1909, 1911) to distinguish it from cliometrics and psychohistory (see Simonton 1983c, 1984b). Catherine Cox (1926), for instance, tried to extend the conceptual approach of the standard IQ tests to obtain intelligence scores for

301 "geniuses," including eight early American presidents (see also Thorndike 1936; Woods 1906). On the basis of biographical information about early childhood achievements, coupled with the fundamental distinction between mental and chronological age, she obtained the following scores: Washington 140, J. Adams 175, Jefferson 160, Madison 160, J. Q. Adams 155, Jackson 145, Lincoln 150, and Grant 130. More recently, several researchers associated with the Institute of Personality Assessment and Research at the University of California at Berkeley founded what they called the Historical Figures Assessment Collaborative (HFAC 1977), a group dedicated to the use of established personality assessment methods in historical studies. For example, these collaborators have illustrated the utility of the California Q-sort (Block 1961). This consists of one hundred personal statements printed on a separate card, which are then sorted by the rater into nine categories from least to most characteristic of the person, with a specified number of cards per pile (to yield something approximating a normal distribution). The collaborative applied this technique to both Adolf Hitler and Woodrow Wilson, proving, in the process, both the utility and the reliability of the approach. The most characteristic Q-sort descriptions of Wilson included "Anxiety and tension find outlet in bodily symptoms," "Is moralistic," "Has high aspiration level for self," and "Is verbally fluent; can express ideas well." Among the least characteristic descriptions were "Regards self as physically attractive," "Has insight into own motives and behavior," and "Is subjectively unaware of self-concern; feels satisfied with self."

The collaborative went one step further and obtained Q-sort descriptions for five other American presidents, T. Roosevelt, Harding, F. D. Roosevelt, Eisenhower, and Kennedy. Correlation coefficients were calculated among the six presidential descriptions, producing fifteen correlations in all. These coefficients gauge the extent to which two presidents have similar personality structures. The two presidents who were the most alike were Kennedy and T. Roosevelt ($r = .66$), followed very closely by F. D. Roosevelt and Kennedy ($r = .63$) and by the two Roosevelts ($r = .58$)—clearly forming a cluster of what James Barber (1977) would label active-positive presidents. Other pairs of presidents are neither alike nor unalike, such as F. D. Roosevelt and Wilson ($r = .00$). And two presidents, Harding and Wilson, actually have personality descriptions ranked in slightly opposite directions ($r = -.13$), an appropriate finding given that Harding was elected in reaction to the excessively serious moralizing of the Wilson presidency. One final peculiarity is that Wilson's personality structure is the least like those of the other five presidents studied. The president who comes closest to him is his fellow progressive T. Roosevelt, the very person whose third-party Bull Moose campaign enabled Wilson to get elected by the narrowest of margins. The collaborative suggested that a cluster or factor analysis might reveal those subgroups of presidents who have like personality configurations. Such analyses would be especially valuable if we had Q-sort descriptions for all thirty-nine presidents, rather than for just six.

Besides the Q-sort, the collaborative explored the application of the Gough Adjective Check List (ACL) to historical figures (Gough and Heilbrun 1965). This measure consists of three hundred personality decriptors and thus has the potential of yielding fine-grained profiles. In addition, because a smaller eighty-one-adjective checklist has proven useful in assessing the public images of world leaders (see, for example, Merenda et al. 1971; Merenda, Shapurian, and Clarke 1974), and because the Gough ACL has proven useful in studying the personalities of contemporary politicians (see, for example, Costantini and Craik 1980), the potential utility of a three hundred-descriptor list for evaluating historical figures appears good. Although the collaborative's illustration concerned the psychiatrists Freud and Jung, this checklist has been adapted for assessments of the personalities of European monarchs (Simonton 1983b, 1984d; compare Thorndike 1936; Woods 1906). More recently, the ACL was specifically used to gauge the character contrasts of the thirty-nine presidents between Washington and Reagan (Simonton 1986e). Descriptions of presidential personality traits were extracted from several biographical sources (such as Armbruster 1982; Bailey 1980, 1981; Boller 1981; *Current Biography* 1940–1983; Whitney 1982) and transferred to index cards. All identifying material was removed and, to further assure the anonymity of the descriptions, the cards were placed in random order. A team of independent judges translated this abstracted information into evaluations on the ACL. Analysis of the final ratings revealed that the thirty-nine presidents could be dependably differentiated on 110 adjectives. A factor analysis collapsed these ratings into fourteen distinct personality dimensions:

1. moderation—moderate and modest versus temperamental and hasty
2. friendliness—friendly and outgoing versus unfriendly and cold
3. intellectual brilliance—having wide and artistic interests
4. Machiavellianism—sly and deceitful versus sincere and honest
5. poise and polish—poised and polished versus simple and informal
6. achievement drive—industrious and persistent
7. forcefulness—energetic and active
8. wit—humorous and witty
9. physical attractiveness—handsome and good-looking
10. pettiness—greedy and self-pitying
11. tidiness—methodical and organized
12. conservatism—conservative and conventional
13. inflexibility—stubborn and persistent
14. pacifism—peaceable versus courageous

Not only did scores on these dimensions display respectable internal-consistency reliability coefficients (with the exception of factor 10, between .70 and .98 with a mean of .87), but the scores also correlate in an expected way with alternative personality indicators. To offer a few examples: forcefulness correlates positively with Maranell's (1970) measures of activeness (.73) and strength (.62), whereas Machiavellianism correlates negatively (−.36) with the latter's gauge of idealism. Winter and Stewart's (1977) assessment of power motivation correlates positively with forcefulness (.80) but negatively with pacifism (−.87) and moderation (−.72), whereas their assessment of achievement motivation is associated with achievement drive (.77). Presidents Barber (1977) calls active are higher in forcefulness (.76) and lower in moderation (−.62), while those he styles positive are higher in friendliness (.61). Forcefulness correlates positively (.86) with Etheredge's (1978a) indicator of interpersonal dominance, while friendliness correlates positively (.64) with his indicator of extroversion. Using Thorndike's (1950) personality assessments for ten presidents, moderation correlates −.75 with general emotionality, friendliness correlates .74 with agreeableness; intellectual brilliance correlates .80 with intelligence; poise and polish correlate .64 with liking for art, music, and beauty; achievement drive correlates .90 with general activity and .72 with liking for responsibility; inflexibility correlates .76 with dominance and −.75 with agreeableness; and pacifism correlates −.69 with dominance and .65 with cooperativeness. Finally, intellectual brilliance correlates .70 with the IQ scores the presidents were given by Cox (1926). The personality profiles for the more recent presidents (Johnson through Reagan) accord equally well with their public images as recorded by activity vector analysis (see Gelineau and Merenda 1981; Merenda et al. 1971; Merenda, Shapurian, and Clarke 1974). The standardized scores are given in table 4.3, where a positive score indicates that the president is high on a trait, a negative score that he is low, and a score near zero that he is about average.

Proceeding through the factors, and concentrating solely on those presidents who departed at least two standard deviations from the mean, we can put forth a number of conclusions. T. Roosevelt and Jackson stand out as the least moderate, Polk as the least friendly. Jefferson exhibited the most impressive intellectual brilliance, Harding the least. The most Machiavellian presidents were Nixon, L. B. Johnson, Van Buren, and Polk. Taylor had the least poise and polish, Grant the lowest achievement drive. T. Roosevelt and L. B. Johnson scored the highest in forcefulness. The chief executives highest in wit were Kennedy, Reagan, and Lincoln; the most physically attractive were Pierce, Fillmore, Kennedy, and Harding. Nixon was by far the most petty, Buchanan and Jefferson the most tidy. The most conservative president was Reagan, the least conservative Jefferson, the most inflexible Tyler, Wilson, and A. Johnson. No president was extreme in pacifism by the two-deviations criterion; the poles are repre-

Table 4.3 Standardized Factor Scores for 39 Presidents on 14 Personality Dimensions Derived from Application of the Gough Adjective Check List

President	Factor													
	1	2	3	4	5	6	7	8	9	10	11	12	13	14
1. Washington	0.5	−0.4	0.3	−0.3	1.1	1.1	−0.0	1.1	0.0	−0.4	1.2	−0.3	0.1	0.1
2. J. Adams	−1.6	−1.5	0.6	−0.7	−0.1	0.9	0.0	−0.8	−0.9	0.6	−0.6	−0.1	0.9	−1.2
3. Jefferson	0.5	0.4	3.1	−0.3	0.2	0.6	−0.1	−0.2	0.3	−1.3	2.1	−2.0	−0.6	1.4
4. Madison	1.0	−0.4	0.6	−0.2	0.6	−0.1	−0.9	−0.3	−0.9	−0.8	0.6	−0.0	−0.6	1.4
5. Monroe	1.0	0.1	−1.4	−1.2	0.1	−0.1	−1.3	−0.7	−0.2	−1.1	−0.3	0.2	−0.4	0.5
6. J. Q. Adams	−0.4	−1.5	1.2	−0.6	0.3	0.2	−0.0	−0.9	−0.9	−0.6	−0.4	−0.3	0.5	−0.6
7. Jackson	−2.0	−0.7	−0.6	−0.2	−1.1	−0.0	1.7	−0.8	−0.6	1.1	−1.7	−1.3	1.4	−1.4
8. Van Buren	1.2	0.7	−0.3	2.3	1.9	−1.0	−1.1	1.3	−0.6	−0.1	−0.1	0.2	−1.0	1.0
9. W. Harrison	−0.2	−0.4	−0.1	0.4	0.1	0.2	−0.4	−0.2	−0.1	0.7	−0.6	0.6	0.3	−0.9
10. Tyler	−1.0	−0.8	0.2	0.0	0.5	0.6	−0.1	−0.7	−0.3	−0.1	−0.7	−0.8	2.3	−0.9
11. Polk	−0.9	−2.1	−0.6	2.2	0.6	1.4	0.9	−1.5	−1.1	1.1	1.4	−0.5	1.8	−0.6
12. Taylor	0.4	0.8	−1.2	−0.9	−2.0	−0.4	−1.0	−0.3	−0.7	−0.1	−0.9	−0.8	−0.7	−1.0
13. Fillmore	1.1	1.0	−0.7	−0.4	0.8	−0.5	−0.8	0.3	2.0	−0.3	−0.1	−0.4	−1.1	0.9
14. Pierce	0.3	1.3	−0.3	−0.3	0.1	−1.0	0.3	0.0	2.2	0.4	0.0	−0.4	−0.7	0.8
15. Buchanan	0.8	0.2	−0.8	−0.2	1.2	−1.5	−0.8	−0.3	0.2	0.9	2.4	1.1	−1.0	0.4
16. Lincoln	1.0	1.0	0.8	−0.5	−1.2	−0.0	−0.7	2.0	−0.7	−1.3	−1.2	0.1	−0.8	0.6
17. A. Johnson	−1.8	−0.7	−1.2	−1.0	−1.9	1.8	0.6	−1.0	−0.7	0.6	−1.0	−1.3	2.0	−1.8
18. Grant	0.2	−0.5	−1.4	−0.6	−1.7	−4.2	−0.4	−0.6	−0.4	0.4	−1.4	−0.1	0.9	−0.3

19. Hayes	0.2	−0.7	−0.1	−0.4	0.6	−0.4	−0.5	−0.6	−0.5	0.2	0.5	1.4	−0.0	0.1
20. Garfield	0.2	−0.1	0.9	−0.0	0.2	0.6	0.2	−0.1	−0.1	−0.6	0.2	−0.1	−0.4	−0.6
21. Arthur	0.8	1.1	0.9	−0.6	1.6	−1.4	−0.6	−0.3	1.4	−0.1	−0.7	−0.1	−1.0	0.4
22. Cleveland	−0.8	−0.4	−0.5	−0.9	−0.6	0.6	0.0	0.2	−0.7	−1.1	0.1	1.1	1.2	−0.8
23. B. Harrison	0.3	−1.2	−0.7	−0.6	0.7	−0.6	−0.7	−1.1	−0.7	−0.4	−0.1	−0.1	−0.3	−0.6
24. McKinley	1.0	0.5	−0.6	0.0	1.1	−0.7	−0.2	−1.0	−0.3	−0.8	−0.9	1.9	−0.9	0.6
25. T. Roosevelt	−2.3	−0.4	0.9	0.6	−0.5	0.6	2.7	−0.3	−0.9	1.7	−1.4	−1.9	0.7	−1.8
26. Taft	1.1	0.8	0.0	−1.0	−1.0	−0.4	−1.9	0.5	−0.5	−0.1	0.6	1.1	−1.0	1.5
27. Wilson	−1.3	−1.2	1.3	−0.4	0.8	0.4	0.8	1.0	−0.2	0.2	−0.0	−1.3	2.2	1.0
28. Harding	1.1	1.5	−2.0	−0.1	−0.2	−1.0	−1.3	−0.7	2.0	−0.1	−0.5	0.2	−1.3	1.6
29. Coolidge	0.6	−1.2	−1.5	0.6	−0.8	0.6	−1.7	1.7	−0.6	0.4	1.3	1.6	0.0	0.8
30. Hoover	0.4	−0.9	0.5	−0.1	−0.2	0.6	0.2	−0.8	−0.6	−0.6	1.8	0.4	0.1	1.3
31. F. Roosevelt	−0.1	1.4	0.9	1.7	0.9	0.1	1.3	1.0	1.9	−1.1	−0.9	−1.1	−0.6	−0.3
32. Truman	−1.5	−0.1	0.2	0.3	−1.9	0.6	0.2	−0.4	−0.7	−0.6	−0.8	−0.8	0.7	−1.3
33. Eisenhower	0.8	1.2	−0.7	−0.9	0.0	0.1	−0.5	−0.2	0.5	−0.6	1.3	1.1	−1.0	0.4
34. Kennedy	0.3	1.1	1.8	0.5	1.3	0.8	0.7	2.6	2.0	−0.8	−0.7	−0.6	−0.7	−1.0
35. L. Johnson	−1.6	0.4	−0.2	2.4	−1.5	0.7	2.2	1.0	−0.9	0.7	0.3	−0.3	0.2	0.0
36. Nixon	−0.8	−1.6	0.4	2.9	0.3	1.0	0.7	−1.0	−0.7	4.3	0.2	−0.5	0.7	−0.8
37. Ford	0.6	1.3	−0.6	−0.8	−0.3	−0.0	0.5	0.3	1.2	−0.1	−0.0	1.0	−0.6	0.2
38. Carter	0.7	0.7	−0.0	−0.5	−0.5	−0.2	1.1	−0.8	0.0	0.4	1.3	1.0	−0.9	1.8
39. Reagan	0.2	1.4	0.4	−0.2	0.4	0.4	0.6	2.4	1.7	−0.6	−0.1	2.2	0.0	−0.6

Note: Factors are defined as follows: 1 = moderation, 2 = friendliness, 3 = intellectual brilliance, 4 = Machiavellianism, 5 = poise and polish, 6 = achievement drive, 7 = forcefulness, 8 = wit, 9 = physical attractiveness, 10 = pettiness, 11 = tidiness, 12 = conservatism, 13 = inflexibility, and 14 = pacifism.
Source: Table 3 in Simonton (1986e).

sented by Carter on the positive end and T. Roosevelt and A. Johnson on the negative end.

These fourteen personality dimensions exhibit interesting correlations with various facts drawn from presidential biographies, including both developmental antecedents and presidential performance criteria (for details, see Simonton 1986e). For example, those presidents who come from large families show more moderation and more poise and polish, but less forcefulness and inflexibility. Evidently, having many siblings to contend and compromise with in childhood contributes to a more conciliatory and socially refined character. The practicing lawyers among the presidents also display more poise and polish; those who attended law school tend to be more Machiavellian as well (compare Green and Pederson 1985).

Machiavellianism is also linked with the president's success as a legislator (see Alker 1981). In particular, the more Machiavellian chief executive tends to sign more acts and to claim more legislative victories, though he suffers more legislative defeats as well. The Machiavellian president pushes many laws through Congress, and even if he does not always win, the losses are offset by a larger number of successes. Another personality asset in the Oval Office is forcefulness, which is associated with the total number of bills signed as well as the total number of administration-sponsored bills that are passed. On the other hand, inflexibility is decidedly a legislative liability. Inflexible presidents employ the veto power more often, only to see Congress retaliate with a high percentage of overturned vetoes. Indeed, presidential inflexibility is equally correlated with the Senate's proclivity to reject executive nominees to the cabinet and to the Supreme Court. It is worth mentioning that none of the fourteen factors is connected to vice-presidential succession. Accidental presidents have the same personality profiles, on the average, as duly elected presidents, a null result that further reinforces the inference drawn earlier that the poor performance of these presidents is due to situational factors.

The personality profiles shown in table 4.3 can be subjected to a cluster analysis in order to discern which presidents have the most similar personalities. The outcome appears in figure 4.1. Presi-

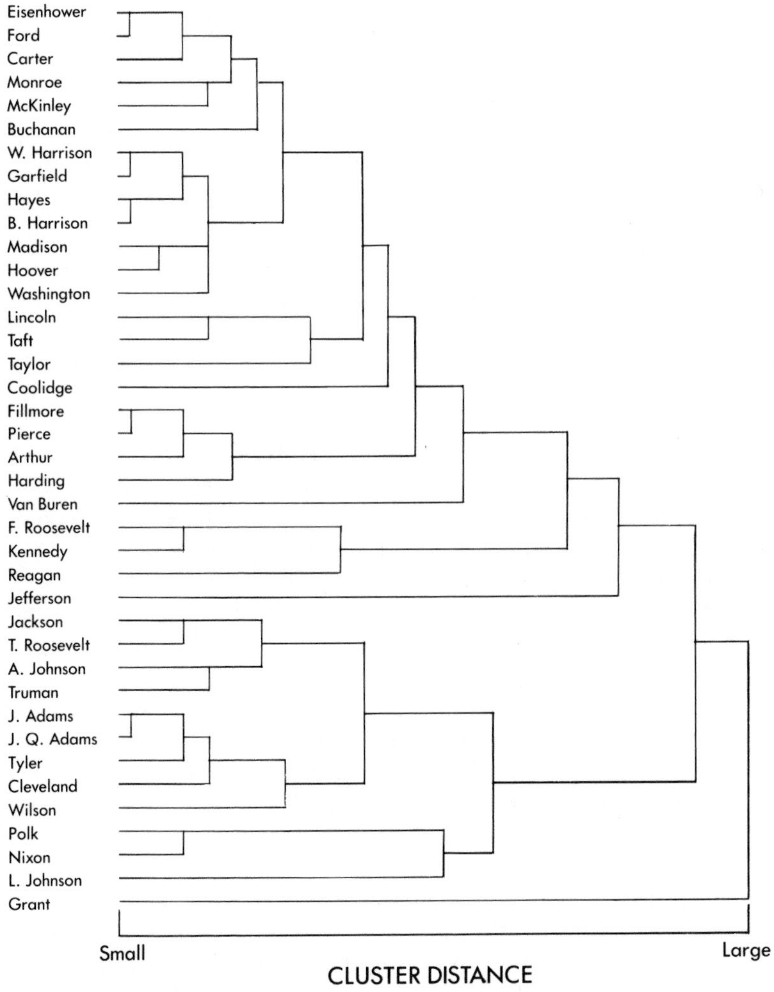

Eisenhower
Ford
Carter
Monroe
McKinley
Buchanan
W. Harrison
Garfield
Hayes
B. Harrison
Madison
Hoover
Washington
Lincoln
Taft
Taylor
Coolidge
Fillmore
Pierce
Arthur
Harding
Van Buren
F. Roosevelt
Kennedy
Reagan
Jefferson
Jackson
T. Roosevelt
A. Johnson
Truman
J. Adams
J. Q. Adams
Tyler
Cleveland
Wilson
Polk
Nixon
L. Johnson
Grant

Small
Large
CLUSTER DISTANCE

Figure 4.1. Dendrogram indicating the similarity in personality profiles for 39 presidents. Most similar presidents grouped together on the left, least similar on the right (from Simonton, 1986e, figure 1).

dents linked on the left-hand side are very similar, whereas those linked only on the right-hand side are quite different. Thus, the sole father-son pair, J. Adams and J. Q. Adams, shows rather similar profiles, as we might expect. The only grandfather-grandson pair, W. Harrison and B. Harrison, shows a bit more difference in personality structure. On the other side, Grant does not join the rest of the presidents until the very last step, suggesting that the former Union general's character departed significantly from other kinds of presidential character. Between these two extremes we see clusters of various degrees of comprehensiveness, depending on the cluster distances. Polk and Nixon form a cluster of neurotic, work-driven chief executives obsessed with their place in history; L. Johnson is the next president to enter this group. Further up is the cluster begun by the Adamses and joined by Tyler, Cleveland, and Wilson, a club of highly determined, self-righteous, and preeminently stubborn chief executives. This cluster is comparable to the one composed by Jackson, T. Roosevelt, A. Johnson, and Truman—presidents equally persistent, yet much more pugnacious.

F. Roosevelt forms a cluster with Kennedy and Reagan of what Barber (1977) calls active-positive presidents, who are energetic and optimistic in the pursuit of their policies. The cluster made up of Fillmore, Pierce, Arthur, and Harding, in contrast, might be considered a cluster of passive-positives, who are upbeat yet lethargic—good-natured but do-nothing. Lincoln, Taft, and Taylor form a curious cluster of relaxed, informal presidents. The set consisting of W. Harrison, Garfield, Hayes, B. Harrison, Madison, Hoover, and Washington might as well be treated with the set composed by Eisenhower, Ford, Carter, Monroe, McKinley, and Buchanan; they both represent well-intentioned but nondescript chief executives. It is interesting that Jefferson, certainly one of the most remarkable presidents ever to enter the White House, is second only to Grant in the distance of his profile from other occupants. This may reflect his own ambivalence as president. Jefferson was a vigorous and optimistic person, yet as president he tried to practice a political philosophy that minimized the influence of the federal government. Such acts as the 1803 Louisiana Purchase reveal how his intrinsic personality disposition could override his ideological commitments.

The above results illustrate some of the utility of adapting standard personality instruments to the examination of presidential character. In lieu of the simple one- and two-dimensional schemes for classifying presidential personalities that have been the vogue (for example, Barber 1977), we can obtain profiles that divulge the rich diversity of American heads of state. Because these profiles are associated with performance criteria, we can surmise that personality has some impact on the general style that a president brings to the Oval Office.

Dogmatism

I now will treat at length one specific stylistic trait, the degree of rigidity displayed by the president. This trait has been assessed using three distinct methods: the surveying of professional historians, the content analysis of speeches, and the application of psychometric instruments to biographical data. In the latter case I will show how presidential performance can be a multiplicative function of individual and situational factors. I begin by discussing a method of assessment different from those seen thus far.

Idealistic Inflexibility. Gary Maranell (1970), a sociologist, had 571 historians, all members of the Organization of American Historians, rate thirty-three presidents on seven dimensions. The sample consisted of all chief executives from Washington through Lyndon Johnson, omitting only W. Harrison and Garfield, whose tenures in office were too brief to admit evaluation. (To permit easy comparisons across dimensions or presidents, all scores were standardized.) Five of the dimensions will be discussed at length in the next chapter, but two are of immediate relevance here (and did not correlate appreciably with the other dimensions in any case). First, the presidents were evaluated on the degree to which their official actions displayed idealism as opposed to practicality. The most idealistic president by far, according to the historians, was Woodrow Wilson (4.23), with J. Q. Adams (1.18), Kennedy (1.14), and Hoover (1.00) distant runners-up. The least idealistic and hence most practical were Polk (−1.44), Coolidge (−1.41), and L. Johnson (−1.01). The second dimension is the extent to which the president's approach to accomplishing his policies or programs exhibited flexibility. The two most flexible presidents were Kennedy (1.61) and Lincoln (1.50), the two least flexible A. Johnson (−2.18) and Wilson (−2.23). As one might expect, these two dimensions are negatively correlated ($r = -.33$). The more idealistic the president, the more inflexible; the more pragmatic, the more flexible. A factor analysis of all seven measures in fact indicated that these two dimenions form a single bipolar factor (Simonton 1981c; Wendt and Light 1976). Therefore, by taking the idealism score and subtracting the flexibility score, we obtain a new variable that gauges what can be called idealistic inflexibility or, in a word, dogmatism.

Wendt and Light (1976) have shown that presidential dogmatism has a number of biographical antecedents. Those presidents who come from more favorable socioeconomic backgrounds tend to be less dogmatic ($r = -.59$). Those who experienced severe childhood deprivations, such as the death of a parent or an extended illness, were disposed to be more dogmatic ($r = .62$). Another inquiry found that the more dogmatic presidents also tended to have been college professors, such as J. Q. Adams and Wilson (Simonton 1981c). An even more curious finding is that presidential dogmatism is a curvilinear, inverted, backward-J function of the amount of formal education received by the president (Simonton 1983a). This curve is depicted in figure 4.2. The most idealistic, inflexible presidents tended to be those who had had either very little formal education (such as A. Johnson, who had virtually no schooling and was an illiterate until his late teens) or a great deal of formal education (such as the sole Ph.D., Wilson). The president with a doctorate was more dogmatic than the unschooled, however. In contrast, the presidents with the most pragmatic flexibility were those who had had some college, but without necessarily graduating. Some amount of college removes the more simpleminded, untested attitudes that a person may have acquired in childhood. What extends our confidence in this conclusion is

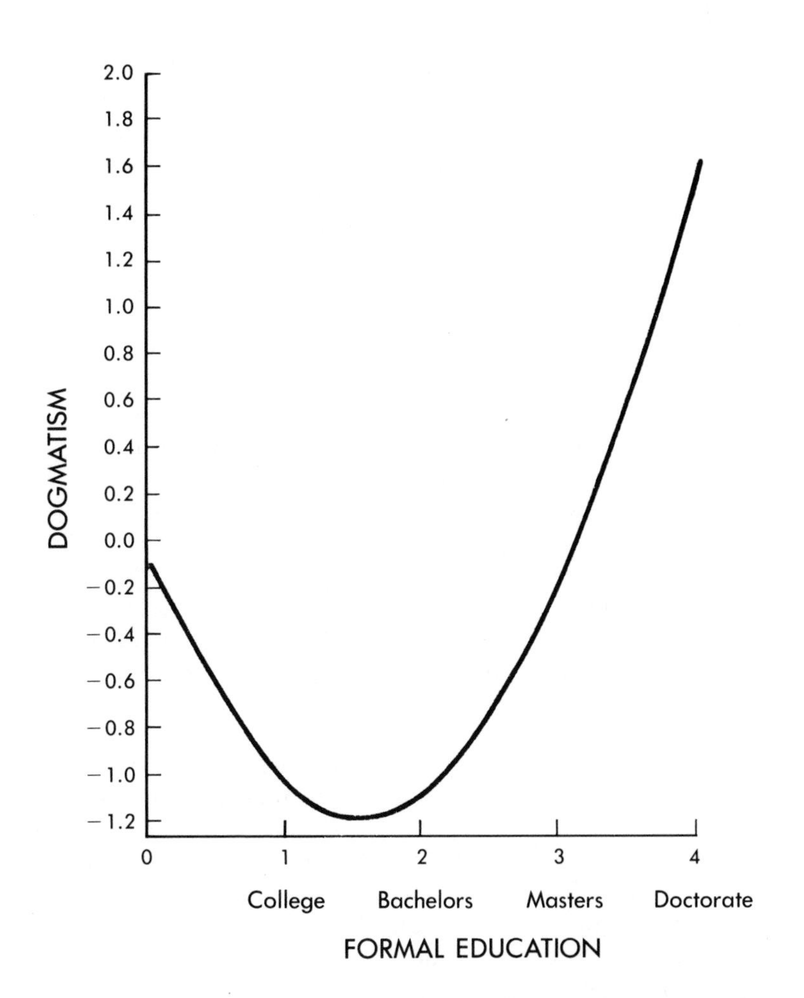

Figure 4.2. Relationship between formal education and dogmatism for 33 American presidents (from Simonton, 1983a, figure 2).

that precisely the mirror image of this curve has emerged in other studies, using different historical figures, of the relation between formal education and creativity, a concept inversely associated with dogmatism (Simonton 1984b, chap. 4). When this result is put together with the impact of being a college professor, we can infer that a long presence in an academic institution, whether as a graduate student or as a teacher, can inculcate an excessive ivory-tower idealism and inflexibility. The highly abstract and impractical theories of the graduate seminar can be a handicap (compare Murphy 1985).

Besides these biographical antecedents, presidential dogmatism correlates with a couple of political behaviors (Wendt and Light 1976). To begin with, Republican presidents have been, on average, less dogmatic than Democratic presidents ($r = .39$), at least for the presidents between Hayes and Nixon inclusive (compare Maranell and Dodder 1970). More significant is the positive correlation between dogmatism and the president's willingness to intervene militarily in foreign affairs ($r = .59$). This result is compatible with what I said earlier about integrative complexity in decision makers being an asset in the avoidance of war. Another study isolated an interesting fact about how presidential dogmatism fluctuates over history (Simonton 1981c): it exhibits a negative autocorrelation ($r = -.32$), signifying that dogmatic presidents tend to alternate with nondogmatic presidents. Actually, this outcome is a little more ambiguous than it seems. A nondogmatic president may succeed a dogmatic president as a reaction to his excessive idealistic inflexibility. No doubt Harding was elected in part for this reason. However, a president of one disposition may succeed one of another disposition because both were elected on the same ticket, and the vice president succeeded on the death of the president. Thus the inflexible and idealistic Andrew Johnson followed the more flexible and pragmatic Lincoln. Clearly, in this case the ticket was balanced in personality. Despite this ambiguity, vice-presidential succession is infrequent enough that we may surmise that a portion of the negative autocorrelation may be due to a reaction setting in. Indeed, I recently determined that even though the dogmatism scores of a president and the vice president who succeeded him are negatively correlated ($r = -.27$), showing that running mates are chosen to be complementary on this attribute, removing instances of vice-presidential succession actually raises the absolute value of the autocorrelation ($r = -.38$). Hence, the notion of reaction is apparently valid. Voters do replace dogmatic presidents with nondogmatic ones, and vice versa.

Ideologues. Although most of the research on presidential dogmatism is of a preliminary nature, the results are suggestive enough to recommend that additional investigations be carried out on this specific presidential style. In the next chapter I will show that this dimension bears a provocative relation to presidential greatness. A series of content analytical inquiries by Tetlock and his associates suggests, albeit more indirectly, that presidential dogmatism may have repercussions for political ideology and rhetorical style as well. In the initial study, Tetlock (1983) classified American senators as liberal, moderate, or conservative according to their 1975 and 1976 voting records. Next, their policy statements were coded on the same integrative complexity dimension that we have repeatedly come across in this chapter. It happened that the statements of the conservative senators were significantly less complex than those of their liberal or moderate colleagues, a differential that survived statistical control for age, education, party affiliation, and years of service in the Senate. Tetlock's study suggests that dogmatic thinking may be the modus operandi of those occupying the right wing of the political spectrum. Yet Tetlock was quick to point out the danger in concluding that dogmatism is the vice exclusively of highly conservative politicians. Two considerations advise caution.

First, the diversity of political opinion in the United States Senate is usually narrow compared with the equivalent legislative bodies of most democratic nations. No communists, nor even true socialists, represent constituencies in the Senate. Because the only extremists elected as senators are right-wing, authoritarians of the left are excluded, granting the conservatives a monopoly on simple-minded policy assertions by default. If we turn to ideologically more varied legislatures, however, the conservatives might discover real competitors in the radical left. To check this idea, Tetlock (1984) turned to the British House of Commons, to content analyze confidential interviews with eighty-nine members of Parliament. The extreme socialists did not differ significantly from extreme conservatives in integrative complexity; both groups expressed opinions that were far more simple, undifferentiated, and unidimensional than those advocated by the moderate socialists and the moderate conservatives.

This outcome is consistent with the ideologue hypothesis, which affirms that dogmatism is actually content-free, favoring no specific ideological stance (Rokeach 1960). In contrast to the rigidity-of-the-right hypothesis that we have so far implicitly assumed, ideologues are characterized by the pattern of their thought processes more than by the orientation of their thoughts. Even so, Tetlock's second investigation also indicates that the left may be a jot more comfortable with integratively complex and multidimensional debate than the right. Although there was no difference between extreme socialists and extreme conservatives, a pronounced contrast did materialize between the moderate socialists and the moderate conservatives. The moderate socialists interpreted key issues in the most complex terms of all. So the ideologue hypothesis may be essentially correct as long as it is accompanied by the proviso that rigidity is more prevalent on the right than on the left.

Yet another interpretation of these findings exists, and this alternative takes us to the second complication. As Tetlock admits, the integrative complexity of policy statements may be more a matter of rhetorical tactics than stable personality disposition. When the M.P.'s were interviewed in 1967, the Labour party was in power, and the conservatives were thus cast into the rather unpleasant role of the loyal opposition. Because the left wing was more in control of government policy, the socialists had to engage in intricate policy formulation (and delicate excuse-making), whereas the conservatives were free to harangue them. This situation is analogous to the contrast we saw earlier between prepresidential campaign speeches and presidential policy pronouncements. The opposition party, too, despairing of swaying government decisions, may use their seats in the public forum as pulpits from which to proclaim their ideals—not to their legislative colleagues but to the people. In a sense, members of the minority party may be perennially running for office in the hope that the forthcoming election will bring better returns. Should the next election return the opposition party to power, a dramatic reversal in rhetorical style ought to result.

To test this notion Tetlock went back to the United States Senate (Tetlock, Hannum, and Micheletti 1984; compare Tetlock, Bernzweig, and Gallant 1985). This time he compared senators in three Congresses dominated by moderates and liberals (the Eighty-second, Ninety-fourth, and Ninety-sixth) to senators in two Congresses dominated by conservatives (the Eighty-third and Ninety-seventh). The chief inference to be drawn is that the integrative complexity of speeches made on the Senate floor is the outcome of both stable cognitive differences between representatives of conflicting ideologies and transient rhetorical style differences dependent on which side is in power. The conservative senators, as assessed by voting behavior, were simpler than liberals and moderates when conservatives were the out-group, but this difference almost vanished when it was the conservatives' turn to organize the Senate. This change was caused, not by the conservatives becoming more complex, but by the liberals and, to a lesser degree, the moderates becoming less complex. Hence, no absolute switching of roles took place. The conservatives at no time displayed an integrative complexity much more pronounced than their rivals'. Also, both across and within sessions the conservatives exhibited more stability in integrative complexity, suggesting that for them this dimension may be closer to a permanent cognitive predilection than to a temporary rhetorical device.

Tetlock obviously has more undergrowth to clear away, yet insofar as this dimension relates to idealistic inflexibility he has identified some useful questions for future inquiry. For instance, to what extent is presidential dogmatism linked with specific ideologies? We have already seen that, on the average, Republican presidents may be more pragmatic and less idealistic than Democratic presidents (at least from Hayes through Nixon), but no firm correlation exists between party affiliation and presidential policy. There are conservative (largely Southern boll weevil) Democrats and progressive (mostly Midwestern and Northeastern gypsy moth) Republicans. Tetlock's studies were predicated on voting records and advocated positions, not party labels.

Individual-Situational Interaction. Another question derived from Tetlock's inquiries has to do with the impact of extrinsic conditions on the president's preferred rhetorical manner. Andrew Johnson and Woodrow Wilson were condemned by Maranell's 571 historians as the two most rigid and impractical chief executives in American history. Especially in Wilson's case, this overflowing dogmatism has often been ascribed to deep-rooted and sturdy personality characteristics (for example, George and George 1956). Nevertheless, both of these presidents were compelled to face a Congress, especially a Senate, that was entirely hostile to their programs. Johnson's Reconstruction plan for the South was killed by the Radical Republicans who distrusted this Southern War Democrat, and relations between the two branches of government degenerated to veto contests and impeachment proceedings. Wilson's pet project, the Versailles treaty with its controversial League of Nations provisions, was also shot down by a Senate controlled by Republicans, a large proportion of whom were isolationists disgusted with recent American interventions abroad. Thus, both Johnson and Wilson may have been victims of the opposition role. The prestige of the presidency notwithstanding, both men represented minority positions in the federal government, an adverse situation that might easily have propelled them into simplistic rhetorical styles. Both endeavored unsuccessfully to outflank their Senate enemies by taking the debate directly to the American people, via implicit or explicit campaign appeals.

I will not be so rash as to say that the high dogmatism ratings of these two unfortunate presidents was totally caused by outside events. Even when out of power and after tempers should have cooled, Johnson sought vindication by election to the Senate and insisted that he be buried with the Constitution he thought he was defending; Wilson persisted in his self-righteous advocacy in the 1920 election, which he perceived as a great, solemn referendum. Still, it remains conceivable that any natural inclination toward rigidity was aggravated by the untoward circumstances into which both were thrown. In more auspicious times both of these serious men had shone as governors, Johnson in Tennessee and Wilson in New Jersey. I am arguing that both individual character and political situation have a say, both separately and in interaction. To illustrate how this might happen, I will conclude with a look at a recent study of the personal and contextual basis of presidential veto behavior (Simonton 1986d). This study strove to explain vetoes and overrides (as recorded in Kimmitt and Haley 1978) by using the personality ratings obtained from applying the Gough ACL to biographical data about presidential character (Simonton 1986c). In particular, this investigation took advantage of the inflexibility measure, which exhibits a high negative correlation with Maranell's (1970) flexibility dimension ($r = -.70$) and thus taps the same character trait.

As observed earlier, the incumbent's propensity to veto legislation as well as the congressional inclination to overturn those vetoes are both a consequence of certain political conditions, such as the magnitude of the mandate the president received in the general election and the degree to which his party controls Congress (Copeland 1983; Lee 1975). Yet we have also noted the impact of personality: inflexible chief executives employ the veto power more often and see more of their vetoes overridden (Simonton 1986c). These situational and individual factors operate not only in isolation, as additive effects, but also in conjunction, as nonadditive (multiplicative) interaction effects. For instance, the incumbent's intrinsic inflexibility interacts with the extent of his party support in Congress in the determination of how many vetoed bills become law despite his explicit objections. If a president is of average inflexibility (that is, has a score near zero on factor 13 in table 4.3), the extent of party control is negatively related to the frequency of overridden vetoes, as we would normally expect. Should the president be a whole standard deviation below the mean level, and thus relatively flexible, the occurrence of overturned vetoes has little to do with the president's support in Congress. In this category belong the seven most flexible presidents in American history (those in table 4.3 with scores of −1.0 or less). At the other extreme, if the incumbent is a standard deviation above the mean in inflexibility, the negative linkage between party control and vetoes overturned becomes more pronounced. And should the president's inflexibility exceed two units above average, the antagonistic relationship between the executive and legislative branches becomes more salient still. A highly stubborn, persistent, hardheaded, and rigid chief executive, unlike more flexible presidents, is highly dependent on the goodwill of Congress to avoid a veto override.

This party control-inflexibility interaction might be styled the Johnson–Wilson efffect after Andrew Johnson and Woodrow Wilson, both of whom were at least two standard deviations above the mean in inflexibility (see table 4.3). This effect demonstrates quite dramatically how substandard performance in the Oval Office may ensue simply because the incumbent is the wrong person in the wrong place at the wrong time.

CONCLUSION

In contrast to the preceding two chapters, which judged presidents from the standpoint of voters and survey respondents, this chapter has identified considerably more individual attributes of the incumbent that may contribute to presidential success, here assessed by performance. Interpersonal dominance and extroversion or introversion, the power, achievement, and affiliation motives, integrative complexity and pragmatic flexibility—these and many other personality traits all have their consequences for decisions made in foreign and domestic policy, decisions that may have repercussions for a president's accomplishments as national leader. Diverse biographical variables—such as prior political experience, previous occupation, level of formal education, and even family background—have a say as well, whether directly (such as the impact of a tenure on Capitol Hill or the incumbent's veto behavior) or indirectly via personality consequences (such as the effect of formal education, socioeconomic class, and childhood deprivations on presidential dogmatism).

Even though individual factors are more conspicuous in our discussion of performance, their greater prevalence need not contradict the conclusions drawn in chapters 2 and 3 that situational factors seem to predominate. To properly weigh the compatibility of the findings in all three chapters we should consider the following four items:

1. Personal traits of the incumbent are likely to be granted more latitude for influence when presidential success is evaluated by performance rather than by reputation with the public. The president has specific powers mandated by the Constitution and by precedent that permit him to control directly the course of his administration, and consequently to translate individual needs, values, and thinking styles into acts that set his presidency apart from those of presidents with different personalities. For example, he can present his case directly to Congress in special messages and State of the Union addresses, in the bills that he sends for consideration, and in the testimony given by administration officials before congressional committees, and he can always resort to the veto when legislation departs from executive philosophy. Even if the capacity to control events does not automatically mean that the president's disposition will leave an imprint on national policies, it is a necessary requirement, and what the incumbent can do he usually will do, especially in modern times when an activist presidency is the norm.

This freedom of expression stands in stark contrast to the status of an incumbent running for reelection or being appraised by survey respondents. Neither the Constitution nor any historical precedent gives the president much power to impress his mind upon the minds of the voters. He cannot demand that they keep well-informed of his administration's accomplishments over the years or that they apply just and objective criteria in their evaluations of executive performance; nor can he veto the opinions of those voters or respondents who are uninformed or excessively subjective. Hence, we would expect that indicators of success that rely on the people will exhibit less compliance with the president's individual attributes than indicators tied more closely to events within the sphere of the office. It is interesting to observe, for example, that the state of the economy figures as a prominent situational factor in the previous two chapters, yet has not been proven to correlate with any personal traits (or even policies) of those who are held responsible by the public, nor is there any convincing evidence that the chief executive even has the power to convert such traits into effective measures. Reagan's economic plans clearly emerged from his personal worldview, but he was not given carte blanche to rearrange the federal priorities according to his wishes, his immense popularity notwithstanding.

2. Almost all of the performance indicators that appear dependent on the president's personal qualities have little relevance for predicting presidential success in the voting booth or the polls. Neither election success nor high approval ratings have yet been shown to be a function of foreign policy orientation (whether extroverted dominance or isolationism), the use of the veto power, the fate of appointments to the cabinet or Supreme Court, or other performance criteria that appear most subject to the incumbent's character. Accordingly, a connection is so far lacking between the performance consequences of individual traits and the effect of performance on the president's standing with the American public. Of course, performance and popularity are not utterly disconnected, and thus in some instances personality can exert an effect, however indirect, on the judgments of the people. A case in point is the power motive, which, by increasing the chances that the incumbent will engage American military might abroad, may increase the probability of rally-around-the-flag events and even war, thereby enhancing the opinions of survey respondents as well as the prospects for reelection.

3. For many performance criteria treated in this chapter, situational factors exhibit a hegemony about as complete as that observed in the previous chapters. Presidential legislative success, in particular, is subject to a host of events and conditions not entirely under the incumbent's control. The ability to get administration bills through the legislative process is largely a function of how strongly represented the president's party is in Congress, a factor that contributes comparably to the likelihood of executive vetoes and legislative veto overrides. Although one might argue that presidential candidates with superior leadership abilities sweep more like-minded representatives and senators into office on election day, this assumes coattails much longer than actually seems to be the case, and presupposes that situational factors do

not also dominate the casting of ballots, a supposition that appears unlikely given what we have discussed in chapter 2.

4. The implications of individual attributes, even where clearly important, are often modulated by contextual variables. In some instances, this modulation weakens the association between personality trait and administrative consequence. Thus, the relation between interpersonal dominance and foreign policy is often undermined by the overwhelming influence of diplomatic precedents and military capabilities, lessening the disagreements that the president and his advisers might otherwise have with regard to policy questions. Similarly, the need for power can be superseded by stronger political realities, pulling a power-complacent chief executive into war and pushing a pugnacious president toward peace, as happened in the cases of McKinley and T. Roosevelt. On the other hand, the larger situational context can increase the import of certain personality dispositions. The link between presidential inflexibility and veto behavior is less obvious when the circumstances are auspicious for the incumbent, but becomes quite apparent when conditions are less favorable to a friendly working relationship between the White House and Capitol Hill. An inherently rigid incumbent can be provoked by powerful antagonists into a self-defeating exhibition of personal weakness—the Johnson–Wilson phenomenon.

The results of the empirical research on presidential performance are not inconsistent with the work on election success and popularity. The findings expand our understanding of the interplay of person and context. The president brings into the White House a definite disposition that unfolds during the course of his administration, but he does not have a free hand to indulge in self-expression. Rather, a host of situational factors set the boundaries and opportunities for the projection of presidential personality on the world of political action. Any given presidential behavior may be the result of individual characteristics, political setting, and the subtle interaction between the two. It is truly a matter of being the right person in the right place at the right time. And if all influences converge to the same beneficial effect, the leader may go down in history as a truly great president.

◆ 5 ◆
HISTORICAL GREATNESS

We come now to the most elusive success criterion of all. Presidential achievement is readily conceived in the terms used in the last three chapters. Just as we may calculate the percentage of votes received in the polling booth or the electoral college, so may we estimate the proportion of survey respondents who give the incumbent president a high approval rating. Furthermore, we can always gauge a chief executive according to performance criteria, whether specific presidential acts or broad stylistic proclivities. In the final analysis, however, these several criteria ideally should converge on the ultimate criterion—the president's place in the history of the nation. Presidents who fail to win reelection, who are unpopular with the American people, and whose performance in the White House is below par should have but a minuscule chance of attaining a high place in posterity's estimation. At the opposite pole, those presidents who earn popularity and reelection through remarkable accomplishments in the Oval Office should receive eventual acclaim as the greats of American political history. Presidents Lincoln and Franklin Roosevelt are often considered to have been truly great presidents, just as Grant and Harding are invariaby considered among the worst.

John Adams, the first president to actually live in the White House, prayed that "none but wise and honest men ever rule under this roof," a passage later inscribed on the dining room mantel by FDR. Numerous incumbents since 1800 have aspired to live up to this hope, even if only a small proportion have come close to the mark. Buchanan strove to be a great president, but he failed, unlike his successor, Lincoln, to meet head-on the chronic crisis between free and slave states. In more recent times, Lyndon Johnson and Nixon each labored earnestly with an eye directed toward history. It is one of the ironies of American politics that the failure of either man to attain a hallowed position in the hearts of fellow Americans may be partly ascribed to their willingness to sacrifice even wisdom and honesty for the sake of the final score in the history books. An almost neurotic obsession with approval quite possibly spurred the downfall of two otherwise extremely gifted politicians (see also Kearns 1976; Mazlish 1972).

The last conjecture leads us to ask how an incumbent should go about becoming a great president. To answer this question we must inquire into the nature of greatness. This inquiry can be divided neatly into two independent parts. We must begin by asking how we can assess the comparative greatness of the thirty-nine presidents. Once we have isolated a suitable measure, the next question is how we can predict which presidents will become great and which not. This second question, besides its intrinsic theoretical interest, has potential practical value. If we can find some way to predict which of two presidential candidates shows the greatest likelihood of joining the list of immortals, what better criterion do wise and honest voters need when casting their ballots in November?

ASSESSING GREATNESS

The difficulty in gauging the comparative greatness of American presidents lies not in a dearth of choices, but in their profusion. One likely place to start is with some measure of popular acclaim (compare Kane 1974, 340–43). Just four presidents—Washington, Jefferson, Lincoln, and T. Roosevelt—have monuments in the nation's capital, though Roosevelt's monument is not particularly conspicuous. These are the same presidents whose portraits are carved on Mount Rushmore. The presidents who have been elected to the Hall of Fame are Washington, Adams, Jefferson, J. Q. Adams, Jackson, Lincoln, Grant, Cleveland, T. Roosevelt, and Wilson. Washington, Jefferson, Madison, Jackson, and Lincoln are the only presidents who have had states or state capitals named after them. The number of counties named for presidents include 31 Washingtons, 26 Jeffersons, 22 Jacksons, and 16 Lincolns, to mention only the top four. Finally, there is certainly an inverse relationship between the face value of United States paper currency and popular acclaim: Washington is on the ubiquitous-one dollar bill, Lincoln on the five, while Grant appears on the less commonly seen fifty (albeit Jefferson got short-changed when he was placed on the two-dollar bill, and who ever gets to see Wilson's portrait on the one hundred thousand-dollar bill?). Certainly, there must be some way of combining these various indicators of popular acclaim into a single overall index of presidential greatness.

But are these adequate ways of measuring a President's true greatness? For a number of reasons the answer is no (see Bailey 1966). For one thing, all of these measures are heavily dependent on the passage of time. The Hall of Fame does not admit living presidents and former presidents, and twenty-five years must elapse after a nominee's death before election can even be considered. It is doubtful whether more monuments will be built in Washington, D.C. (most memorials nowadays, such as the Kennedy Center for the Performing Arts, serve functional purposes, and, in any event, all the best spots for monuments around Capitol Mall are already occupied). Even Franklin D. Roosevelt has yet to be honored that way, though a memorial park is on the drawing board. Mount Rushmore is unlikely to have new faces added; all counties, states, and state capitals already have been named; and all the low-denomination bills have been claimed (three- and four-dollar bills being improbable indeed). Thus, these measures have no value in discriminating the relative greatness of recent presidents.

Such indicators are of low discriminating power even with respect to the earlier chief executives. The majority of presidents are simply lumped into the category "obscure" without any attempt to differentiate among them. Fewer than one-third of the presidents have been elected to the Hall of Fame; fewer than one-quarter have had their portraits placed on paper currency; fewer than one-seventh have had state capitals named after them or their portraits carved on Mount Rushmore; and fewer than one-tenth have had monuments to their memory placed in full view of the tourists who walk down Capitol Mall. Both Fillmore and Van Buren are unsung and unpraised by these standards; yet does that imply that they were equally inferior presidents? Probably not. The differences in greatness of the thirty-nine presidents can be distinguished better than by assigning a mere handful to the "illustrious" category and all the rest to the category of nonentities.

Another difficulty concerns the reason that a president is memorialized. Grant is not on the fifty-dollar bill and in the Hall of Fame because of his achievements as chief executive, for he is uniformly rated as one of our worst presidents; any kudos he receives are given for his accomplishments as Union general. Even a president as great as Jefferson may be given a boost from his many other claims to fame. Jefferson himself, in the epitaph he wrote, boasts only that he was "author of the Declaration of American Independence, of the statute of Virginia for religious freedom, and father of the Univerity of Virginia"—omitting any mention of his presidency altogether. Popular acclaim may be far too global an indicator of presidential greatness.

An alternative is to gauge the eminence or fame of a president by counting how often the president appears in standard reference works or even by measuring the amount of space devoted to him in histories and biographical dictionaries. By depending on scholarly works, such a measure would be better informed, and it would also permit finer distinctions among the presidents, even among the top ones. For example, Cox's (1926) study ventured to rank some pre-twentieth-century presidents as follows: Washington, Lincoln, Jefferson, Grant, J. Adams, Jackson, Madison, and J. Q. Adams (see Cattell 1903). Though this type of measure has been extensively applied to the study of leadership and even creativity (Simonton 1984b), it has its deficiencies. As the Cox rankings indicate, for example, citation eminence ratings do not specify how a president actually became famous, and thus a mediocre chief executive like Grant can be ranked highly. So in this respect these scholarly measures are no better than those based on popular accliam. In yet another respect the citation measures are actually inferior. An investigation into the eminence of monarchs has discovered that the most eminent ones tend to be either very good or very bad, both as leaders and as human beings (Simonton 1984d). In other words, there are actually two ways of making it in the history books—by becoming either famous or infamous. The notorious will not be elected to a Hall of Fame or have a monument dedicated to their memory, yet scholars may devote much time to discussing their demerits. Harding is better known than several superior presidents, like Polk and Cleveland, because, I think, of the scope of the scandal that grew in his admininstration (see Maranell 1970).

A third method of assessing greatness probably does the best job of circumventing the drawbacks of using popular acclaim or citation eminence. Historians can be asked to score the presidents directly on dimensions specific to presidential greatness.

Rating the Presidents

In 1948 Arthur Schlesinger, Sr., asked fifty-five authorities in American history to rate the presidents using five grades—great, near great, average, below average, and failure. These experts were provided no specific guidelines as to what constituted greatness, the definition was left up to them. The results were published in 1949, ranking all presidents between Washington and F. D. Roosevelt, excluding only the short-termed W. Harrison and Garfield. The six greats were, in order, Lincoln, Washington, F. D. Roosevelt, Wilson, Jefferson, and Jackson, followed by the four near greats, T. Roosevelt, Cleveland, J. Adams, and Polk. At the bottom of the heap landed Grant and Harding.

In 1962 Schlesinger conducted a follow-up poll, increasing the number of rated presidents from twenty-nine to thirty-one by adding Eisenhower and Truman, and increasing the number of authorities to seventy-five. Except for the demotion of Jackson to the rank of near great, the outcome was fairly similar to that of the 1948 poll. Truman was placed among the near greats, whereas Eisenhower found himself with the average chief executives. For a considerable time these Schlesinger polls represented the more or less definitive ranking of the American presidents.

Yet many historians dissented from the rankings (and Schlesinger himself did not agree with the details of either poll). Most notable among the dissenters was Thomas A. Bailey, a historian who wrote a comprehensive critique on the subject of rating the chief executives in *Presidential Greatness* (1966). Bailey outlined some of the sources of presidential reputations, including many that have no business entering into the judgments of historians (such as the impact of prepresidential careers). He discussed at length some of the criteria by which presidents should be most justly evaluated. Bailey finished by offering his own assessments of the best and worst among the American presidents. Although he did not do anything more than locate each president in broad categories such as those in the Schlesinger polls, Tom Kynerd (1971) ventured to translate Bailey's explanatory and qualifying remarks into a detailed ranking of the thirty-one presidents from Washington to Eisenhower (again omitting W. Harrison and Garfield). The three unequivocal greats, in order, were Washington, Lincoln, and F. D. Roosevelt, followed by three near greats, T. Roosevelt, Jefferson, and Wilson. There were a baker's dozen average presidents, ten below-average presidents, one near failure, J. Q. Adams, and one patent failure, A. Johnson. Bailey's rating looks different from Schlesinger's, for Bailey composed his own rating in reaction to what he saw to be major biases in the earlier polls. Nonetheless, all three ratings place Washington, Lincoln, and F. D. Roosevelt at the top of the list.

Bailey was not the only scholar to single-handedly rate past White House residents. Clinton Rossiter did so, too, in *The American Presidency* (1956). While he did not strictly rank the presidents one by one, he distributed them among the five broad categories of great, near great, average, below average, and failure. As before, neither W. Harrison nor Garfield was rated; Rossiter opted not to evaluate Taylor as well, even though he had served over a year as chief executive. There were eight great presidents: Washington, Lincoln, F. D. Roosevelt, Jackson, Wilson, T. Roosevelt, Jefferson, and Truman. Below come six near-great presidents, seven average, five below average, and four failures, Pierce,

Buchanan, Grant, and Harding. The standing of Andrew Johnson among the near greats is perhaps the strangest peculiarity of Rossiter's system, for Johnson is rated as a very low average in the Schlesinger polls and as a disastrous failure by Bailey.

Yet another one-man rating is that of Eric Sokolsky whose *Our Seven Greatest Presidents* (1964) was written in response to the Kennedy assassination. As with Rossiter and Bailey, no ranking is given, but merely the general groupings great, very good, adequate, poor, and failure. Sokolsky's assignment of Grant and Harding to the failure category raises no eyebrows, yet his awarding of great and very good status is a bit unconventional in places. The greats are Jefferson, Jackson, Lincoln, T. Roosevelt, Wilson, F. D. Roosevelt, and Kennedy. Washington, J. Adams, Polk, Cleveland, and Truman make up the very good presidents. The two surprising ratings are the demotion of Washington from great to very good and the elevation of Kennedy to great. As Kynerd (1971) suggests, Sokolsky's assessment of Kennedy may not have been utterly objective. But Sokolski, like Rossiter and Bailey, based his ratings on some explicitly stated criteria; any slippage with regard to JFK might be attributed to the emotions of the moment.

In 1970 Gary M. Maranell published a new rating of the presidents that purported to be an extension of the Schlesinger polls. The author was being modest, for Maranell's study was a vast improvement on anything done up to his time. Maranell surveyed, not just fifty-five or seventy-five, but 571 American historians. Even more significant, perhaps, was the fact that he specified precisely what he wanted the presidents to be rated on. The presidents were not to be rated on a single, ambiguous, global dimension like "greatness," but on seven distinct dimensions that bear some relation to greatness, though each in a different way and degree. The seven dimensions were the general prestige accorded to the president today; the strength of action that he displayed in directing the government; his presidential activeness with respect to his administration; the idealism (as opposed to practicality) of his official actions; the flexibility of his approach to accomplishing his programs; the administration accomplishments of the president; and, as a kind of control variable, the amount of information each respondent possessed about the president. The presidents were assigned precise (standardized) scores on the seven dimensions in lieu of crude rankings or elementary groupings. Maranell's poll covered the presidents from Washington through Lyndon Johnson (omitting the hapless W. Harrison and Garfield once again.)

The results of the Maranell poll are strikingly similar to previous ratings, especially for those variables that are most comparable to greatness. Thus, on the first dimension, general prestige, the six most favored presidents are Lincoln, Washington, F. D. Roosevelt, Jefferson, T. Roosevelt, and Wilson, the five least favored Fillmore, Buchanan, Pierce, Grant, and Harding. Of all the seven dimensions, general prestige probably comes closest to the idea of pure greatness, for the other dimensions yield more diversified ratings (see also Maranell and Dodder 1970). In the case of presidential strength of action, the highest are F. D. Roosevelt, Lincoln, Jackson, T. Roosevelt, Wilson, Jefferson, Truman, and L. B. Johnson; the lowest are Coolidge, Buchanan, Fillmore, Pierce, Grant, and Harding. Roughly the same group of presidents secured a high place in presidential activeness: F. D. Roosevelt is still enshrined in the top place, but Lincoln drops to eighth place and Kennedy climbs to sixth place; at the low end, Coolidge manages to wedge himself between the notorious pair, Grant and Harding. In administration accomplishments, Grant and Harding again form a couple at the bottom of the list, and the top spots are occupied by the familiar Lincoln, F. D. Roosevelt, Washington, Jefferson, T. Roosevelt, Truman, and Wilson.

One special asset of the Maranell evaluations is that the numbers he assigns to each president on the dimensions carry significance beyond mere rank order. The intervals between the scores inform us of the difference between any two presidents on a given dimension. Looking at presidential activeness, for example, we can say that F. D. Roosevelt stands head and shoulders above those presidents immediately below him on the scale, T. Roosevelt, Jackson, L. B. Johnson, and Truman. Though these four are separated from each other by approximately 0.1 points, the first-place claimant surpasses the second-place by four times that amount.

The most ambitious and most recent survey is that conducted in 1981 by Robert K. Murray and Tim H. Blessing (1983) as part of their presidential performance study. Eight-hundred forty-six respondents provided greatness evaluations; all those polled were Ph.D.-holding historians in American academic departments. With the usual exceptions of W. Harrison and Garfield, every president from Washington to Carter was assessed, thirty-six in all. Four presidents were classed as great: Lincoln, F. D. Roosevelt, Washington, and Jefferson. Near greats were T. Roosevelt, Wilson, Jackson, and Truman. Five presidents precipitated to the bottom of the heap, namely, A. Johnson, Buchanan, Nixon, Grant, and Harding. The Murray–Blessing scores are in line with earlier ratings, but with a new addition to the collection of failed presidents, Nixon. Murray and Blessing went on to compare their ratings with two other recent polls, albeit less extensive and elaborate ones. The first was a survey of forty-nine experts that appeared in the *Chicago Tribune Magazine* in 1982. This poll discriminated the "ten Best" presidents from the "ten Worst." In the former category can be found Lincoln, Washington, F. Roosevelt, T. Roosevelt, Jefferson, Wilson, Jackson, Truman, Eisenhower, and Polk; in the last are Carter, Tyler, Coolidge, A. Johnson, Fillmore, Grant, Pierce, Buchanan, Nixon, and Harding. The second survey was an unpublished poll of forty-one experts executed by David L. Porter that listed Lincoln, Washington, F. D. Roosevelt, Jefferson, and T. Roosevelt among the all-time great, with Nixon, Buchanan, and Harding anchoring the bottom. For the most part, the *Chicago Tribune* and Porter polls yielded ratings that did not appreciably differ from those of Murray and Blessing.

Once we allow for the expansion of the supply of presidents that have to be rated, all of the polls, from Schlesinger's 1948 survey to the 1981 Murray–Blessing survey, tend to concur on the relative greatness of the past presidents. It should be apparent, then, that having historians rate the presidents is about the best conceivable way of assessing presidential greatness. Whether we end up with ranks or with interval scales, we obtain measures that can make fine distinctions between presidents at either end of the scale. Although the Murray–Blessing (1983) study is more current, the type of scaling found in the Maranell (1970) survey remains perhaps the best of the lot. Besides polling a large number of historians, the survey required the respondents to rate the presidents on less global dimensions than overall greatness. Nevertheless, in the next section we will learn that several of the seven dimensions in the Maranell poll are so intimately intertwined that they measure pretty much the same thing.

The Historical Consensus

An abundance of presidential ratings does not help us much if the historians do not agree among themselves. It is hard to evaluate precisely the degree of consensus merely by looking at the diverse rankings and ratings, for the impression they give is quite mixed. On the positive side, there appears to be some unanimity on who are the best and worst presidents, in broad groupings at least. Lincoln and F. D. Roosevelt are at or near the top on almost all assessments, and Washington, Jefferson, Wilson, T. Roosevelt, Jackson, and Truman are all placed close to the upper ranks. Grant and Harding usually vie for the bottom of the barrel, though occasionally they must jostle with A. Johnson, Coolidge, Pierce, Buchanan, and Fillmore for the unenviable position as dregs. Never has a historian ventured to put Lincoln at the bottom of the list, nor is Harding ever elevated to the top. So the ratings are not utterly capricious. On the negative side, the specific rankings of the presidents may vary from one rating to another. In some ratings Lincoln stands highest, in others F. D. Roosevelt, and in yet others Washington. The rankings of the mediocre presidents are especially unstable from one rating to the next. Of course, no measure in the behavioral and social sciences is flawless, and so it may be expecting too much to seek consensus in the nitty-gritty details as well as in the overall perspective. Even so, we should assess in an objective, quantitative fashion the exact extent of the consensus.

Kynerd (1971) made such an assessment in a paper that compared the ratings of Schlesinger, Bailey, Rossiter, and Sokolsky. The comparison was executed statistically, by the computation of correlation coefficients between separate ratings. The outcome is instructive. The highest correlation is that between the two

Schlesinger rankings (r = .96), as we should expect. The second highest correlation is that between the Sokolsky and the Rossiter ratings (r = .93), two scorings that also correlate highly with the second Schlesinger poll (r = .95 and .89, respectively). When viewed as reliability coefficients, these rather high correlations are much more respectable than most social science instruments, such as intelligence tests, personality inventories, and attitude scales (see Simonton 1981a; Simonton 1984b, chap. 1). Bailey's desire to offer an antidote to the Schlesinger results seems to have worked, for his ratings (as interpreted by Kynerd) exhibit the lowest correlations with the remaining assessments: .73 with Schlesinger's 1948 poll, .75 with Schlesinger's 1962 poll, .76 with Sokolsky's, and .80 with Rossiter's. Nevertheless, it cannot be overemphasized that these correlations, albeit noticeably smaller, are honorable. In no case does a correlation approach a small or zero value, and certainly a negative correlation between two ratings has never been found. This is not to say that we can conclude that one measure is as good as any other. Kynerd demonstrated that the Schlesinger ratings, unlike those of Bailey, are biased by party membership, the Democratic presidents getting the better deal. But with suitable precautions we can safely affirm that an impressive consensus does indeed underlie the five ratings analyzed by Kynerd.

The Maranell (1970) evaluations present a somewhat different problem. Because there are seven dimensions rather than just one, we must inquire first as to their relations. It is convenient that Maranell himself addressed this issue by calculating correlations among the seven dimensions. Five of the dimensions correlate so highly with one another that it is obvious that they are all assessing pretty much the same thing. These five are general prestige, strength of action, presidential activeness, administration accomplishments, and the respondent's amount of information. Prestige, as an example, correlates .95 with strength, .89 with activeness, .98 with accomplishment, and .79 with information. Strength correlates .97 with activeness, .97 with accomplishment, and .84 with information. These correlations are high, competing with the reliabilities calculated by Kynerd for the earlier ratings. Even the respondent's knowledge correlates no lower than .79

with the other four measures. These five dimensions therefore appear to be tapping a single underlying factor of greatness. The greater the president, the higher his prestige, strength, activeness, and accomplishment, and the more historians learn about him in order to comprehend the progression of American history. In comparison, none of these five dimensions correlates highly with the two remaining dimensions of idealism and flexibility. Presidential idealism correlates most highly with prestige (r = .17), flexibility with accomplishment (r = .16), but neither of these correlations is statistically or substantively significant. As observed in chapter 4, however, idealism and flexibility are sufficiently correlated in a negative direction (r = −.33) to form a second factor called dogmatism, or idealistic inflexibility. The seven dimensions of the Maranell survey may in practice consist of two more inclusive dimensions, greatness and dogmatism.

This inference has been endorsed by factor analytic studies (Simonton 1981c; Wendt and Light 1976). Two and only two factors emerge. The first, defined by the dimensions of prestige, strength, activeness, accomplishment, and information, accounts for 84 percent of the common variance in the correlation matrix. The factor loadings of these dimensions on the first factor range from .840 to .998—extremely high values. The second factor is more poorly defined, accounting for only 16 percent of the common variance. It is a bipolar factor consisting of idealism with a positive loading and flexibility with a negative loading. We thus have a primary greatness factor and a secondary dogmatism factor, just as we surmised from inspecting the correlation matrix. Concentrating on the greatness factor, we can create a new rating by merely summing up the scores a president receives on the five dimensions. (Wendt and Light 1976 omit the information dimension, but its omission or inclusion has no impact on the results.) The factor scores on this composite greatness scale are reliable, for coefficient alpha is .98, and therefore we are justified in treating it as a new, cohesive rating.

It may seem odd to partition global greatness into several distinct dimensions only to collapse them together; yet the combined measure is superior to the holistic assessment because we know better what criteria went into its definition. At the same time, we can prove that this composite measure reflects the same historical consensus that was behind the pre-Maranell assessments. In particular, the greatness measure correlates .94 with Schlesinger's 1948 poll, .93 with his 1962 poll, .88 with Rossiter's rankings, .94 with Sokolsky's, and .72 with Bailey's (Simonton 1981c). Again, Bailey's cantankerous rankings come out on the low end of these comparisons, yet the correlation stays high. This greatness measure also correlates well with various indicators of popular acclaim, including a portrait on Mount Rushmore ($r = .52$), a monument in Washington, D.C. ($r = .52$), and election to the Hall of Fame ($r = .48$), as well as how early a coin was struck with a presidential profile ($r = .57$) and how low a denomination of currency is graced with a presidential portrait ($r = .40$)(Simonton 1986c; see also Nice 1984). On a more scholarly level, the greatness measure correlates .69 with having an entry in the *Macropaedia* of the *Encyclopaedia Britannica* (15th edition) (Simonton 1981b). The top scorers are F. D. Roosevelt, Lincoln, T. Roosevelt, Jefferson, Wilson, and Washington; at the bottom are Grant, Buchanan, Fillmore, Pierce, and Harding (Simonton 1981c).

Not only do the seven dimensions hang together as a single greatness measure, but the agreement among the historians is such that the ratings more or less transcend ideological bias. Maranell, in a companion study (Maranell and Dodder 1970), checked to see whether the political orientation of an American historian affected his presidential evaluations. Schlesinger's evaluations contained a hidden liberal slant, but Maranell had a good many more respondents, and this might lessen the danger of bias. The special focus of this check was how a president's prestige score depended on whether the survey respondent was liberal or conservative, as indicated by party preference. By and large, the separate ratings are remarkably alike, with a correlation of .95. Hence, ideological commitments exert minimal influence on the magnitude of consensus. The president who elicited the biggest contrast between liberal and conservative historians was F. D. Roosevelt. Not surprisingly, FDR was assigned a lower prestige score by the conservatives than he received from the liberals. Liberals placed him almost two standard deviations above the mean, whereas conservatives put him at just below one standard deviation above the mean. Even so, we should not overlook the fact that conservative historians considered FDR to be safely among the top 20 percent of American presidents on the prestige dimension.

Maranell came across another contrast between liberals and conservatives that is much more provocative. Ideological disposition evidently affects how a historian links idealism and flexibility with greatness. For liberal historians, great presidents, whether measured by prestige, strength, activeness, or accomplishment, are both idealistic and flexible. The opposite is true for conservative historians, who are more inclined to rate a president highly if he is pragmatic and inflexible. Hence, while liberals and conservatives concur in their overall greatness ratings, the discrepancies that appear may be credited to dramatically opposed attitudes about having idealistic and flexible leaders in the Oval Office.

The survey outcome of Murray and Blessing (1983), when likewise subjected to quantitative comparisons, reveals a comparable consensus on differential greatness. Murray and Blessing themselves scrutinized how the ratings were affected by various characteristics of the respondents, including the historian's age, sex, geographical region, specialty area, academic affiliation, and professional status. These demographic and scholastic factors normally accounted for between one and five percent of the variance in each president's rating. With only one exception (Cleveland), well over 90 percent of the variation in a president's score is free from the most obvious kinds of rater bias. In addition, Murray and Blessing showed, albeit in a qualitative fashion, that the professional status of the respondent had no consequence for a president's evaluation. Scores given by the seventy-five historians with the highest status were virtually identical to those assigned by the remaining 771 respondents. The correlation between the elite and hoi polloi is .996 (Simonton 1986c).

All this is not to say that the consensus among the 846 historians was near-perfect for each president. Some chief executives elicited noticeable disagreement from the historians and accordingly can be considered controversial figures in American political history. Murray and Blessing actually performed the valuable service of calculating controversiality scores for the thirty-six presidents.

A controversial president was one whose greatness ratings exhibited a large variation across respondents, whereas the dispersion of scores for an uncontroversial president was tiny. The three least controversial presidents were Lincoln, F. D. Roosevelt, and Washington. According to this rating, their membership in the exclusive club of great presidents is necessarily secure. The most controversial president was Nixon, followed by L. Johnson, Hoover, Jackson, J. Q. Adams, and A. Johnson. The disagreement sparked by Nixon and LBJ may be partly attributable to their recentness. We are perhaps too close to the events of these two administrations to confidently judge, for example, the comparative weight of the Watergate scandal and the diplomatic triumphs of the Nixon presidency, or the long-term effects of America's involvement in the Vietnam War and the institution of the Great Society programs under the Johnson presidency. In the case of Hoover and the nineteenth-century presidents, however, the dust should have had time to settle. Because these presidents tend to have received extreme scores on Maranell's idealism and flexibility dimensions, we can speculate that differences in controversiality reflect the contrasting perceptions of liberal and conservative historians. In any event, I must stress that the historical consensus is still so potent that even controversial presidents are firmly in place on the greatness scale. Jackson need not worry about being dumped among the mediocre presidents, nor can Nixon hope for a promotion to the above-average spot.

The Murray-Blessing ratings are compatible with the two nearly contemporary surveys by the *Chicago Tribune* and Porter; the correlations are .96 and .98, respectively, while the *Chicago Tribune* and Porter ratings correlate .98 with each other (Simonton 1986c). Furthermore, the Murray–Blessing rating correlates .95 with the first Schlesinger poll, .94 with the second Schlesinger poll, .85 with Rossiter's, .89 with Sokolsky's, .81 with Bailey's, and, respectively, .94, .94, .86, .96, and .79 with the prestige, strength, activeness, accomplishment, and information dimensions of Maranell (Simonton 1986c). The only low correlations are with the Maranell dimensions of idealism and flexibility (.11 and .22, respectively) and with Murray and Blessing's own controversiality scores (−.14). The corresponding coefficients for the *Chicago*

Tribune and the Porter surveys are practically identical (Simonton 1986c).

The size of the overall historical consensus can be better appreciated if we perform a factor analysis on all measures at once, including all seven Maranell dimensions and the Murray–Blessing controversiality ratings, sixteen measures all told (Simonton 1986c). As found in earlier studies (Simonton 1981c; Wendt and Light 1976), just two factors emerge. The first factor defines a clear greatness factor, for virtually all ratings display large loadings on this dimension. Only presidential idealism, flexibility, and controversiality have negligible correlations with the greatness factor. With just two exceptions, the remaining thirteen loadings are in the .90s, and often approach the maximum value of unity. Maranell's information dimension has a loading of .80, which implies that the amount of information a respondent has about the president in question is at best an indirect indicator of greatness. The second exception reveals Bailey's refusal to conform absolutely to the historical consensus; his loading is still around .80. This greatness factor, furthermore, accounts for 85 percent of the explained variance.

The Bailey rating is the only measure putatively assessing greatness that loads to any noteworthy degree on the second factor, a dimension that looks like the dogmatism factor found in previous analyses of the Maranell data. Appended to this factor is the Bailey assessment and the Murray–Blessing controversiality rating. At one pole of this factor we have those presidents who are idealistic, inflexible, highly controversial, and unfavorably perceived by Bailey; at the other pole we have those presidents who are pragmatic, flexible, not very controversial, and positively valued by Bailey. The foundation of Bailey's dissent seems to be that he prefers to play it safe by refusing to regard highly any president who might be a subject of debate among other historians. However, we should not focus too much attention on Bailey when interpreting the second factor, for the highest loadings involve flexibility and controversiality, followed by idealism. Thus, this dimension pertains to presidents who are controversial because they stuck to their guns, their rigidity often assisted by an inordinate idealism. Consistent with this interpretation is the finding of

Table 5.1 Standardized Greatness Scores from Nine Presidential Ratings

President	Schlesinger 1948	Schlesinger 1962	Rossiter	Bailey–Kynerd	Sokolsky	Maranell–Simonton	Porter	*Chicago Tribune*	Murray–Blessing
1. Washington	1.5	1.5	1.2	1.6	0.6	1.2	1.6	1.6	1.9
2. J. Adams	0.7	0.7	0.5	−0.6	0.6	0.4	0.8	0.3	0.6
3. Jefferson	1.2	1.2	1.2	1.2	1.4	1.2	1.4	1.3	1.5
4. Madison	0.1	0.4	−0.9	−0.7	−0.2	0.1	0.5	0.1	0.2
5. Monroe	0.4	−0.2	−0.9	0.9	−0.2	−0.0	0.1	0.2	0.2
6. J. Q. Adams	0.5	0.3	−0.2	−1.5	−0.2	−0.1	0.0	−0.0	0.1
7. Jackson	1.1	1.1	1.2	1.0	1.4	1.2	1.1	1.1	1.0
8. Van Buren	0.0	−0.1	−0.2	0.6	−0.2	−0.4	−0.0	0.0	−0.3
9. W. Harrison	—	—	—	—	—	—	—	—	—
10. Tyler	−0.8	−1.0	−0.2	−0.2	−0.2	−0.9	−0.9	−0.9	−0.8
11. Polk	0.6	0.9	0.5	−0.1	0.6	0.4	0.9	0.8	0.4
12. Taylor	−1.2	−0.9	—	−0.8	−1.1	−1.0	−0.8	−0.7	−0.7
13. Fillmore	−1.1	−1.1	−0.9	−0.3	−1.1	−1.4	−1.0	−1.2	−0.9
14. Pierce	−1.4	−1.3	−1.6	−1.1	−1.1	−1.4	−1.4	−1.4	−1.1
15. Buchanan	−1.3	−1.4	−1.6	−1.2	−1.1	−1.2	−1.6	−1.5	−1.3
16. Lincoln	1.6	1.6	1.2	1.5	1.4	1.7	1.7	1.7	2.0
17. A. Johnson	−0.5	−0.8	0.5	−1.6	−0.2	−0.2	−1.2	−1.1	−1.2

18. Grant	−1.5	−1.5	−1.6	−0.9	−1.9	−1.2	−1.3	−1.3	−1.4
19. Hayes	0.2	0.2	0.5	0.8	−0.2	−0.8	−0.1	−0.3	−0.4
20. Garfield	—	—	—	—	—	—	—	—	—
21. Arthur	−0.2	−0.6	0.2	0.2	−0.2	−0.8	−0.5	−0.5	−0.5
22. Cleveland	0.8	0.6	0.5	0.1	0.6	0.1	0.3	0.5	0.1
23. B. Harrison	−0.7	−0.4	−0.9	−0.4	−1.1	−1.1	−0.6	−0.6	−0.7
24. McKinley	−0.4	0.1	−0.2	0.7	−0.2	−0.3	0.2	0.7	−0.2
25. T. Roosevelt	0.9	1.0	1.2	1.3	1.4	1.4	1.3	1.4	1.3
26. Taft	−0.1	0.0	−0.2	0.0	−0.2	−0.1	−0.2	−0.1	−0.2
27. Wilson	1.3	1.3	1.2	1.1	1.4	1.2	1.2	1.2	1.2
28. Harding	−1.6	−1.6	−1.6	−1.4	−1.9	−1.4	−1.7	−1.7	−1.6
29. Coolidge	−0.9	−1.2	−0.9	−1.0	−1.1	−1.1	−1.1	−1.0	−0.9
30. Hoover	−0.6	−0.3	−0.2	−1.3	−0.2	−0.1	−0.3	−0.2	−0.4
31. F. Roosevelt	1.4	1.4	1.2	1.4	1.4	1.9	1.5	1.5	1.9
32. Truman	—	0.8	1.2	0.4	0.6	1.1	1.0	1.0	0.9
33. Eisenhower	—	−0.7	0.5	0.3	−0.2	−0.2	0.6	0.9	0.5
34. Kennedy	—	—	—	—	1.4	0.8	0.4	0.4	0.4
35. L. Johnson	—	—	—	—	—	0.8	0.7	0.6	0.6
36. Nixon	—	—	—	—	—	—	−1.5	−1.6	−1.3
37. Ford	—	—	—	—	—	—	−0.7	−0.4	−0.6
38. Carter	—	—	—	—	—	—	−0.4	−0.8	−0.6

Source: Adapted from table 1 in Simonton (1981c) and table A1 in Simonton (1986c).

another study that controversial presidents exhibit exceptional achievement drive, forcefulness, pettiness, and inflexibility, but are deficient in moderation, friendliness, and wit (Simonton 1986e).

The first factor, the greatness dimension, most interests us here, for this factor shows that all the ratings of the presidents measure essentially the same thing. To realize all the better the extent of historical consensus, we should directly inspect the greatness scores that the presidents have earned in the diverse ratings (see Simonton 1986c). Direct comparison is facilitated by inverting scores whenever necessary so that all ratings move in the same direction and by standardizing all scores to a zero mean and a unit standard deviation (making the scores directly comparable to the motivational and personality ratings displayed in tables 4.2 and 4.3). Table 5.1 presents the standard scores for the two Schlesinger rankings, the Rossiter, Bailey, and Sokolsky ratings (based on the numerical codings in Kynerd 1971), the Maranell assessments collapsed into a single greatness dimension (from Simonton 1981c), and the three most recent evaluations by Porter, the *Chicago Tribune*, and Murray and Blessing.

No matter which column we examine, a better than average president has a positive score and a worse than average president a negative score; a score near zero indicates relative mediocrity. Moreover, a chief executive more than one point (standard deviation) away from the zero mean, in either direction, can be taken as exceptional. Thus, five presidents consistently show standard scores of 1.0 or more on every greatness measure. These undeniably great presidents were, in chronological order, Jefferson, Jackson, Lincoln, Wilson, and F. D. Roosevelt, with Lincoln and FDR the two brightest stars in the constellation. Antipodal to these five are three presidents who show a rating of −1.0 or less no matter what measure we look at. Again in chronological order, these unquestionably inferior presidents were Pierce, Buchanan, and Harding, the latter truly last. In both categories there appear close rivals for the top and bottom spots in history. Washington and T. Roosevelt narrowly miss a consistent standard score of unity or better, and hence can be counted among the near great. Coolidge and especially Grant exhibit a similar near miss at the low end of the scale, making them near failures. Nixon is condemned to a tentative position in the same group, for the three ratings recent enough to evaluate his presidency are all in concordance about his markedly substandard status. Last, and least in terms of distinctiveness, I should mention those chief executives whose scores are neither good nor bad but uniformly run-of-the-mill. In this class of utterly ordinary chief executives belongs Taft, whose rating without exception hovers around zero, singling him out as the most dependably middling president in American history. This result may fit the observation made in chapter 4 that Taft had the lowest power and achievement drives of any modern president.

The presidential rating game, as it is sometimes derisively called (see Peskin 1977), is not without its critics, to be sure (for example, Amlund 1964; Bailey 1966; Hoxie 1976). Nevertheless, it should be manifest by now that the rating of presidents cannot be faulted for lack of consensus. Quite the contrary; the correspondence among the diverse assessments is extraordinary. The assertion that Lincoln and F. D. Roosevelt were great presidents and that Harding was a presidential failure is grounded in a consensus so solid that the remark apparently represents an objective acknowledgment of reality more than a subjective judgment.

PREDICTING GREATNESS

Now that we are confident that presidents can be reliably differentiated on greatness, can we locate variables that will allow us to predict the greatness rating before the historians are ever polled? At the time of this writing political commentators and scholars are debating whether Ronald Reagan will go down in history as a great chief executive. If we can isolate the predictors of greatness, this debate can be settled without going to the trouble of surveying hundreds of historians and political scientists some years hence. Potential predictor variables can be classified into two categories: those that could be used to predict a politician's presidential greatness even before he enters the White House, and those that could be used to translate the actual performance of his administration into an ultimate greatness assessment. One set of predictors has to do with promise, the other set with accomplishment. After presenting an inventory of potential predictors in each category, I will discuss two equations that actually predict presidential greatness with rare precision.

Biographical and Personality Correlates

Several psychologists have tried to uncover personality variables that might predict a president's reputation among historians. The first such effort was by David Winter (1973), who wanted to show that his measure of power motivation correlated with presidential greatness. As described in chapter 4, his indicator of a president's need for power was based on a content analysis of inaugural addresses delivered by twentieth-century presidents. The resulting measure was correlated with the Maranell (1970) survey results for the eleven presidents between T. Roosevelt and L. B. Johnson (see also Winter 1985). Because the power motive is tied closely to the achievement motive for this special collection of people, Winter examined the correlations between power motivation and Maranell dimensions after first partialling out achievement motivation. These partial correlations were large for the five dimensions that make up the greatness factor (r between .44 and .54) but small for the two dimensions that define the dogmatism factor (r = .16 and .19). (The partial correlations between the seven dimensions and achievement motivation controlling for power motivation were uniformly negligible.) Hence, a high need for power expressed in a president's inaugural address may help us predict his probable greatness. Given that the criteria of greatness involve strength of action and presidential activeness, this relation is not surprising. In any case, if we inspect table 4.2 again, we are reminded that T. Roosevelt, Truman, and Kennedy all displayed uncommon power drives, whereas Taft, Coolidge, and Hoover did not.

Wendt and Light (1976) studied fifteen presidents between 1876 and 1972. They combined the Maranell dimensions into a single composite greatness measure (omitting the information dimension), and replicated Winter's chief conclusions. The amount of power imagery in a president's first inaugural address correlated even better with greatness (r = .74), the relation between greatness and achievement imagery again being smaller (r = .57). They also discovered that greatness was associated with the president's affiliation with the Democratic party (r = .70). Although this correlation might be ascribed to political bias on the part of the 571 historians participating in the Maranell poll, another interpretation is possible. Since Democratic presidents are more disposed toward a power orientation (see chapter 4), some of their success in the historians' judgments may be due to concrete personality contrasts with Republican chief executives. Becoming a successful president may require an exceptional drive toward the fulfillment of power needs. This is not to say that the historians are unbiased, but rather that the bias takes a form other than political partisanship: historians may prefer activist presidents to less obtrusive ones (Hoxie 1976). A similar preference holds for absolute monarchs as well, indicating that historians favor those leaders who give them much to talk about in their narratives (Simonton 1984d).

In a more recent inquiry into presidential motivation conducted by Winter and Stewart (1977), affiliation needs were considered along with achievement and power needs. The association between the power motive and assessed greatness, again determined by the Maranell ratings, was even stronger when both achievement and affiliation drives were statistically controlled. In particular, the need for power correlated .63 with general prestige, .74 with strength of action, .68 with presidential activeness, .66 with administration accomplishments, and .59 with the respondent's information. Yet the affiliation motive is associated with the first four of these greatness indicators in a *negative* direction. Those White House residents with a conspicuous desire to be with others, to win social approval, are less likely to join the ranks of the great. The specific partial coefficients are −.52 for general prestige, −.72 for strength of action, −.65 for presidential activeness, and −.63 for administration accomplishments. Evidently, a politician who is obsessed with getting along with others is likely to become a blank spot in the pages of American history. If the pages are not empty, it will be for the wrong reasons, for, as observed in chapter 4, high-affiliation presidents are somewhat scandal-prone. Hence, the motivational prescription for a grand presidency is patent: elect power-needy leaders who care not an iota about making friends, or enemies. That Ford, the genuine "nice guy" in the White House ("Mr. Sunshine" in Lionel Hampton's campaign song), exhibited low power needs but high affiliation needs may contribute to an explanation of why he was the only accidental president in this century not to be reelected. His unconditional pardon of his predecessor, which adversely affected his reelection chances, was a gesture typical of a leader who places social concord and goodwill over personal aggrandizement.

Another investigation adopted a line of attack altogether different from the preceding one (Simonton 1981c). First, it studied all thirty-three presidents that Maranell (1970) had evaluated, not just the eleven or fifteen most recent ones. Second, biographical variables were inspected in addition to personality traits per se. These biographical variables included numerous family background characteristics (such as birth order and family size), educational experiences (such as level of formal education and scholastic honors), personal traits (such as height and age), occupations (such as lawyer or soldier), and aspects of political careers (such as years in public office and specific offices held). The information used was discovered in various presidential fact books (for example, Kane 1974, 1977; Taylor 1972). While over a hundred potential predictors were correlated with the Maranell general greatness factor, only three variables came out with high correlations. First, the most highly esteemed presidents tend to be tall ($r = .40$): Lincoln and F. D. Roosevelt stood (albeit the latter with leg braces) literally head and shoulders above Van Buren and Benjamin Harrison. Second, great presidents are likely to come from small families ($r = -.37$); Lincoln and FDR once again illustrate this point, each having fewer than three siblings, in contrast to men like Buchanan and Taft, who had nine or more siblings. Third, on the average, the greater chief executives publish many books before assuming the presidency ($r = .42$). Teddy Roosevelt published about a dozen books prior to assuming the duties of the office, some popular history, like *Oliver Cromwell*, others just plain popular, like *Ranch Life and the Hunting-Trail.* This third correlate is a bit peculiar, and may reflect yet another bias in the presidential ratings; because historians love to read books, they may be prejudiced in favor of those presidents who provide them with plenty of material for scholarly research. An alternative explanation stems from the fact that that fluency is associated with many varieties of leadership (Bass 1981), including charismatic leadership (Cell 1974). Perhaps the prepresidential book publication correlate is tapping a broad verbal and ideational fluency that supports effective leadership (see Simonton 1985a). Politicians who are capable of composing book-length manuscripts may also be somewhat more intelligent than average, and this superior intellect may contribute to greatness.

All of the biographical correlates were based on their straightforward zero-order correlations with assessed greatness. In the next section we will find that one of the best predictors of greatness is the duration of the president's administration, and so it behooves us to partial out this factor. After all, how long a president serves is subject to a host of influences, such as how long the president lives, that have little bearing on greatness as a leader. Thus it is of value to ask: taking two presidents who had tenures of equal length, are there any biographical variables that still predict differential greatness? This question turns out to have a dramatic answer, for partialling out how long a president serves deletes family size and height as predictors, leaving only the prepresidential publication record ($r = .38$). Hence, two of these biographical correlates may enjoy at best an indirect effect on the president's reputation; height, for example, as we saw in chapter 2, may contribute to the incumbent's reelection chances, and thereby to a long tenure in office. Nonetheless, a new predictor emerges too. Those presidents who were professional soldiers prior to entering office, such as Taylor, Grant, and Eisenhower, made inferior chief executives, on the average ($r = -.44$). In 1948 Eisenhower avoided recruitment as a presidential candidate with this excuse: "The necessary and wise subordination of the military to civil power will be best sustained . . . when lifelong professional soldiers, in the absence of some obvious and overriding reasons, abstain from seeking high political office." The negative correlation might suggest that Ike ought to have remembered this remark when the next election rolled around four years later.

The quest for biographical predictors has not been overwhelmingly successful. Nevertheless, all of the studies described above were exploratory only, with no pretensions to being definitive. Numerous relevant variables remain to be defined and tested, and many definitions can probably undergo substantial improvement. This is particularly true of variables that assess political experience. Yet it must also be acknowledged that there really may not be many direct biographical predictors. Rather, greatness may depend mostly on what takes place during a president's administration, any one biographical factor influencing the result only insofar as it impresses itself on events.

Administration Correlates

While the number of biographical correlates of presidential greatness is small, a large number of administration events and policies have been linked with greatness assessments. Wendt and Light (1976), again using only fifteen presidents and assessing greatness using the combined five dimensions from the Maranell (1970) survey, demonstrated that the greatest presidents tended, in descending order, to emphasize international rather than isolationist foreign policies ($r = .71$), to enjoy positive press relations ($r = .66$), to have been the targets of assassination attempts after their election ($r = .59$), to have wars declared or sanctioned by Congress ($r = .57$), to exercise the veto power more frequently ($r = .52$), to engage the United States in more military interventions abroad ($r = .48$), and to experience a higher rate of cabinet turnover ($r = .41$). Presidents T. Roosevelt, Wilson, F. D. Roosevelt, and Truman exemplify, each with his own exceptions, this template for greatness.

This cluster of attributes is particularly interesting because many of them can be linked with specific personality antecedents, particularly a strong power motivation and an inclination toward intellectual simplicity. Earlier I mentioned that the need for power was related to a president's engaging the U.S. in a war, to his serving as an assassination target, and to a high rate of turnover in the White House cabinet (Winter 1973). This personality variable was also associated with effective press relations (Wendt and Light 1976). In addition, high integrative complexity is negatively related to both isolationism in foreign policy and a tendency to fall back on military force to resolve international conflicts. Accordingly, the cluster of administration events that go along with higher assessed greatness may constitute nothing more than proxy variables for underlying motivational and cognitive factors.

This last remark should be kept in mind as we contemplate the findings of a second investigation (Simonton 1981c). All thirty-three presidents assessed by Maranell were scrutinized, and a large number of administration events were tabulated by utilizing, in conjunction with the fact books mentioned above, American history compendia (such as Caruth 1979; Kull and Kull 1952; Morris 1976; *Webster's* 1971) and general reference works (such as *Encyclopaedia Britannica*, 15th ed.). In partial replication of the preceding study, the greatest presidents were found to initiate more military interventions ($r = .42$), to submit a war message to Congress ($r = .40$), to have Congress declare war ($r = .43$), and to lead the nation through more years of war ($r = .60$). Great chief executives also display a higher likelihood of getting shot at by a would-be assassin ($r = .63$). Furthermore, the greater the president the more major acts he signs ($r = .48$), the more Supreme Court justices he nominates ($r = .36$) and the more nominated justices actually serve on the bench ($r = .51$). The great president thus attains positive relations with Congress. The political conditions for the great president are in fact conducive to cooperative interactions between executive and legislative branches, for the great president usually has a party majority in the House ($r = .46$). He is also likely to have entered the White House by defeating an incumbent president, a rare achievement ($r = .36$), and *not* to have been defeated for renomination to run for a second term ($r = -.42$).

Apropos of this correlate, presidents stand taller in the eyes of posterity if they served a long tenure in the nation's highest office ($r = .64$). Most of the highly rated presidents, such as Washington, Jefferson, Lincoln, and F. D. Roosevelt, were elected to at least two full terms in the White House, whereas most of the lesser presidents, such as Pierce and Harding, served one term or less. Finally, one other crucial correlate must be noted: the truly great presidents manage to avoid administration scandals ($r = -.35$).

The two chief executives who most consistently rank lowest in the ratings, Grant and Harding, were both victims of this merciless tendency.

Before we begin to interpret the foregoing findings, we must underline the danger implicit in the fact that the length of time in office shows the largest correlation with assessed greatness. A long tenure means that numerous other events will occur, if only by chance. As noted in the previous chapter, for instance, the supply of Supreme Court vacancies can be ascribed largely to chance; accordingly, the longer a president serves the more appointments he will be able to make, on the average. Likewise, a long stay in the Oval Office will increase the odds of a president signing more history-making bills, and of having to intervene militarily abroad. Though these events may look like accomplishments on which a president can base his reputation as an active, strong chief executive, they can just as well be seen as mere repercussions of tenure duration, and therefore epiphenomenal to the actual level of leadership demonstrated. To show how misleading such event counts can be, one study of European monarchs proved that the single best predictor of a ruler's eminence was a straight count of historical events that occurred under his or her reign; the chief predictor of this event tally was how long the monarch reigned; and the principal predictor of reign length was simply how long the king, queen, or regent lived (Simonton 1984d; see also Sorokin 1926). Assessed leadership, intelligence, and morality exerted a minimal influence on the ultimate historical rating. Hence we are compelled to ask what happens if we equate presidents' lengths of tenure by introducing the appropriate statistical controls. If we partial out administration duration, what will remain to predict presidential greatness?

When we control for time passed in the White House, the main correlates of historical standing are reduced to four variables. The greatest presidents are more likely to be assassinated ($r = .38$), to survive an assassination attempt ($r = .46$), to guide the United States through more years of war ($r = .43$), and not to be disgraced by a conspicuous administration scandal ($r = -.38$). Consequently, the picture is fairly like that of the power-motivated and intellectually uncomplicated chief executive, with the proviso that the president have low affiliation needs. The high need for power raises the probability of war and assassination attempts; the low need for affiliation minimizes the chances that the incumbent will look the other way when cronies appointed to high office abuse the public trust (Winter and Stewart 1977). And an incumbent low in integrative complexity may be more likely to become a wartime commander-in-chief.

David C. Nice (1984) has also demonstrated the manifest connection between serving as a wartime commander-in-chief and a president's historical acclaim. In addition, he has pointed to a second, purely political predictor that we have yet to mention, the degree of party system aging. Great presidents may head a major realignment of the American people along new issue cleavages, whereas the mediocre presidents merely continue the inherited party system, with its ideological commitments and constituencies. The great may revolutionize politics, while the small indulge in politics as usual. As Nice saw it, political alignments were revamped just five times in American history: by Washington in 1789, Jackson in 1828, Lincoln in 1860, McKinley in 1896, and F. D. Roosevelt in 1932. In the first three elections the victorious presidential candidates were the focus of new political parties (Federalists, Democrats, and Republicans, respectively); in the last two elections established parties were reconstituted and thus revived (as in FDR's New Deal coalition). By comparison, presidents like Monroe, Buchanan, B. Harrison, and Hoover came into office via a mature, even senile, political structure. In any event, Nice's expectation was confirmed: as a party system aged, the presidents it planted in the White House scored lower in greatness, whether measured by the Schlesinger or the Maranell polls. In contrast, the most highly esteemed chief executives tended to enter office during extensive realignments. If not the strict focus of that party restructuring, the great president, such as T. Roosevelt, was at least in on the ground floor. Another fact mentioned above seems consistent with this finding: the greater presidents tend to be those who win election by defeating an incumbent president, an accomplishment that may reflect a major realignment of political forces (Simonton 1981c). Thus the success criterion of chapter 2 is apparently linked with the criterion of the present chapter.

Party system aging is similar to war inasmuch as it suggests that great presidents come forth during momentous times. The nation's leader must have the opportunity to prove his mettle, and this requires a crisis, whether foreign or domestic. It may even be true that all presidents are essentially the same in raw character and skill but that some are made great by their times. "There are no great men," Admiral Halsey observed, "only great challenges that ordinary men are forced by circumstances to meet." War with rival states offers a unique chance to make the big time; a decrepit political system on the verge of collapse provides another. In both cases the incumbent is expected to rally the majority of the people around a new grand cause, whether it be a war to end all wars or a New Deal for the "forgotten man." In both cases, too, there is some uncertainty whether the president actively generates the situation that grants him the latitude to manifest greatness; the president frequently seems to be the pawn of circumstances not entirely at his bidding. Though the role of a president's power motivation and integrative complexity may be cited in assigning responsibility for engaging the United States in a war, the uncertainty inherent in the party system aging factor remains problematic.

This difficulty extends to the definition of terms as well. A party realignment is less readily discerned than a state of war (see, for example, Archer et al. 1985; Gans 1985; Ladd 1985; Margolis 1985). Combat casualties inform us all too directly that a war is in progress; whether a restructuring has taken place demands a more subjective opinion. Did Ronald Reagan's landslide victory over Walter Mondale in 1984 represent the remaking of the American party system? The hard facts may not support such a claim (Axelrod 1986), yet I suspect that should Reagan go down in history as a great president, future historians will look for a realignment, whether or not one happened in fact. This subjectivity may have permitted a comparable bias to affect the choice of the five dates taken to demarcate notable realignments in the past. Peering backward through time, a historian may strain harder to spot realignments attributable to those presidents already labeled great. If so, the correlation between system aging and leader greatness would be a historiographic artifact. Fortunately, we do not have to settle this question. It turns out that party system aging lacks utility as a predictor in the equations discussed in the next section (Simonton 1986c).

Prediction Equations

In the preceding two sections we have listed numerous variables that correlate with the assessed greatness of a president. Some of these variables, such as the power motive and height, regard characteristics that a leader possesses even before inauguration day; others, such as war and assassination, concern what transpires after he takes the oath of office. The problem now before us is determining which of these variables is crucial for predicting an incumbent's ultimate glory in history. In the language of path analysis, some of these correlates may exert direct effects on a president's standing in the history books; others may have only an indirect effect (by affecting directly or indirectly a direct effect); still others may reflect only a spurious connection with assessed greatness (that is, both the correlate and greatness may be consequences of a more fundamental common cause) (Kenny 1979). The accepted procedure for determining the direct effects is to perform a multiple regression analysis, for in a properly specified regression equation the indirect and spurious effects will prove insignificant and drop out of the picture. The result should be an equation that maximizes prediction precision while preserving parsimony in the number of predictors required. Simply expressed, a multiple regression equation predicts the most variance with the fewest variables.

In the first investigation to use this technique (Simonton 1981c), the criterion of success was the greatness factor extracted from a factor analysis of the Maranell (1970) survey. Hence, the derived equation was founded on thirty-three presidents from Washington through L. B. Johnson, excluding only W. Harrison and Garfield. First, the administration correlates were permitted to enter the regression equation, and only those variables that made a significant contribution to the predicted variance were retained. The equation that resulted accounted for 68 percent of the variance in greatness with only four predictors: the duration of the president's administration; the number of years he served as a wartime commander-in-chief; whether he was the target of an unsuccessful assassination attempt; and whether his administration was plagued by a major scandal, this variable relating negatively to greatness. The next step was to permit biographical correlates to enter the equation to see whether any items from an incumbent's preadministration résumé enhanced the prediction of greatness. Only one predictor from this set, the incumbent's prepresidential book publication record, significantly improved the predictive power of the equation. The five-variable equation handled three-quarters of the variance in rated greatness, a laudable degree of predictive success given how few predictors were needed.

The correspondence between rated and predicted greatness using merely these five predictors did not vary according to historical period, and thus the equation was transhistorically invariant (compare Bailey 1966; Hoxie 1976). In only two instances was the discrepancy (or residual) between observed and expected scores sufficiently substantial to require comment. Both Washington and Kennedy were more favorably perceived by the historians than was predicted by the equation. Washington probably earned extra kudos for his unique position as the first president. His contemporaries were not the only admirers to endorse Henry Lee's 1799 epitaph "First in war, first in peace, first in the hearts of his fellow countrymen." In 1842 Lincoln, still a young politician, said, "To add brightness to the sun or glory to the name of Washington is alike impossible." Some historians, like Bailey (1966), have gone so far as to maintain that, if anything, Washington receives less credit in the polls than he deserves.

Kennedy's case is more interesting, for when Maranell's respondents were asked to fill out the questionnaires in March of 1968, the assassination of this promising president must have been fresh in the minds of everyone. Indeed, JFK's successor, LBJ, was the incumbent and his brother Robert Kennedy was a candidate for the presidency. By the time many of the questionnaires were returned, both Martin Luther King and Robert Kennedy had been shot to death, highlighting the sorrows attending the assassination of notable leaders. It is not callous to conjecture, therefore, that JFK received a big sympathy vote because of what may be styled a tragedy effect (Simonton 1984b, chap. 6). Historiometric research has demonstrated that illustrious persons gain luster if they die unusually young (Lehman 1943; Mills 1942; Simonton 1976); even more polish is probably applied if the victim died tragically for a noble cause. "Martyrdom is the only way in which a man can become famous without ability," George Bernard Shaw quipped. This is not to say that JFK displayed no capacity as president, but only that more perspective is needed, so that historical judgment will not stumble over rubble left from the fall of Camelot. In 1970, when Maranell's survey was published, historians may still have been intoxicated by such laudatory pieces as Sokolsky's *Our Seven Greatest Presidents* (1964) that were quick to name Kennedy's membership in the Olympian group.

The results of polls of the past decade, especially the publication of the Murray–Blessing survey in 1983, made it possible to test the prediction that Kennedy's reputation would decline with time to level off at a rating closer to that of Cleveland (compare Simonton 1981c). The first study to take advantage of these new ratings confirmed this forecast (Simonton 1986c). The goal of this investigation was to devise a prediction equation that would be maximally independent of the specific presidential ratings used, and therefore would obtain an equation with the best chance of predicting the greatness ratings in future surveys of historians. This quest for invariant predictors began by scanning the data for variables that correlate with *every* greatness rating presented in table 5.1 (with the Maranell assessment broken down into its five components). Years in office was the most prominent correlate of greatness, with correlation coefficients ranging between .43 and .59, and a correlation of .57 with the state-of-the-art Murray–Blessing judgments. The association between reputation and duration of tenure held no matter how the latter variable was defined, whether as (in order of descending effectiveness) years in office, number of Congresses, days Congress was in session, or reelection to a second term.

Another robust correlate was the number of years the nation

was at war during the president's tenure in office. This variable correlated between .38 and .65, including a .50 correlation with the rating assigned by the Murray–Blessing respondents. Though the relevance of war did not require a specific definition either—war declaration, battle counts, and other indicators were positively associated with greatness (see also Nice 1984)—the number of war years emerged as the strongest and most consistent correlate. A third variable, administration scandal, correlated with every one of the thirteen greatness criteria but one, the Maranell information dimension ($r = -.02$). Recognizing that this dimension has a tenuous connection with greatness and, more important, that historians would be expected to scrutinize scandalous presidencies in some detail, the existence of this single exception is not at all problematic. Consequently, three correlates appeared as particularly strong candidates as predictors of greatness: years in office, years of war, and freedom from administration scandal. F. D. Roosevelt is the embodiment of the great president by these yardsticks (over a dozen years in office, the nation's war leader during World War II, with no scandals during his presidency), whereas Harding is the prototypical failure (only a couple of years in the White House as a peacetime chief executive, with such devastating scandals as Teapot Dome).

These three correlates were among the five isolated in the earlier inquiry (Simonton 1981c). But what happened to the other two predictors, unsuccessful assassination attempts and the pre-presidential publication record? The last variable may indeed betray a certain bias in the hearts of historians toward fellow authors, for the number of publications prior to entering the presidency correlates most highly with the information scale of the Maranell survey. Nonetheless, book output cannot be considered a universal predictor inasmuch as it fails to correlate with the ratings of Rossiter, Bailey, and the Schlesinger 1948 poll. Authorship is associated with the three most up-to-date assessments by Porter, the *Chicago Tribune,* and Murray–Blessing, a point that will get our attention again shortly.

The status of failed assassination attempts is more problematic as a predictor. Even though this variable correlates positively with the composite greatness measure extracted from Maranell, it is by no means a consistently useful correlate. In fact, of the thirteen greatness criteria, an unsuccessful attempt on the life of an incumbent correlates only with the Maranell and Rossiter ratings. Further confusion is caused by the manner of defining the variable in the earlier study (Simonton [1981c] counted apparent assassination attempts on the president-elect, as in the cases of Lincoln and FDR) and by the intimate conceptual relation between successful and unsuccessful assassination attempts (which differ, after all, by the merest stroke of luck). Moreover, once we statistically control for years in office, death by assassination emerges as a significant correlate of greatness (Simonton 1981c). Such control makes perfect sense given the link between greatness and a long tenure in the White House. Because assassinated presidents serve a shorter time, their ratings are hurt; yet if we take those presidents who served an equal length of time, those who were assassinated receive higher ratings. In other words, if an incumbent must leave office before finishing out his term, it is far better to succumb to an assassin's bullet than to die naturally. As it happens, when we partial out the impact of years in office it is successful assassination, not its failure, that springs forth as the most reliable correlate of greatness by the diverse criteria presently available. The first-order partial correlation between assassination and the thirteen greatness indicators is significant in every case but one (Rossiter, $r = .30$), whereas failed attempts are nonsignificant in every case but one (the Maranell activeness dimension, $r = .39$). Therefore, a fourth correlate can be added to the list. A great president guards against corruption and graft, leads the nation through military crisis, and serves as the American head of state for many years; if tenure duration is brief, he has the excuse that he was assassinated. Adding this qualification permits Lincoln to be classed among the great despite the fact that he was just barely into his second term when Booth shot him in Ford's Theatre.

Given these four potential predictors, the next step in the analysis was to develop the multiple regression equation that best predicts greatness (Simonton 1986c). To accomplish this task, three criteria of greatness were employed, namely, the ratings earned in the three most recent polls by Porter, the *Chicago*

Tribune, and Murray and Blessing. By focusing on the last three columns of table 5.1, we can devise a prediction equation that holds across the thirty-six presidents between Washington and Carter (omitting W. Harrison and Garfield). At the same time, by using more than one greatness assessment, we lessen the chance that the prediction equation capitalizes on idiosyncratic aspects of a given rating. And, in fact, when the four stable correlates—years in office, war years, scandal, and assassination—are allowed to enter regression equations for the three most recent greatness assessments, all four variables prove to be statistically significant according to each criterion. This outcome essentially confirms the earlier inquiry (Simonton 1981c), with the sole reservation that actual assassination has been substituted for attempted assassination. But has some other predictor been inadvertently left out? Perusing the zero-order matrix for predictors does not guarantee that a possibility will not be overlooked, for some variables may only enter the picture once the effects of other factors are already accommodated.

Consequently, the residuals from the three regression equations were correlated with the over two-hundred variables that remained as potential predictors, including both administration performance criteria and such personal attributes as personality, political experience, prior occupation, education, and family background. Only one variable had a statistically significant correlation with the residuals of all three equations: having entered office as a national war hero—as Washington, Jackson, Grant, and Eisenhower did—is a fair predictor of greatness. This predictive utility holds despite the lack of a single zero-order correlation between war heroism and any of the thirteen greatness indices; its relevance emerges only when the other four predictors serve as suppressor variables (Nunnally 1967). In any case, new residuals were calculated, and the correlations with remaining variables again were surveyed. No other variable exhibited a significant relationship, with one quasi exception. The number of books published before entering the presidency was a significant predictor of the Murray–Blessing ratings ($p < .05$), but was of only marginal significance for the Porter and *Chicago Tribune* ratings ($p < .1$). Because a robust prediction equation was the desideratum, this variable was not inserted. Still, the insertion of presidential authorship does not affect in any substantial degree the direction, magnitude, or significance of the effects of the five variables that were retained.

We thus end up with three five-variable prediction equations. These equations account for about 78 percent of the variance in presidential greatness. Moreover, the regression coefficients for the independent variables hardly differ across the three greatness measures. Whether we look at Porter, the *Chicago Tribune*, or Murray-Blessing, the primary predictors are years in office, years of war, and scandals, the secondary predictors assassination and war heroism. Given that the Murray–Blessing ratings are the best of the three, we can use the equation for those ratings to typify the overall results. Then we can accurately predict greatness via the following equation:

$$\begin{aligned}\text{Greatness} = &-1.24 + 0.17\ (\text{years}) + 0.26\ (\text{war}) - 1.70\ (\text{scandal}) \\ &+ 0.89\ (\text{assassination}) + 0.82\ (\text{hero})\end{aligned}$$

Here "years" is the number of years the president served; "war" is the number of those years that the nation was at war; "scandal" equals 1 if the administration was plagued by a cabinet-level scandal (as under Grant, Harding, and Nixon) and equals 0 otherwise; "assassination" equals 1 if the president was assassinated in office (namely, Lincoln, Garfield, McKinley, and Kennedy) and 0 otherwise; and "hero" equals 1 if the president had been a war hero (for example, Washington, Jackson, Grant, and Eisenhower) and equals 0 otherwise.

The intercept tells us that a president enters office with a greatness score of -1.24 points. Because the greatness ratings were without exception standardized (see table 5.1), this signifies that on inauguration day the incumbent has a score more than a standard deviation *below* the (zero) mean. Even if the new chief executive moves into the White House as a war hero, his initial rating will be substandard ($-1.24 + 0.82 = -0.42$). Each year that a president spends in the Oval Office adds another 0.17 points to his predicted score, so after four years an incumbent will be halfway to mediocrity; if he is a war hero the scale will be tipped only a bit toward the positive end of the scale ($-0.42 + 4 \times 0.17) =$

0.26). Hence, something more dramatic must transpire if a president wants to join the ranks of the great. A president who serves just one full term as a wartime commander-in-chief is halfway to greatness, and another four years as a peacetime chief executive will establish greatness for sure. An alternative is to be killed by an assassin, which adds as many points as over five years as a peacetime president or two years as a wartime president. There are consequently three principal routes to greatness: the Washington–Jackson method of entering the White House as a war hero and serving eight years; the Wilson–FDR technique of entering office without the war hero advantage and serving two terms or more, a portion of which as the nation's war leader; and the Lincoln approach, in which the president still leads the country in war but assassination substitutes for a long sojourn at 1600 Pennsylvania Avenue.

All of these accumulated points, however obtained, are to no avail should the president's administration suffer a scandal of substantial proportions. A single scandal can undermine eight years in the White House and status as a national war hero, as Grant sadly demonstrates. Even assassination could not have retrieved his reputation, and had war broken out during his administration, it would not have appreciably raised his low grade. Posterity is even harsher with Harding, given his short tenure and his lack of any war leader credentials. The equation shows that nothing could have rescued Harding from the bottom of the pile.

It must be emphasized that the prediction equation presented above is extremely robust. Besides being built almost entirely from variables that correlate with all greatness criteria from Schlesinger's 1948 poll to that of Murray and Blessing, the equation holds for the three most recent surveys and thus is confirmed for thirty-six presidents. Hundreds of variables were given the chance to become predictors, including various indicators of election victory and popularity, diverse assessments of motivation and interpersonal preference, and about a hundred separate ways of assessing presidential performance, including legislative successes and failures (see Simonton 1986c). Yet only five passed the tests. Even more important, the equation is transhistorically invariant; it holds just as well for nineteenth-century presidents as for twentieth-century presidents (Simonton 1986c). No systematic tendency exists for one or another predictor to expand or shrink in predictive value from 1789 to 1980 (see also Simonton 1981c). When we acknowledge the obvious truth that any historian willing to evaluate the presidents on greatness will presumably know roughly how each president stands on these five predictor variables, it is reasonable to surmise that the above prediction equation constitutes the actual criteria that historians employ, however intuitively, to rate chief executives of the United States of America.

Granting this last inference, we may use the equation to predict scores for presidents whom the historians did not evaluate (compare Simonton 1981c). For instance, respondents are not asked to assess W. Harrison and Garfield, but if they had the ratings would have been low anyway, −0.39 and −0.26 respectively. Both suffer from want of years in office, the hero of Tippecanoe somewhat more (one month versus nine months); where Harrison gains from his military exploits, Garfield acquires more points for his assassination. Reagan's greatness score is only slightly above mediocrity (0.12) if we assume that he serves eight full years in office and avoids war, scandal, and assassination.

The prediction equation can be improved upon, albeit but modestly. Although personality variables, such as power and affiliation needs, were included in the batch of potential predictors, none of these proved valuable as direct antecedents of assessed greatness. Yet certainly the list of personality traits can be considerably expanded. In chapter 4 I described a study of presidential personality that applied the Gough Adjective Check List to biographical data, extracting fourteen distinct dimensions on which the thirty-nine presidents may vary (Simonton 1986e). Perhaps one or more of these personality dimensions may facilitate the prediction of greatness. It happens that just one dimension correlates consistently with assessed greatness by whichever criterion we choose—intellectual brillance. When correlated with the available greatness indicators, the correlations range from .43 (with Bailey) to .70 (with Sokolsky), with a .59 correlation with Murray–Blessing. If this variable is added as a sixth predictor in the regression equation, intellectual brillance proves its worth as a predictor, but without materially altering the relevance of the original five predictors. Interestingly, intelligence is the one individual-difference attribute to consistently correlate with leadership in the several forms it may take (Simonton 1985a). It is also interesting to report that the prepresidential publication record, which has marginal utility as a predictor, is totally devoid of value once intellectual brilliance is in the equation. Because intellectual brilliance is associated with authorship, the latter variable may have been functioning as a proxy variable for the former in the earlier equation (Simonton 1981c).

The six-variable prediction equation explicates fully 82 percent of the variation in the Murray–Blessing ratings, a truly impressive figure indeed. The prediction equation is:

$$\text{Greatness} = -1.10 + 0.15\ (\text{years}) + 0.21\ (\text{war}) - 1.44\ (\text{scandal}) + 0.73\ (\text{assassination}) + 0.87\ (\text{hero}) + 0.26\ (\text{intelligence})$$

Here "intelligence" is intellectual brilliance measured in standardized form, and the other predictors are defined precisely as before. If the president in question is of average intellect relative to other presidents so that the value of the sixth predictor equals zero, then the final term drops out and we are left with an equation comparable to the earlier one. On the other hand, a president one standard deviation above average gains 0.26 points toward the final greatness score, whereas a president one deviation below average loses that many points. The addition of this sixth predictor definitely gives Jefferson a boost. At a White House dinner in honor of a group of Nobel laureates, John F. Kennedy offered the toast: "I believe that this is the most extraordinary collection of talent, of human knowledge, that has ever been gathered together at the White House, with the possible exception of when Thomas Jefferson dined alone." As can be discerned in table 4.3, Jefferson scored over three standard deviations above the zero mean, which adds almost a standard deviation to his greatness score ($0.26 \times 3.1 = 0.81$).

Others are more intellectually handicapped, most notably Harding, who is two whole deviations below the norm, costing him 0.52 points in greatness. Harding often complained that he could not always comprehend the speeches his ghostwriters expected him to deliver. He was notorious for banal wisdom and empty alliterations such as "America's present need is not heroics but healing, not nostrums but normalcy," and he possessed so little economic sense that he advocated that the U.S. adopt a protective tariff in order to help European industries get back on their feet after the First World War! At least Harding was aware of his own limitations, once confessing to a White House secretary, "My God, this is a hell of a place for a man like me to be!" The historians agree, and Harding's lack of even passable intelligence, in conjunction with the scandals that sprang up about him, consigns him to the nadir of American political history.

It is instructive to compare the observed greatness scores according to Murray and Blessing with the predicted scores according to the six-variable equation. This comparison appears in table 5.2. Also shown are the residuals obtained by subtracting the predicted from the observed greatness rating. Once more we learn that William Harrison and Garfield would not have been deemed great presidents had the historians rated them; in Garfield's case, however, the inclusion of intellectual brilliance as a predictor brought him up to the level of ordinary chief executives. Garfield was among our brighter presidents; he graduated with highest honors from Williams College and went on to teach Latin, Greek, and higher mathematics at what was eventually to become Hiram College. Ronald Reagan, who received a score in intellectual brilliance only slightly above the norm, is still predicted to be an average president under the stipulations presented earlier. As expected, Kennedy is not quite as overrated as he once was (Simonton 1981c). One reason is that his reputation has fallen in the thirteen years between the Maranell (1970) and Murray–Blessing (1983) polls; the other reason is that the present six-predictor equation incorporates intellectual brilliance when, as is evident in table 4.3, JFK stands beside our most brilliant presidents. The nation's first president, however, still exhibits a residual overappreciation, albeit not nearly as much as previously (Simonton 1981c). Allowing for the impact of war-hero status diminished the discrepancy between predicted and observed scores, especially when we consider that Washington's reputation with historians grew between 1970 and 1983.

Table 5.2 Observed Standardized Murray–Blessing Rating, Predicted Score Using the Six-Variable Equation, and the Residual Errors of Prediction

President	Observed	Predicted	Residual
1. Washington	1.87	1.03	0.84
2. J. Adams	0.59	0.29	0.30
3. Jefferson	1.52	1.73	−0.21
4. Madison	0.23	0.90	−0.67
5. Monroe	0.19	−0.24	0.42
6. J. Q. Adams	0.13	−0.17	0.30
7. Jackson	1.02	0.82	0.20
8. Van Buren	−0.32	−0.57	0.25
9. W. Harrison	—	−0.24	—
10. Tyler	−0.83	−0.44	−0.39
11. Polk	0.42	−0.04	0.46
12. Taylor	−0.70	−0.33	−0.37
13. Fillmore	−0.86	−0.86	0.01
14. Pierce	−1.11	−0.56	−0.55
15. Buchanan	−1.27	−0.69	−0.58
16. Lincoln	1.99	1.30	0.68
17. A. Johnson	−1.23	−0.80	−0.43
18. Grant	−1.35	−0.81	−0.54
19. Hayes	−0.38	−0.53	−0.15
20. Garfield	—	−0.05	—
21. Arthur	−0.53	−0.33	−0.20
22. Cleveland	0.12	−0.02	0.14
23. B. Harrison	−0.66	−0.66	0.00
24. McKinley	−0.16	0.37	−0.53
25. T. Roosevelt	1.34	1.14	0.20
26. Taft	−0.23	−0.48	0.25
27. Wilson	1.22	0.86	0.36
28. Harding	−1.60	−2.68	1.08
29. Coolidge	−0.87	−0.63	−0.24
30. Hoover	−0.36	−0.35	−0.01
31. F. Roosevelt	1.91	1.78	0.13
32. Truman	0.92	0.96	−0.04
33. Eisenhower	0.48	0.81	−0.33
34. Kennedy	0.36	0.52	−0.15
35. L. Johnson	0.58	0.68	−0.11
36. Nixon	−1.30	−0.76	−0.54
37. Ford	−0.60	−0.86	0.26
38. Carter	−0.63	−0.50	−0.13
39. Reagan	—	0.22	—

Source: Table 5 of Simonton (1986c).

All in all, we possess the capacity to predict presidential greatness with an exceptional degree of precision. The five-variable equation yields expected scores that correlate .88 with the actual scores obtained by Murray and Blessing (Simonton 1986c). In addition, the predicted values correlate .88 with the Porter and *Chicago Tribune* ratings, .84 with the Maranell greatness composite, .80 with Schlesinger's 1948 poll, .79 with Schlesinger's 1962 poll, .77 with Sokolsky's, .73 with Rossiter's, and .72 with Bailey's. This equation is perhaps the most useful, for all of the independent variables are easily measured with virtually no ambiguity. If we acquire a reasonable estimate of how intelligent a president is in relation to other presidents, the six-predictor equation can be used. The correlation between predicted and observed values in this case is .91, an even more remarkable figure (Simonton 1986e). Earlier in this chapter we registered the fact that the dozen greatness assessments alternative to the Murray–Blessing survey exhibit correlations usually in the .80s and .90s with the Murray–Blessing ratings. Consequently, using merely five or six facts we can produce greatness scores about as well as by polling hundreds of experts: the six-predictor equation actually performs better than Rossiter, Sokolsky, Bailey, and the Maranell activeness and information dimensions. Again, even though the regression weights were based on the Murray–Blessing data alone, the expected scores in table 4.3 correlate .89 with Porter, .88 with the *Chicago Tribune*, .87 with Maranell, .84 with Sokolsky, .83 with either Schlesinger poll, .77 with Rossiter, and .72 with Bailey. Given that the equation replicates across alternative greatness indicators (as well as distinct historical periods), we could hardly expect better predictive success. We can with some justice claim that we know what it takes for a president to enter the annals of lasting fame.

Those critics suspicious of quantitative methodology may doubt whether we have yet identified the core antecedents of historical acclaim. Perhaps the central factors are more subtle than those hitherto investigated. Maybe so, but every attempt has been made to tap every potential variable that contains a modicum of empirical substance. As a case in point, the qualitative theories of Barber (1977) and Burns (1978), both briefly mentioned in chapter 1, have been empirically scrutinized and found wanting. An effort was made to gauge the presidents on Barber's two dimensions of active-passive and positive-negative, but judges were unable to attain a reliable consensus using his definitions of these dimensions (Barber 1977, 12-13). Instead, Barber's own classifications were adopted, even though fewer than half of the chief executives were placed into one of the four quadrants of his typology ($N = 17$). The presidential greatness ratings were then regressed on the two dimensions plus their product term (the active-passive times positive-negative interaction effect). Nothing emerged that was even close to statistical significance. Those presidents whom Barber considered to be active-positives received assessments from historians no better than those of presidents in the other three groups.

Burns' theory of transactional versus transformational leadership presents more problems. Burns, unlike Barber, made no systematic effort to categorize a respectable number of American chief executives, and his constructs are far more difficult to define, especially if we wish to avoid the same sort of halo-effect artifacts that may confound Nice's (1984) notion of political realignment. Nonetheless, Machiavellianism, which should be associated with being a transactional leader (see Alker 1981), has already been shown to exhibit no correlation whatsoever with historical greatness (Simonton 1986e). Taking the biographical data already collected for the earlier examination of presidential personality (Simonton 1986e), a team of seven independent raters assessed all thirty-nine presidents using the Presidential Style Q-Sort devised at the Institute for Personality Assessment and Research at the University of California at Berkeley by Kenneth Craik and his colleagues. Several items on this inventory appear prima facie germane to Burns' ideas. In particular, reliable measures were obtained for such attributes as "Rarely permits himself to be outflanked," "Skilled and self-confident negotiator," "Places political success over effective policy," "Willing to compromise," and "Exhibits artistry in manipulation" for the transactional president, and "Characterized by others as a world figure," "Able to visualize alternatives and weigh long-term consequences," "Understands implications of his decisions; exhibits depth of comprehension," "Believes he knows what is best for the people," "Is innovative in his role as an executive," and "Initiates new legislation and programs" for the transformational president. None of these attributes correlated with the diverse indicators of historical approbation. Indeed, nearly fifty ways of characterizing presidential style could be reliably differentiated, not one bearing any connection with the chief executive's reputation with scholars. This null effect does not disprove Burns' theory, but it should cause us to wonder about its relevance to an empirical examination of presidential success. In general, constructs linked with either Barber or Burns add absolutely nothing to the predictive power already contained in the above equations.

INTERPRETATION

At this juncture in our discussion of presidential greatness two conclusions have been fixed beyond a reasonable doubt. First, to select posterity's acclaim as a criterion of presidential success does not require us to resort to indicators of inferior reliability. On the contrary, a solid, imposing historical consensus exists on the greatness of those who have resided at the White House. Second, nothing prevents us from constructing equations that precisely predict the greatness scores the presidents receive in the surveys of professional historians. Indeed, prediction equations containing but a half-dozen variables can anticipate the actual ratings with an accuracy on a par with asking experts to respond to questionnaires. From the standpoint of sheer technical efficiency, therefore, we have no reason ever to consult the historians again.

Of course, more is involved in understanding presidential greatness than simply reconstructing the ratings. We must know just why that particular set of predictors proved so central. What is it about years in office, war years, scandal, assassination, war heroism, and intellectual brilliance that permits these six variables to predict over four-fifths of the variance in assessed greatness? It is one thing to predict greatness, quite another to comprehend the basis of greatness. As I see it, there are two rival explanations of this phenomenon, the personal and the attributional (Simonton 1981c, 1984b, 1986c).

The personal account assumes that great presidents, such as Lincoln and F. D. Roosevelt, were truly great leaders, even great men, because unique personal traits set them apart from more mundane chief executives. By the same token, the failures of American history, such as Grant and Harding, lacked the personal qualities essential for leader achievement. The attributional interpretation is just as plausible, if not more so. A historian responding to a survey questionnaire is engaged in a special variety of person perception. In particular, the historian is attempting to make a dispositional attribution about each president's leadership characteristics using whatever information is at hand. This attributional process is governed by the same principles and biases that have been documented in the literature on social cognition (Fiske and Taylor 1984). Unlike the personal account, which asks what a president did to deserve to be called great, the attributional interpretation concentrates our attention on the information-processing strategies and heuristic methods that a historian uses to infer the attribute of leader greatness.

Naturally, the historians themselves would claim that the personal account is the right one. Moreover, as we have seen, early research on the correlates of presidential greatness sought to ground the historians' ratings in concrete presidential personality traits, most notably power, achievement, and affiliation motives. In particular, the great president is said to be a leader exceptionally high in power needs and usually low in affiliation needs. These motives are supposed to account directly for the observed pattern of predictors. If the power motive can be held responsible for a president becoming a wartime commander-in-chief and even for being assassinated, and if the affiliation motive is a hidden cause of administration corruption, then presidential greatness may indeed be the ultimate outcome of a constellation of personality traits. Even the war-hero predictor may be only a proxy index of power motivation. The main addition to the motivational prescription is that the president should be bright if he aspires to greatness, but the cognitive attribute of intelligence fits in nicely with a personal account anyway. Indeed, the place of intellectual brilliance in achieved greatness can be deduced from a genius theory of political leadership (Simonton 1984b).

To be sure, only five out of the six predictors can be explicated in these terms, for no one has shown how personality may provide the basis for a long tenure in office. Even so, it may be argued that the predictive value of years in office may merely indicate that great presidents are more likely to get reelected. Given that wartime chief executives are reelected (Simonton 1986c), if the power motive creates a proclivity for engaging the United States in war (Winter and Stewart 1977), then tenure duration may be a result of a personality trait (though this is partly balanced by the supposed tendency of power-driven presidents to be assassinated). It is possible to make a preliminary case that the six predictors of greatness reveal the quality of political leadership exhibited by the president. Chief executives who serve many years, lead the nation through many years of war, avoid scandals, are assassinated, enter offices as a national war hero, and exhibit extraordinary intelligence may really be better leaders. They have what it takes in terms of both motives and mind.

Nevertheless, we can counterpose several facts that do not live comfortably with the foregoing interpretation. With the exception of intellectual brilliance, no personality variable contributes to the prediction of assessed greatness, whether directly or indirectly. Specifically, power, achievement, and affiliation motives, interpersonal dominance and extroversion orientations, and dogmatism (idealistic inflexibility) predict neither greatness nor the predictors of greatness (Simonton 1986c). As a case in point, power motivation fails to predict the number of years a president serves as wartime commander-in-chief and the odds that an incumbent will be assassinated. Even biographical factors, including items drawn from the president's political résumé, have minimal predictive worth. Tests for potential individual-times-situational interactions have not improved this state of affairs one iota (Simonton 1986c).

Moreover, a detailed analysis of the predictors divulges some peculiarities that have little affinity with a dispositional attribution. Why is it that the number of years of war is a primary predictor, rather than whether the president delivered a war message to Congress? Certainly the president has more control over the initiation of a war than over how long a war lasts once begun—for wars have a momentum all their own (Houweling and Siccama 1985)—and thus the delivery of a war message should more accurately mirror any power inclination (see Nice 1984). Presidents can be dragged into wars they did not desire, as happened to McKinley in 1898 and Wilson in 1917, whereas other presidents deliver a war message to Congress only to have it fall on deaf ears, as John Adams learned in 1797. A president can even receive credit as a war leader for a conflict that he did not start; Nixon's reputation was apparently enhanced by his leadership during the Vietnam War. In a similar vein, if years in office reflects the fact that superior presidents are reelected while inferior presidents are thrown out, then why is it that reelection did not emerge as a direct predictor of presidential greatness? An indicator (years in office) cannot replace the underlying construct (reelection) so long as both are measured with equal reliability coefficients, and the reliabilities for these two variables are both unity. The historians are consequently doing something more than merely rubber-stamping the opinions of the voters.

Such puzzles inspire the alternative suggestion that assessments of presidential greatness inform us more about how people make political attributions than about how well presidents actually perform in office. Several findings can be cited in support of this hypothesis.

Historiometric research on the eminence of political leaders tends to endorse an eponymic position (Simonton 1984d). That is, the place of political figures in the eyes of posterity is primarily determined by their value as names for epochs of history. Leaders are essentially symbols—convenient names for the events of the past. Thus, long-tenured leaders tend to be more famous than short-tenured leaders, for the longer a leader serves the more events can be tallied under his or her name. Furthermore, war tends to generate the sort of events most favored by historians who like to spice up narratives with invasions, battles, sieges, and similar events that justify William Cullen Bryant's condemnation of history as "the horrid tale of perjury and strife, / Murder and spoil." Although a leader's personal qualities may enter into the determination of his or her eponymic value, these attributes operate in a peculiar fashion. For instance, a leader's morality bears not a positive linear relationship with historical distinction but rather a curvilinear inverted-U relation: eminence is attained by being either famously moral or infamously immoral (Simonton 1984d). What is crucial is that the leader's personal traits, like the events of the leader's reign, make him or her stand out in the crowd, against the backdrop of nondescript nonentities.

Apropos of this finding, it is provocative to report an incidental discovery: although the dogmatism measure derived from the Maranell (1970) measures of idealism and inflexibility did not correlate with the greatness measures in a linear manner, dogmatism does feature a curvilinear relationship. When greatness (Maranell factor 1) is regressed on the linear and quadratic functions of idealistic inflexibility versus pragmatic flexibility (Maranell factor 2), the quadratic term has a positive and statistically significant regression coefficient (Simonton 1986c). The same outcome ensues when any of the three most recent greatness measures (Porter, *Chicago Tribune*, and Murray–Blessing) are regressed on the bipolar dogmatism measure. Uniformly, across all measures, those presidents with the highest assessed greatness tend to be either the most dogmatic (idealistically inflexible) or the least dogmatic (pragmatically flexible).

The research I reviewed in chapter 3 on the president's approval rating in polls of the American people implies that presidential popularity is not always dependent on personal attributes and behaviors. International crises, economic fluctuations, and other sources of news, good and bad, affect the way Americans perceive the leadership qualities of the incumbent without regard for how much his administration is objectively responsible for the events (for example, Brody and Page 1975). Similar statements can be made about election success as well, as shown in chapter 2 (see Rosenstone 1983). In general, contemporary leaders are symbols that receive credit or blame for the state of the nations they lead, and past leaders, presidents not excluded, may serve a comparable function. As Leo Tolstoy expressed it in *War and Peace* (1865–1869), "the so-called great men are labels giving names to events, and like labels they have but the smallest connection with the event itself" (344).

An Attributional Model

In light of the above arguments, I can propose an attributional model that affirms that the six predictors are most informative about how historians and laypersons alike make judgments about personal attributes under conditions of limited knowledge (see also Simonton 1986b, 1986c). The proposed model may be expressed in terms of six propositions.

Proposition 1. Greatness is attributed to a leader to the extent that a generalized social schema for leadership is activated by information about the leader.

Two critical features must be noted about this proposition, for they apply to the remaining propositions as well. First, the proposition makes no reference whatsoever to historians. This deliberate omission represents the view that the attributional model is descriptive of how people tend to perceive a leader, independent of their professional status. In the last chapter of this book, I will generalize this model to account for attributions of presidential leadership according to all four success criteria. Second, the proposition says nothing about presidents because the attributional model describes how observers make judgments about that broad class of actors called leaders. There is empirical evidence that the chief predictors of leader fame parallel the six predictors of presidential greatness (Simonton 1984a). For instance, besides reign length and war, the differential eminence of hereditary monarchs is associated with violent death and intelligence (Simonton 1984d). The national-war-hero criterion also figures in the attribution of "charisma" to various kinds of leaders, such as prime ministers, dictators, and presidents (Cell 1974). Thus, the question of what makes a president great is subsumed under the larger issue of why greatness is ascribed to certain leaders.

Proposition 2. The leadership schema includes the three semantic components of strength, activity, and goodness.

The second proposition attempts to define an abstract social schema applicable to all types of leaders. Though this schema is probably quite complex, I will concentrate on probable semantic components suggested by research using the semantic differential technique (Osgood, Suci, and Tannenbaum 1957). An atlas of semantic profiles for 360 English words reveals that *leadership* has high and positive loadings on all three classic dimensions of potency (strong versus weak), activity (active versus passive), and evaluation (good versus bad) (Jenkins, Russell, and Suci 1958). Accordingly, an actor occupying a leadership role, such as the American presidency, may be considered great to the degree that the individual projects an image of strength, activity, and goodness. Conversely, failures are judged weak, passive, and bad. We know already that historians, when rating the presidents, consider criteria such as these. Maranell's (1970) dimensions of "strength of action," "presidential activeness," and "idealism versus practicality" roughly parallel strength, activity, and goodness, for example. Likewise, Barber (1977), in constructing his fourfold typology, employed the two central axes of active versus passive and positive versus negative, the last having an approximate correspondence with the evaluation factor. Moreover, it is quite clear from reading Schlesinger's (1949, 1962) speculations that strength, activity, and goodness are thought to set the great presidents apart from the failures. Hence, activation of the social schema for leadership may depend on inferring these three qualities from information about the leaders. Finally, this generalized schema captures the key features of how the layperson may conceive the ideal chief executive: the archetypal president is seen as both competent and trustworthy (Kinder et al. 1980; see also Merenda 1964).

Proposition 3. The attribution of strength, activity, and goodness to a leader is founded on that information which has the highest cognitive availability.

When historians respond to a questionnaire, it is improbable that they all go to their libraries, check out monographs on each president, and, cloistered for weeks, systematically extract all data pertinent to the schema for leadership. Even the most conscientious among them will rely on memory. Consequently, whatever information is most readily retrieved from the store of expert knowledge will carry the most weight in activating the social schema. If a fact pertinent to assessing the goodness of a president happens to be recalled, then that fact will be highly influential even if it is not necessarily the most representative or direct. In taking this information-processing shortcut, historians are acting the same way that other people do when making social judgments. Observers lean very heavily on the availability heuristic, a principle that, though convenient, often leads the social inference process astray (Tversky and Kahneman 1974).

Proposition 4. Cognitive availability is more important than objective causal relevance in making the three dispositional attributions of strength, activity, and goodness.

The availability heuristic is not the only cognitive inclination that may elicit misguided attributions. Observers, when judging actors, are also prone to commit the fundamental attribution error (Ross 1977). That is, observers are so biased in favor of attributing dispositional causes to behaviors that situational influences and constraints are largely overlooked. This bias stays even when the observers should know better (Johnson, Jemmott, and Pettigrew 1984). Available information will provide the framework for judging a leader's strength, activity, and goodness even if that information is not the most germane by more objective standards. Because the observer seeks a dispositional attribution, data will be exploited more because it has been retrieved from memory than because it is especially relevant. The fundamental attribution error explains why the incumbent's approval rating in the polls is affected by current events that can have very little to do with the incumbent's real performance. Here we are merely postulating that the historians behave no differently. In a sense, a respondent is a respondent and a poll is a poll, whether we have voters evaluating the performance of the present incumbent or historians rating the greatness of past incumbents. Naturally, if we were to ask the historians directly whether they commit the fundamental attribution error, or whether they rely too heavily on the most cognitively available information, they would deny any such biases. Even so, observers are not particularly adept at identifying the information that can be objectively demonstrated to have guided their inferences (Nisbett and Wilson 1977).

Proposition 5. Information with the highest cognitive availability is that which had the highest salience when the information was originally attended to and processed.

Events or characteristics that are the most salient are most likely to grab attention, to receive extensive processing, including consolidation in long-term memory, and thus to exert an inordinate influence on subsequent information processing, such as social inference (see McArthur 1981). Hence, when a historian peruses American history, certain facts will stand out more than others, and this difference in perceptual prominence will be translated into a difference in cognitive availability later on.

Proposition 6. The most salient information includes the six predictors of years in office, war, scandal, assassination, war heroism, and intelligence.

The six predictors of greatness contained in the equation given earlier represent the collection of salient items specified in the preceding proposition. Indeed, these variables uniformly represent the sort of information that can be found in even the briefest biographical entries. War, scandal, assassination, and becoming a national war hero are all rare and dramatic events. Duration of tenure becomes a salient fact not only because of the conspicuous place reelection campaigns have in American political narratives, but because the longer a president holds office the more historical events can be tallied under his name. Intelligence may be considered a salient fact as well, especially for the experts who are the survey respondents, all of whom are highly intelligent themselves. We may argue, too, with only a modicum of cynicism, that true intellectual brilliance is all too rare in the American presidency, making its occurrence an occasion of high social salience (Simonton 1984a, 1985a)

It is imperative that we realize that proposition six does not claim that the six predictors represent the only salient features to be recorded by each historian. For the attribution model to be valid, we need but hold that these constitute the main *systematic* facts on which all past presidents vary. Each president's biography certainly contains other conspicuous items, but these items are unique to each president. For instance, that George Washington was the first president, who, as he himself remarked with some trepidation, walked "on untrodden ground," is no doubt a prominent fact, which may be partly responsible for the high rating he receives in the polls. Nonetheless, that item is not the kind of information on which all presidents can exhibit meaningful variation. In a similar vein, Abraham Lincoln's preservation of the Union and Franklin Roosevelt's New Deal legislation represent salient but idiosyncratic items of information. In the parlance of factor analysis, we may say that the six predictors embody the common factors behind the different greatness ratings of all the presidents, whereas for each president there exist certain unique factors that adjust the summary scores still further. After all, the six predictors leave almost one-fifth of the variance in assessed greatness unaccounted for (Simonton 1986c). We might venture to say that Miller's (1956) "magical number" of 7 ± 2 applies to the number of basic facts that are readily available about each president during the inferential process. The predictors then would fill six places, leaving the seventh for some particular fact about each president. It is interesting to note that, on the average, seven criteria would each explicate about 14 percent of the variance, a proportion in approximate accord with the 18 percent of the variance left after subtracting what can be credited to the universal criteria.

Predictions

The above attributional model is quite complex and would require a long series of studies, with varied methodological approaches, to be fully validated. For example, we might quiz historians, using survey techniques, to discover which information enjoys the most cognitive availability, and we might apply content analysis to biographical materials to learn what data appear to be portrayed in the most salient manner. At this point, however, let us concentrate on those portions of the model that lend themselves to simulation in a laboratory experiment. Although this requires that certain parts of the causal sequence that runs from proposition six back to proposition one will be simply postulated (albeit on the basis of considerable research in social cognition), what remains approachable still yields several interesting and empirically verifiable predictions. These can be cast as the following hypotheses and corollaries:

Hypothesis 1. When given scores on the six predictors for anonymous leaders and requested to assess these leaders on greatness, naive raters will assign the given information the same weight, both in sign and in approximate magnitude, as the predictors receive in the equation predicting actual presidential greatness.

Raters are considered naive if they know neither the hypotheses being tested nor the identity of the leaders they are given to evaluate. If hypothesis one is valid, two corollaries should hold as well:

Corollary 1A. Naive raters given the same information will make the same attributions of greatness, and thus achieve a firm consensus.

Corollary 1B. Naive raters given scores on the six predictors for each president will approximately reproduce the greatness ratings that the historians have given the same presidents.

Obviously, if judges are granted the same information, and if they all assign that information the same weight, then their attributions should be highly congruent, as corollary 1A states. Yet corollary 1B is much bolder. If the attributional model is justified, then observers who are totally ignorant of the presidents they are assessing—and who do not even know that they are rating American presidents—will nevertheless reconstruct the ratings the presidents actually received in the surveys.

Corollary 1B is perhaps the most crucial prediction of the model. If naive raters can reproduce the historians' judgments under such restrictive circumstances, we have more conclusive evidence that the six predictors are directly involved in the historians' attributional processes. While we know that historians are likely to be highly aware of these six pieces of data and that these six facts allow us to predict the historians' ratings with exceptional precision, we still cannot definitely establish that these items are what the historians really depend on. But if naive judges, given just six articles of information, draw the same inferences as the historians, this gap in the argument will be considerably narrowed. Moreover, if corollary 1B is substantiated, an important connection will have been made between laboratory experiments in social cognition and information-processing behavior in the real world. Although there have been attempts to make this link, some in the realm of judging presidents (for example, Anderson 1973; Kinder et al. 1980), few if any studies make direct quantitative comparisons between the predictions of a theoretical model and real-life data. Should college students successfully generate the historians' ratings, the proposed attributional model will boast an external validity seldom realized in laboratory experiments.

Hypothesis 2. If naive raters are given information beyond that contained in the six predictors, their ability to duplicate the historians assessments will deteriorate.

This prediction is derived from the model's affirmation that attributions are made on few predictors simply because few items of information are sufficiently available to feed the inferential process. Presumably, if we provide naive raters more facts than they actually need to use, they will employ these facts, and thereby lower the correspondence between raters' and historians' dispositional attributions. If this decline does not occur, the model would have to be modified accordingly. For example, should no change take place in the degree of agreement, we could argue that the six predictors are more directly tied to the social schema for leadership. Nonetheless, indirect evidence indicates the plausibility of hypothesis two. Bailey (1966) is unique in claiming to have carefully applied forty-three distinct yardsticks in his own ranking of the presidents. Even if the results we reported earlier cast doubt on his claim to have utilized so many criteria, his final ratings, as observed earlier in this chapter, are the least consistent with the overall historical consensus.

Hypothesis 3. The impact of the six predictors on the greatness attributions is mediated by the three semantic components of strength, activity, and goodness.

If the dispositional attribution of greatness demands the activation of the hypothesized social schema, and if that schema is defined, at least in part, in terms of strength, activity, and goodness, then these three semantic attributes should be functions of the six predictors. One weakness in the attributional model is that it does not specify exactly which semantic components are dependent on which predictors. We are obliged to rely primarily on common sense. For instance, it seems reasonable to conjecture that war leaders will be perceived as more strong and active, and that assassinated presidents, presumed to be victims of evil conspiracies (see McCauley and Jacques 1979), might be judged as more good. Even though the attributional model does not detail which semantic components mediate which historiometric predictors, the mediational hypothesis yields two explicit predictions that are empirically testable.

Corollary 3A. The three semantic components of strength, activity, and goodness explain a significant proportion of variance in the greatness attributions.

Under the assumption that the raters achieve consensus on their semantic judgments, regressing assessed greatness on evaluations of the three hypothesized cognitive mediators should produce a multiple correlation (R^2) at least as high as that found when the original six variables are employed as predictors.

Corollary 3B. No shared variance exists between the greatness attributions and the six predictors once effects of the three semantic variables are statistically controlled.

If the implications of years in office, war, scandal, assassination, war heroism, and intelligence are utterly mediated by attributions of strength, activity, and goodness, then these six variables will have no additional predictive power once the three semantic mediators are already in the equation for inferred greatness.

An Experimental Test

The foregoing predictions were tested in a recent laboratory experiment (Simonton 1986b). Like most social psychological experiments, the raters were college students. These raters were naive to both the identity of the leaders being rated and the hypotheses being tested. Actually, two nearly identical experiments were conducted. In study 1 the raters evaluated anonymous leaders (who were all presidents), in line with the assumption that the attributional model applies to political leaders generally, not just to American chief executives. In study 2 the raters knew they were assessing presidents; otherwise there was no difference in the information received. In both studies the raters were given data on how thirty-nine leaders (or presidents) scored on years in office, war years, scandal, assassination, war heroism, and intelligence predictors. Additionally, in some experimental conditions the naive judges were given distracting information known not to influence the historians' assessments of greatness. To assure that the raters would be truly naive, the presidents were listed in a random order on the questionnaire.

The results were startling: with only minor qualifications the hypotheses were strongly confirmed. The implications of the six predictors for the ultimate attribution of leader greatness are largely mediated by the three semantic criteria of strength, activity, and goodness. For example, war-hero presidents tended to be seen as stronger, assassinated presidents as more active, and presidents with scandalous administrations as less good. Years in office emerged as an important predictor for all three semantic components, a prominence consistent with the fact that tenure duration is one of the most dependable predictors of leader eminence. Furthermore, the data support the conclusion that cognitive availability determines what information enters the inferential process; naive raters given more information than was contained in the six predictors tended to use it, to the detriment of performance. As expected, the naive raters gave the six predictors the same weight, in sign and rough magnitude, as the historians who responded to surveys gauging presidential greatness. The only real exception to this congruence in information processing had to do with war, toward which college-age raters are more ambivalent than professional historians; although the naive judges were willing to assign a positive (albeit tiny) weight to war when rating presidents, the weight was negative when the judges were rating unspecified leaders, betraying an antipathy for warmongers who could quite possibly have been enemies of the United States (all the judges were American-born).

This difference notwithstanding, the similarity in information processing between undergraduate and scholar was enough to generate by far the most provocative discovery in the experimental simulation: naive judges, totally ignorant of whom they are rating but granted information on the six criteria, are able to reproduce accurately the greatness ratings that the presidents actually received in the polls. In particular, the ratings assigned by the naive raters using just a half-dozen pieces of information correlated .84 with the ratings given by the Murray–Blessing respondents who, presumably, had access to a wealth of pertinent facts (not the least being the actual identity of the presidents being rated). This concordance approaches the upper bound set by the variable reliabilities. Furthermore, the degree of correspondence between naive judge and knowledgeable expert did not depend on the ability of college students to guess who they were rating. For one thing, raters in study 1, who thought they were rating a mixed batch of leaders of diverse nationalities and periods, gave the same greatness evaluations as raters in study 2, who were explicitly told that they were assessing presidents ($r = .88$). Even when we delete those presidents who are most easily identifiable from the meager facts provided (such as those who did not serve exactly four or eight years in office), the naive raters can still accurately reproduce the survey results.

It somewhat stretches the imagination to think that college students can identify the thirty-nine presidents on the basis of just six items of information or that, having miraculously done so, they can do an equally good job of reconstructing the historians' assessments. The average undergraduate simply has virtually no knowledge about the vast majority of presidential administrations. Indeed, if students could so precisely duplicate the ratings of experts from merely a half-dozen facts about thirty-nine anonymous leaders, there would be no reason even to survey historians and political scientists! When the public was asked to pick the three greatest presidents in a 1975 Gallup poll, the ratings that resulted correlated only .57 with comparable ratings produced in 1977 by having members of the U.S. Historical Society identify the ten best presidents (Nice 1984)—and even this degree of correspondence is exaggerated because of methodological artifacts that, when corrected, imply a zero relation between the ratings (Simonton 1986b). Therefore, the naive raters' reproduction of the Murray–Blessing survey results is probably independent of any putative proficiency the raters might have at deciphering which president was behind which set of facts. The congruence is most probably ascribable to the fact that the same fundamental inferential processes were applied to the same items of information.

Admittedly, the empirical outcome was by no means perfect; there is room for refinement of the attributional model. We have no other theory, however, that can explain how a handful of college students, with the smallest number of facts to go on, can reconstruct the results of a survey of 846 professional historians. Until an alternative explanation materializes we are left with the following tentative generalization: historians who consent to rank the American presidents are engaged in a special type of person perception. In particular, such respondents are perforce producing dispositional attributions based on a restricted quantity of factual information. In processing the limited data, historians clearly employ no specialized strategies or heuristic methods. On the contrary, the survey respondents think just as observers generally think when making complex social inferences under conditions of extreme uncertainty. Hence, a comprehensive model of why some presidents are deemed greater than others may become nothing more than a subtopic of social cognition. The phenomenon of presidential greatness may thus be better integrated into the most recent conceptions of leadership: leadership represents a social relationship between leader and follower that depends more on the follower's perceptions than on the leader's acts (see, for example, Lord and Alliger 1985). An individual is labeled a leader when other group members attribute to that person the putative personal qualities of strength, activity, and goodness.

Pronouncing leadership an attributional more than a personal phenomenon is not equivalent to denouncing the phenomenon as trivial. Observers act on the basis of their attributions, and those acts may have critical practical ramifications. One example is the tendency for accidental presidents to be unfairly perceived as lacking leadership capacities and thus to experience more problems getting their appointive and legislative decisions approved by Congress (see chapter 4). Another is the fact that presidential popularity remains a secure predictor of an incumbent's reelection chances despite the loose tie between a president's approval rating and his objective performance in the Oval Office (see chapter 3). The attribution of presidential greatness may constitute the prime prerequisite for actual greatness.

CONCLUSION

Can the personal and attributional interpretations of historical greatness be reconciled? Are they of necessity mutually exclusive? While a conclusive answer is beyond reach given our present understanding of the phenomena, we can speculate on a possible reconciliation. On the one hand, the essential claim of the attributional model is probably correct: historians base their greatness assessments on a small collection of facts, which are selected because they are salient and memorable, not because they are the most pertinent to evaluating presidential performance. On the other hand, some if not all of the factors that contribute to a high rating may have some correlation, however modest, with particular personal characteristics of a president. An administration scandal defines a salient event that historians are quite likely to recall (and in this case, probably justly) when judging a president's strength, activity, and goodness, and hence greatness. At the same time, it may still be true that chief executives who thirst for friends and pats on the back are more likely to be too trusting when boon companions appointed to federal office embezzle from the public treasury. Similarly, power-hungry presidents may indeed be more disposed to involve the nation in war and to become assassins' targets. Nonetheless, only if such personality attributes actually translate into salient historical events will they affect the historians' perceptions of the presidency under scrutiny. And this contingency is the crux of the matter, for the causal arrow from potential to accomplished effects is by no means secure. Chance and a host of other factors intervene.

The impact of assassination is a case in point. While power-seeking incumbents may, for whatever reason, have a tendency to expose themselves to murderers, that disposition does not suffice. Besides the necessity that the president somehow provoke an assassin to take aim—an event that has only happened about a half-dozen times in American history—the assassin must get off a lucky shot. If the would-be assassin misses, the presidents' reputation is unaffected. But if he hits his target, by chance more than by expertise, the president's rating is improved. It seems capricious to decide a president's greatness according to the marksmanship of his potential killer and the tightness of security arrangements at a particular instant in history. Nonetheless, we have evidence that not only historians, but observers generally, form utterly opposed impressions about events decided only by the flip of a coin. McCauley and Jacques (1979), in a stimulating Bayesian analysis, showed that people believe that presidential assassinations are the result of conspiracies, whereas unsuccessful attempts on the life of a president are taken as the work of lone assassins. Ronald Reagan survived the wound inflicted by John W. Hinckley, Jr., and no one debates whether a grand plot was behind the event, yet theories still abound about all the possible (and impossible) conspirators who supposedly participated in Lee Harvey Oswald's assassination of JFK. We have no evidence that conspiracies are intrinsically more successful than solitary attempts. It is the outcome, nevertheless, that determines all, not the cause, a reality that introduces a whimsicality to any greatness assessment that uses assassination as a measure.

Analogous remarks can be put forth for the other predictors of greatness. The length of a president's stay in the White House, even if partly the result of some personality asset, is subject to chance intrusions, such as the incumbent's physical health, assassination, and the quality of the opposition candidate at election time. Monroe's reelection by just one vote less than unanimity in the electoral college—and the casting of that lone dissenting vote simply to reserve the honor of unanimous election to the first president—tells us more about the lull in sectional strife during the Era of Good Feelings than about the leadership qualities of this average president. And should we grant that power-seeking presidents will be on the prowl for a war to commit the nation to, that does not mean that they will succeed. As observed in chapter 4, Teddy Roosevelt, the Rough Rider, would have been quite pleased to serve in a major war as commander-in-chief rather than as a colonel, yet he failed so miserably that he received a Nobel Peace Prize instead. He was president a few years too late, or about a decade too soon. The weak correlation between affiliation desires and the propensity for scandal is insufficient to explain the incidence of corruption and graft in the executive branch. From table 4.2 we can see that Harding's affiliative needs were not at all outstanding, whereas Nixon's affiliation score, though high, was exceeded by both Kennedy and Ford. Indeed, Ford, the most affiliative president in history, was "Mr. Clean" par excellence. So pure luck must throw grit into the machinery linking motive and consequence. Harry S Truman, another modern executive with strong affiliation drives, noted, "The only thing you have to worry about is bad luck," with the addition "I never have bad luck." Grant, Harding, and Nixon did.

Although personality traits may make a modest contribution to the administration events that affect the attribution of presidential greatness, their effect can be strengthened, weakened, or even obliterated by extraneous factors that have nothing whatsoever to do with presidential character. We cannot at this point specify the relative influence of trait and circumstance on the course of a presidency, but Machiavelli's statement in *The Prince* (1513) is perhaps an overestimate of the role of chance: "Fortune is the arbiter of one-half of our actions, but . . . she still leaves us to direct the other half, or perhaps a little less" (35). But whatever influence traits may exert, social-cognitive processes settle which events prove to be central to the historians' perceptions. The six variables that consistently and accurately predict rated greatness include a few that no historian would dare to justify. Of the six, only scandal can be found among the forty-three criteria that Bailey (1966) claimed determined his judgments. Some of Bailey's supposed criteria, such as whether the president kept the peace, are plain wrong: even Bailey rated wartime chief executives more favorably. No historian has ever claimed that his greatness ratings depend on the president getting himself assassinated or having been a national war hero, yet these factors are sound predictors nonetheless. Hence, historians may not be the best judges of the criteria they employ in global assessments of presidential greatness; such judgment requires a degree of access to higher-order cognitive processes that is in all likelihood lacking (Nisbett and Wilson 1977). The attributional model alone may adequately explain why a half-dozen dramatic facts are singled out for attention and assigned such prominence in the historians' assessments. That naive raters, given the six predictors, can reconstruct the survey results gives this conclusion strong endorsement. Therefore, in the last analysis, studies of presidential greatness tell us more about how persons judge successful leadership than about how leaders actually achieve success. In the next chapter, I will propose that this inference applies just as well to the success criteria that were the subject of the preceding three chapters.

◆ 6 ◆
POLITICAL LEADERSHIP

What makes for presidential success? Why are some presidents more esteemed than others, whether by contemporaries or posterity? Is there any useful advice that we might offer a candidate or incumbent set on bringing the highest caliber leadership into the White House? The preceding four chapters provide the necessary basis for addressing these questions. From a brief summary of the empirical research, I will turn to a broader theoretical appreciation of the relative significance of individual and situation in promoting political leadership. The book ends with a short discussion of the potential usefulness of the findings I have inventoried.

EMPIRICAL SUMMARY

The material presented in the foregoing chapters can be consolidated by organizing the findings differently. Rather than treat the results according to the particular criterion of success, we can group the chief conclusions according to the predictor variables. These factors behind presidential success can be classified as individual effects, situational effects, and individual-situational interaction effects. Reviewing the empirical findings in this way, we can better spot which variables, if any, are useful for predicting success by two or more criteria.

The Person

Personality differences among the presidents leave an impression on their comparative successes as chief executives. Motivational contrasts are especially central. Presidents who are driven by an excessive need for power and seek domination and prestige usually enjoy good relations with the press, pick a cabinet characterized by expertise more than by camaraderie but force frequent cabinet changes, and provide favorite targets for assassination attempts; in foreign affairs, power-motivated incumbents are less likely to reach accords with other nations, are somewhat trigger-happy, and by peaceful or violent means manage to expand the U.S. sphere of influence. Closely related to the power motive are interpersonal dominance, Machiavellianism, forcefulness, and achievement drive, each with its own set of performance correlates. The American head of state who prefers a dominant position in his interpersonal relationships likewise favors a foreign policy that gives the United States a preeminent role in world affairs. Machiavellianism and forcefulness are both associated with the incumbent's accomplishments as chief legislator; Machiavellianism and achievement drive are both related to the president's success in the voting booth, at least prior to running for president. Shrewd, energetic, and ambitious leaders become successful politicians.

Curiously, it is difficult to untangle the power and achievement motives in presidents, though each disposition sometimes leaves its own distinctive mark on the course of history. For example, achievement-motivated White House residents are more inclined to negotiate peace-facilitating concords with other nations, and are less acquisitive when it comes to territory. Presidents with a strong desire to excel, however, do not necessarily like their job; for them the presidency is a chore, a burden taken on more out of duty than out of love. In contrast, power-hungry presidents seem to enjoy the job much more, are active and vigorous in fulfilling its responsibilities, and, perhaps as a consequence, have a stronger likelihood of going down in history as great. Teddy Roosevelt, a clear example, said toward the end of his second term, "No President has ever enjoyed himself as much as I have enjoyed myself, and for the matter of that I do not know any man of my age who has had as good a time."

By the criterion of historical greatness, a potent affiliation motive hampers an incumbent. Affiliative presidents tend to be more passive and to appoint cabinet members on the basis of congeniality rather than expertise. A president of such a disposition, however amiable and attractive, constantly courts the danger of scandals erupting in the administration. Nonetheless, social, friendly, even extroverted incumbents do have an advantage in the domain of foreign policy: they seek out peace-nurturing or conciliatory agreements with other world powers. In fact, when extroversion is coupled with dominance, we obtain a world-integrating leader. The United Nations is a reminder of FDR's extroverted dominance. For the most part, however, great presidents are usually high in power, low in affiliative needs.

Presidents differ not only in what drives them, but in how they think. Integrative complexity, or the capacity to make fine differentiations and comprehensive integrations of information, is linked to election success, to skill in averting war during tense international crises, to nonisolationist foreign policy preferences, and to a commitment to less extremist political ideologies. Dogmatism is associated with the incumbent's going down in history as a controversial chief executive. Curiously, presidents deemed great by historians score either high or low on the dogmatism dimension—they are either idealistic and inflexible or pragmatic and flexible. The most general cognitive attribute is intelligence, which exhibits an ambivalent connection with presidential success. More intelligent presidents tend to enter office with a diminutive share of the popular vote and may not even receive a popular majority, as Woodrow Wilson discovered twice. Bright chief executives thus lack a strong mandate from the people. At the same time, the more intellectually brilliant the president the greater the odds of his going down in history as one of the all-time greats. Much of the esteem in which Jefferson is held can be ascribed to the likelihood that he was the only undoubted genius ever to live in the White House.

Besides variations in motivational and cognitive traits, presidents bring into office diverse biographical experiences, which can have repercussions for presidential success. Family background offers many examples. Only children are more frequently channeled into the vice-presidential slot than into the top place on the party ticket (a letdown that paternal namesakes suffer too); middle children have more favorable odds of winning reelection, whereas the reelection chances of incumbents whose fathers were also politicians are less favorable; and great presidents tend to have grown up in small families. Jackson, Lincoln, Franklin Roosevelt, and Truman all had two or fewer siblings. The chief executive's physical attributes are not without consequence either. Most notably, the probability of reelection as well as the prospects for being considered a great president increase with each inch of the president's height. More than figuratively does Lincoln stand head and shoulders above the crowd.

Occupational choices project their own set of effects. For example, a career in academe is associated with both presidential dogmatism and less likelihood of reelection. The impact of a military career is more beneficial: former army generals have an edge in gaining the top spot on the ticket, and national war heroes may be more popular with contemporaries and have a head start toward a superior place in history. A presidential candidate's political résumé is even more important. For instance, presidents with extensive legislative experience on Capitol Hill do not have to resort as often to the executive veto. Cleveland and Franklin Roosevelt, who had plenty of practice vetoing bills as state governors but no experience receiving vetoed bills as legislators, hold the records for using the veto power. Candidates who lack broad exposure to the American people, who have never before been considered for the nation's highest office, are seldom granted a long stay on Pennsylvania Avenue; dark-horse presidents, from Pierce to Carter, tend to be one-term custodians. Last of all, we must recall the many ways that Democratic presidents generally differ from their Republican rivals. On average, Democrats are more power-motivated, can summon more support in the House, have better chances of reelection, serve longer, and receive higher ratings in some polls of historians.

Although a large number of individual traits distinguish the effective from the ineffective chief executive, they seldom explain as much variance as situational factors. Hence, the primary determinant of presidential success still may be the context in which the president assumes and exercises the duties of the office. One example of a situational factor is the state of the economy, a national condition that affects the president's approval rating in the polls, his reelection chances, the likelihood that his vetoes will be respected by Congress, and maybe even the desire of the public for more authoritarian leadership. The influence of war is even more pervasive, for it is the sole variable that has a prominent place in all four perspectives on presidential success. It affects the president's popularity, his reelection prospects, and the probability that his vetoes will be sustained, and has an additional and significant effect of raising the president's greatness rating. Again and again it has been shown that great presidents have had the opportunity to prove themselves as the wartime commander-in-chief, Lincoln, Wilson, and FDR offering the most outstanding examples.

Yet another situational factor is the proportion of Congress controlled by the president's own party. The more extensive that control, the better the incumbent's legislative box score, the less often he has to resort to the veto, the less often Congress succeeds in overriding those vetoes, and the higher the likelihood that the incumbent will be renominated and reelected. In this list of broad situational factors we must include the vice-presidential succession effect; accidental presidents experience more cabinet turnover, see more of their nominees to the cabinet and Supreme Court rejected by the Senate, have more of their vetoes overturned in Congress, and more often suffer the final insult of being denied renomination for a second, full term. Tyler was the first to endure the hazards of an unforeseen succession, and Ford may not be the last.

Finally, we must note the peculiar impact of time, the situational variable par excellence. On the one hand, the incumbent's approval rating in the polls declines over the course of his administration, the drop being particularly precipitous after the honeymoon period following inauguration. Additionally, the probability of a veto override increases in the latter part of the term. On the other hand, a long tenure in the White House is positively correlated with such things as the quantity of legislation signed into law, the number of justices appointed to the Supreme Court, and, most crucial, the president's ultimate acclaim in the annals of American history. This apparent contradiction is but one of many instances where something conducive to presidential success by one criterion may be detrimental by another. Contemporaries and historians do not employ identical yardsticks when gauging a president's adequacy, and among contemporaries, professional politicians and the public may disagree. Historical greatness, political leadership, and popularity in the surveys and voting booths are not interchangeable. Nonetheless, the disagreement on the implications of the passage of time may dissolve for presidents who fall to an assassin's bullet. All assassinated presidents except Kennedy were murdered shortly after their inauguration, when we would expect them to stand at the height of their popularity. This is in line with the fact that assassinated presidents are more highly esteemed by posterity despite their abbreviated tenures.

Person-Context Interaction

Individual and situational factors operate not merely in isolation, but in conjunction. Three such individual-situational interactions suffice as illustrations. First, the president's birth order, by affecting his social development, may interact with the political zeitgeist, especially the key issues and crises of the day, to determine whether his time has come in history. Thus, an international conflict may favor the first-born, whereas more settled periods call forth the middle child. Second, if a presidential candidate's dreams are to be realized, a match must occur between his own beliefs and those of the electorate on election day, at least insofar as spatial theory accounts for voter preferences. Third, whether presidential inflexibility translates into excessive use of the veto depends in part on the degree of support the incumbent's party can claim on Capitol Hill—what I have styled the Johnson–Wilson effect. In all of these interactions good timing is essential,

good for a conclusion

for success depends on a compatibility between the characteristics of the president and the circumstances under which he must exercise leadership.

A fourth type of interaction effect is perhaps less interesting but may be also more broadly important. The situation often mediates the effects of individual traits to weaken the correlation between presidential personality (or expertise) and executive success. The repercussions of presidential motivations offers a good illustration. A high need for power may be associated with a proclivity to get the nation involved in military conflicts, but this inclination is frequently overridden by situational considerations. Peace-minded presidents have been dragged into wars, and warlike presidents have been unable to provoke other nations to counter aggression with aggression. Likewise, in the design of foreign policy, the national interest, the distribution of power, precedent, and other contextual influences frequently enter the equation with such overwhelming force that any personal biases toward dominance or extroversion, no matter how potent, are left without effect. Sometimes the primary situational moderator is plain chance, or luck. Even if power-seeking incumbents are more likely to become targets of assassination attempts, only under rare circumstances would a potential assassin even get in position for an attempt; more rarely still would that attempt prove successful, with benefits for the incumbent's reputation. Similarly, even given the likelihood that highly affiliative presidents are in danger of having scandals erupt, some incumbents are more unlucky in their appointments than others. In all of these examples, the situation, whether constraint or circumstance, decides when the individual can leave an imprint on history and when that individual, even though the nation's leader, is largely irrelevant.

THEORETICAL INTERPRETATION

One criterion for evaluating the worth of a scientific enterprise is its ability to make accurate predictions about the phenomenon of interest. When this test is applied to the empirical research just reviewed, one judgment cannot be firmer: we can predict presidential success with an acceptable and sometimes imposing precision. On the basis of a small collection of predictors, the victor in the electoral college can be forecast almost without mistake. The incumbent's popularity in polls of the American people likewise can be accurately predicted using a handful of variables. The actual performance of an administration, given the abundance of available indicators, is necessarily more difficult to foresee. Even so, we possess many reliable clues to the direction that a president's foreign policy may take, and we can predict some aspects of the incumbent's legislative activities, especially his reliance on the veto power, with relatively little error. Most surprising, perhaps, is the ease with which we can forecast presidential greatness using a half-dozen clear-cut predictors. The equations predict a president's historical place so well, in fact, that we hardly need to consult the historians. Therefore, no matter which criterion of presidential success we look at, high-quality predictions are feasible.

The predictive value of the empirical research notwithstanding, we still have a long road to travel before we can fully explain the foundations of presidential success. One difficulty is that the work on most success criteria has been more empirical than theoretical in inspiration. The goal has been largely to glean the raw facts of presidential leadership rather than to present or verify a comprehensive theory. Even when a theoretical outlook can be said to have guided the researcher, the perspective is usually focused on the single substantive issue. The effects of birth order on personality development may be germane to Adlerian individual psychology, but this factor is otherwise rather narrow in theoretical significance. To be sure, many respectable theories have been formulated and tested in the extensive literature on presidential popularity, but here we have an embarrassment of riches, for a consensus has yet to emerge on the favored theoretical interpretation of the fluctuations in public opinion (see Monroe 1984). Any theory that attempts to integrate research on all four success criteria will necessarily receive less acceptance than a theory in the far more circumscribed domain of incumbent approval ratings.

Another difficulty that any ambitious theorist must confront is that much empirical research remains to be carried out before all the facts that should be part of any theory's foundation are in. Even in well-researched areas we often know for sure only that certain variables are correlated, with little solid evidence on the causal arrows that connect antecedents to consequents, and separate direct from indirect or spurious effects. For example, while we know that electoral success depends on the compatibility between candidates and the public on the salient issues in a given election year, it has proven difficult to ascertain the extent to which the candidates persuade voters to adopt their attitudes, the candidates follow the voters, the candidates misrepresent their opinions to the voters, and the voters distort their views of preferred candidates according to nonpolicy criteria (see Campbell 1983; Glass 1985; Markus and Converse 1979; Marshall 1984; Page and Jones 1979). In the case of the association between presidential popularity and legislative success, it is not easy to determine whether senators and representatives heed chief executives with high approval ratings, or incumbents with a high victory rate on Capitol Hill gain credit with survey respondents (see Rivers and Rose 1985; Zeidenstein 1985).

A final difficulty standing in the way of a truly unified theory is that the four success criteria seldom concur in their assessments of presidents. Presidential greatness judged by historians and political scientists bears no relation to the incumbent's popularity, whether measured by the electoral or popular vote, reelection, or the degree of support received in Congress (Simonton 1986c). Not only are there too many independent ways of assessing objective performance, but few performance indicators have been directly tied to a president's standing with either the populace or the experts. For instance, although presidential motivation has been connected with certain preferences in foreign policy, those policy inclinations have not been shown to affect directly the incumbent's standing with the public in surveys or elections, his ability to accomplish his legislative programs, or his ultimate status with later historians and political scientists. Accordingly, it may be necessary to have as many theories as we have success criteria, not a very welcome prospect.

All of these difficulties notwithstanding, I will attempt to outline a general psychological theory that coordinates much of the empirical literature. Consistent with the goals laid down in chapter 1, this theoretical framework will concentrate on explicating the impact of individual and situational factors on political leadership. The theory seeks to be as general as possible, so that it will be applicable to other exemplars of political leadership, not just those in the White House.

Assumptions of the Theory

The proposed theory can be taken as an elaboration of the attributional model presented in the previous chapter (see also Simonton 1986b, 1986c). The modifications aim primarily at extending its utility, so that it may be applicable to the interpretation of data from all four research areas.

Leadership Schema. As in proposition one of chapter 5, we begin by assuming that people engaged in assessing presidential success (whether or not they are also in a position to facilitate it) are involved in making a dispositional attribution. The incumbent or candidate is specifically undergoing evaluation, conscious or not, on leadership. This supposed personal quality is judged by comparing the actor with a standard, a leader schema, that defines an ideal or archetypal leader (see Kinder et al. 1980; Merenda 1964). Earlier, we postulated, on the basis of semantic differential studies, that this leader schema contained three important semantic components, strength, activity, and goodness (proposition two). In support of these three criteria is the fact that people expect the ideal president to be strong and courageous, to rid the country of economic ills and to develop positive relations with foreign powers, and to be honest and not to exploit the office for personal advantage (Kinder et al. 1980). The presidential role is also perceived to demand that its occupant display drive, forcefulness, firmness, determination, courage, and decisiveness (strength); initiative, persuasiveness, enthusiasm, extroversion, and mental and physical alertness (activity); and a sincere interest in people, diplomacy and consideration, and good moral judgment (goodness) (Merenda 1964). However, I have no wish to shackle the theory to a single conception of what this schema entails, for such a commitment without further corroborative research would be irresponsible. In lieu of requiring leaders to be strong, active, and good, we could just as well demand that a leader be active and positive (Barber 1977) or competent and trustworthy (Kinder et al. 1980)—closely related standards that vary slightly in emphasis.

We must be especially careful not to define the hypothesized schema narrowly in terms of particular presidential acts, such as cabinet appointments, veto behaviors, or policy preferences. I maintain that an abstract schema is applicable to all manifestations of political leadership, whether we are speaking of presidents, prime ministers, dictators, or monarchs. The impressive overlap in the predictors of monarchal eminence and presidential greatness appears to endorse this claim (Simonton 1984d); equally supportive is the fact that the picture of the ideal president corresponds closely to that of the American self-made company president, indicating a broadly conceived schema as applicable to the business world as it is to the political arena (Gelineau and Merenda 1981). Consequently, we must select a conception that can cover all cases. In addition, while we would expect the generalized semantic components to be linked with specialized criteria that are largely limited to the role demands of a particular office, such as the presidency, the more specific criteria are likely to be more volatile over time (see also Kinder et al. 1980). Probably all observers of the presidency, whether they lived in the formative years of our nation or in modern times, value competence, but observers from different eras would base this dispositional attribution on different particulars. Nowadays, how the incumbent manages the domestic economy, a criterion of minimal import during the first several administrations, provides heavy input for this attribution. Similarly, moral integrity in private life was probably a far more prominent indicator of goodness or trustworthiness in the more Puritan days of our republic than it is in these more permissive times. In any case, empirical data support the contention that generalized conceptions of the ideal president are stable for long periods, at least fifteen years (Gelineau and Merenda 1980; compare Morrow, Merenda, and Clarke 1974). Therefore, the restriction that the schema be abstract rather than concrete gives us an ideal or archetype having transhistorical, even cross-cultural, relevance.

Let us operate under the assumption that observers of actors in positions of political leadership apply the same schema when making assessments, for the ideal or archetype is part of the cultural heritage (and may even possess a sociobiological substratum). Observers of all kinds compare a given leader against this schema when making attributions of leadership quality. If the observer happens to be a voter, this comparison will determine how he or she is likely to vote in a primary or general election (see Merenda and Clarke 1968); for instance, a study conducted a month before the 1980 general election found that the public image of the incumbent, Carter, correlated less highly with a generalized image of the ideal president ($r = -.11$) than did the public image of the challenger, Reagan ($r = .72$), thus anticipating the election outcome (Gelineau and Merenda 1981). Likewise, if an observer is a survey respondent, the same assessment will guide the approval rating given the incumbent. In these two cases, which correspond to the observers who provide the success criteria in chapters 2 and 3, the public is making the judgment and acting accordingly, with consequences direct—election defeat or victory for a candidate—or indirect—inferior or superior performance ratings for the incumbent, with ramifications for his ability to capture a renomination, to get administration bills through Congress, and the like (see Kinder and Fiske 1986).

The success criteria treated in chapter 4, although more objective, remain dependent on observer reactions. The observers now are fellow political leaders, mostly senators and representatives in the federal legislature (both congressional leaders and the rank and file), but also including cabinet officers, presidential advisers, national party leaders, and even foreign heads of state. Presumably, one consideration that a senator must weigh in approving an executive appointment to the Supreme Court or cabinet, besides the personal merits of the appointee, is the incumbent's stature as a leader; incumbents disrespected by this assessment submit nominees that start off with less credibility. Moreover, because the incumbent is probably involved in self-attributions, basing his self-esteem on his own assessment of his success in living up to an ideal, we can obtain a feedback loop insofar as the president adjusts his executive behaviors accordingly.

In chapter 5 we discussed yet another type of professional observer, the scholars, mostly historians and political scientists, who are called upon to rate past presidents of the United States. These experts may apply an abstract touchstone to each chief executive when making the attribution of leader greatness.

Even though all classes of observers are presumed to use the same basic notion of the archetypal president, the expert judgments alone have no repercussions whatsoever for the leaders being rated. For the most part, historians are rating not contemporaries but deceased personages from the past. The writing of epitaphs cannot affect the process by which leadership is exercised, so that historians and political scientists, in the retrospective opinions they publicize, do not affect the phenomenon under assessment. This lack of feedback contrasts immensely with the power enjoyed by other observers of the political scene, whether the voting public or political colleagues on Capitol Hill. Many of the variables discussed in chapters 2, 3, and 4 show the pathways by which the attribution of leadership affects the leader's practice of leadership, which then reenters the attributional procedure. A voter's application of the leader schema determines whether a candidate will earn his or her vote. The outcome of the election itself then provides additional facts on which to base future assessments; the victor, by virtue of winning, is deemed superior in leadership to the loser, and the larger the margin of victory the more impressive the mandate to display leadership. In like fashion, a survey respondent's judgments, when aggregated in approval ratings in the polls, affect the way future respondents are likely to perceive the incumbent. This feedback effect operates both directly, to the extent that the public follows the opinion polls, and indirectly, insofar as the incumbent's political colleagues weigh the president's popularity when deciding whether to support administration policies. But the two-way causal interaction between attribution and performance seems to be especially powerful and immediate in the case of those fellow politicians with the capacity to make or break the incumbent. If the president's colleagues believe in his leadership, his room for manifesting leadership will be increased accordingly, as a variety of self-fulfilling prophecy. Once doubt sets in about the match between incumbent and ideal, the prophecy can turn negative; expectations diminish the latitude for displaying leadership, which further detracts from the incumbent's performance as the nation's chief executive. Such a downward spiral was apparent in the failing administrations of Tyler, Andrew Johnson, Wilson, Nixon, and Carter.

Information Availability. For purposes of argument, we have posited that the same leader schema is employed by all observers of political actors, whether the assessors are laypersons or professionals. This assumption would seem contradicted by what we have learned in the preceding chapters inasmuch as it implies that all four perspectives on presidential greatness would agree on ratings. Naturally, we could explain away this divergence at once if we simply assumed that observers in distinct groups had contrasting pictures of the ideal leader. Rather than do so, however, let us presume that the dispositional attribution of leadership leans heavily on information with the highest cognitive availability—just as we postulated in proposition three in chapter 5 (Kinder and Fiske 1986). We then must ask ourselves what kind of data is likely to be most available when leadership attributions are in the making. It is evident that observers do not have direct access to motives, values, or other dispositional characteristics, but must make inferences on the basis of the public acts of political leaders (see Jones and Davis 1965). However germane the power motive may be to a leader's strength, for instance, we cannot acquire this datum directly in the normal state of affairs, and consequently strength attributions must be founded on events that seem indicative of that trait.

Such indirect inferences are rather precarious, for many acts are deliberately intended to mislead, to create the desired impression. In chapter 2 we recorded how campaign rhetoric is devoted to such impression management, with special stress on making the candidate out to be competent and trustworthy, or strong, active, and good. This unreliability be what it may, observers seldom have access to unfiltered or unmanipulated information. That is one reason that the Watergate tapes were so damaging to

Nixon's reputation, for rarely do observers obtain such intimate knowledge of the private man behind the public image.

Given the lack of direct access, it is equally clear that observers of politics are privy to quite different sources of information on which to ground their attributions. Voters and survey respondents necessarily get almost all of their data from television, newspapers, and magazines. Political colleagues, in comparison, are granted more privileged types of information. A legislator on Capitol Hill, for instance, may have had personal contact with the president on numerous occasions, and certainly will have carefully read specific administration legislative proposals. As a consequence, when senators gauge the caliber of an incumbent, the latter's personal persuasiveness, as well as the quality of his administration programs, will figure in their attributions in a manner impossible for lay assessors. Historians rating past presidents are in yet another position altogether, for, unlike evaluators who must judge contemporaries, the experts enjoy the advantage of historical hindsight. Historians are gifted with knowledge of how the story ended—whether the incumbent was reelected or assassinated, how a military conflict or economic policy eventually turned out, and so forth. A historian today can look at Richard Nixon very differently from the voters who cast their ballots in 1972.

Different access to pertinent information explains why only two of the four perspectives on presidential success show concordance. The incumbent's standing in the polls is respectably correlated with reelection prospects, as we would expect given that voters and survey respondents would be making attributions of leadership according to identical schemata and more or less the same data. This informational factor may contribute as well to the correlations observed between certain tests of presidential performance. Presidents who are more likely to have cabinet nominees rejected in the Senate are also more likely to have Supreme Court nominees succumb to the same fate; furthermore, the rate at which a president sees his regular vetoes overturned correlates positively with the Senate's tendency to reject cabinet nominees and negatively with the administration's legislative box score.

Because these success criteria all reflect the president's skill at persuading the same set of observers, members of Congress, we must expect some agreement. When the federal legislators hold the incumbent in high regard, then they should be more willing to approve appointees and proposals, whereas when the members of Congress all have a low opinion of the president, executive performance deteriorates proportionately. Because senators and representatives have access to the same data, their judgments should synchronize, yielding the observed correlations among the several performance indices.

One might counter with the argument that the correlations do not point to an attributional process at all; rather, the performance variables gauge presidential leadership far more directly. Superior leaders may send only the very best nominees to the Senate for approval and only the most well-conceived bills or veto messages to both houses of Congress; inferior leaders may be less competent and thus deserve the rejection of their nominees, bills, and vetoes. Such phenomena as the vice-presidential succession effect strongly endorse the attributional interpretation, however. If good feelings between president and Congress were totally dependent on the incumbent's leadership skills and utterly independent of the legislators' leadership attributions, then the substandard performance of accidental presidents could be ascribed to demonstrated deficiencies in political expertise or personality—yet such powerful deficiencies have not been isolated. Furthermore, the attributional interpretation is far more consistent with the finding that the low performance of accidental presidents holds only during the unelected term in office, disappearing once the incumbent is elected to serve a second, full term in his own right. This makes sense if we suppose that certain components of the leader schema, such as perceived strength, are reinforced when an incumbent receives an electoral mandate, and therein the newly elected but formerly accidental president looks better in comparison with the ideal. On the other hand, it is hard to conceive how election at the head of the ticket suddenly gives the accidental chief executive more leadership capacity than he had when serving out the remaining years of his predecessor's term.

The vice-presidential succession effect also rules out an explanation based on the extent to which the incumbent's party controls Congress. Even though both the legislative box score and the rate of overturned vetoes are a function of such control, the accidental president almost always comes from the same party as his predecessor, and the difference in performance between elected and unelected terms cannot be attributed to corresponding shifts in party representation. The odds of having appointees rejected are also not related to the degree of party control. Consequently, the correlations observed among some performance indices may tell us more about how senators and representatives evaluate the leadership qualities of an incumbent than about how presidents truly differ in innate political acumen. The very fact that an accidental president had been willing to subordinate himself to his predecessor by taking secondary spot on the ticket, coupled with his unprepared assumption of the presidency sans popular mandate, may elicit undeserved dispositional attributions of weakness and passivity.

Attention, Memory, and Value. Not all pertinent information accessible to a given observer is actually available to that observer for assessing a politician's placement along a scale of leadership. So we are thrust back on the question of what determines which data have the highest cognitive availability. The following three influences may be most important (see also Kinder and Fiske 1986):

1. As expressed in proposition five in the preceding chapter, salience is assumed to have a major impact. Salient events attract the most attention and have a higher likelihood of being engraved in memory, and thus have better chances of being recalled during information processing such as that done when grading a president on leadership. Once again, we would think that the salience of a given datum would vary according to the perspective of the observer; each class of observers has its own characteristic baseline to which an event is compared in determining how much that event stands out above the background noise of fleeting reality. The current state of the economy and present international crises may grab the attention of people at large, whereas the historian may find the same items of merely transitory interest compared to

truly exceptional events, such as war, scandal, and assassination, that may change the course of history.

2. Salience cannot be the sole factor affecting the different cognitive availability of various articles of information, for we have seen many examples where salient facts are omitted from consideration. In particular, we would expect the temporal proximity, or recency, of a datum to determine how available it is when leadership attributions are being formed or revised. In our review of the literature on presidential popularity, we recorded how approval ratings appear to be most dependent on what has taken place in the last few months, making an administration only as good as its last performance. The principle of temporal proximity applies even to historians, despite the fact that these observers make a profession out of studying the past. Even though certain events are intrinsically more salient than others, the more remote an event is, independent of salience, the greater the probability that it will be ignored or discounted in the narration of history (Simonton 1975, 1984d; Taagepera and Colby 1979).

3. The preceding influences assume that the cognitive availability of various pieces of information is unaffected by personal interests, for salience and temporal proximity are more or less objective aspects of events. However, we will also suppose that a certain subjective bias figures in the retention and recall of information: availability is facilitated by a fact's hedonic relevance (see Jones and Davis 1965). Something that leaves an impact on an observer's personal well-being, whether beneficial or adverse, will equally impress itself on the mind, thereby becoming the sort of information that is most likely to be considered in leadership attributions. Thus, the state of the economy yields statistics with decided hedonic relevance, but certain economic items in the news are more relevant than others; this difference in relevance is reflected in which items most affect assessments of the incumbent. I should emphasize that the term *hedonic* is used not in the restricted sense of physical pleasure and pain, but rather in a larger sense of any broad psychological utility or value.

Attributional Bias. The last core assumption of the proposed theory is related to proposition four of the attributional model presented in chapter 5: cognitive availability is more crucial in determining which data sway the leadership attributions than the objective causal relevance of the datum in question. This is because observers are generally disposed to commit the fundamental attribution error. That is, observers, when judging an actor, are so set on making dispositional attributions using whatever information is at hand that they tend to overlook the circumstances, even the causes, behind a given fact. Information is presumed to be germane to judgments about personal characteristics merely because it is available. Many illustrations of this proclivity can be found in this book. Election success depends far too much on the most recent economic reports considering the tenuous causal link between administration policy and the long-term material well-being of the masses. Events in the news move presidential popularity up and down from one poll to the next regardless of how much the incumbent can be held personally accountable for them, whether they be labor strikes at home or crises abroad. In the domain of administration performance, the vice-presidential succession effect is just one of several examples where the incumbent is evaluated, with dramatic repercussions, according to extraneous circumstances. The variables that predict a president's historical greatness so precisely include a number that appear largely irrelevant to inherent executive leadership. The most conspicuous example is the high esteem a president receives just for getting himself assassinated.

We might speculate that the proclivity to extract excessive dispositional implications from situationally determined events is accentuated to the extent that those events invite the application of the representativeness heuristic (Tversky and Kahneman 1982). An incumbent taking action in time of international crisis, especially during war, is automatically placed in the prime position to display behaviors deemed representative of leadership. A wartime commander-in-chief would thus behave more like the archetypal leader than would a peacetime incumbent, and his stature in the eyes of the public, political colleagues, and historians would rise accordingly. Thus, the more schema representativeness a given event features, the higher the odds that it will sway the attribution process without regard to its situational foundation. Nonetheless, for the purposes of the present theoretical argument, we need not explain why observers indulge in the fundamental attribution error, as long as we are justified in assuming that they indeed do so.

Implications of the Theory

In setting down the foregoing assumptions, several implications of the proposed theoretical framework were conveyed as well. For example, the vice-presidential succession effect was interpreted in terms of the leadership attributions made by the legislators on Capitol Hill, and the patterns of correlations among the several criteria of presidential success were explicated in terms of the difference in access to information on the part of observers. Now I will delineate many other ways in which this theoretical framework aids our appreciation of the empirical findings reported in each of the four core chapters.

Election Success. It is apparent that many of the variables contributing to election victory, whether individual or situational in nature, entail applications of a leadership schema (see Kinder et al. 1980). The significance of campaign expenditures, regional exposure, and prior success in emerging victorious in the presidential primaries can largely be interpreted as data that improve a candidate's image on such schematic components as strength and activity, or competence. The momentum that is often established by success in the initial primaries illustrates how this attributional process can engender a positive feedback loop. The victor, by the salient act of winning, secures a higher standing in assessed leadership, which affects those observers waiting their turn to vote in the next round of primaries. Voters tend to prefer candidates whom they expect to win partly because being perceived as a winner contributes to a higher leadership rating; in the opposite causal direction, preferred candidates are expected, from their higher estimated leadership, to have better chances of success in the voting booth.

Much campaign rhetoric is tailored to a special image of the candidate, an image that highlights the central components of the leadership schema. If audience response can shape the expression of policy statements as a virtual illustration of Skinnerian verbal conditioning, certainly we have justification for maintaining that experienced politicians (and their campaign advisers), during the course of many campaigns, acquire a shrewd sense of what rhetorical devices work best, such as confirmation forms and symbols of strength and competence. Moreover, many of the individual attributes that may figure in the nomination process may have import only insofar as they project the proper image of the ideal leader. Experiments have indeed shown that personal appearance may sway voter preferences via the image of leadership that it projects (Rosenberg et al. 1986). The candidate's height may contribute to an aura of strength, and status as a national war hero may communicate strength, activity, and goodness. The apparent best age for winning candidates may reveal a more complex input into the leadership attributions: youth may be associated with strength and activity, advanced years with competence and trustworthiness, such that a politician in his mid-fifties may have the best appearance on all desirable attributes (see Beard 1874; Oleszek 1969).

The several instances in which the individual traits of candidates interact with the specific situational realities of the election year require more subtle interpretation. The hypothesized role of the economy in setting the preferred magnitude of leader authoritarianism may indicate that certain political circumstances shift the relative weights assigned to the separate semantic components of the leader archetype, hard times favoring strength. The dovetailing of birth order and political zeitgeist likewise suggests that the milieu may affect the standards by which the candidates' characteristics are assessed; during times of war and international crisis, strength becomes the desideratum of the day, whereas in more peaceful times the other components will receive more equal attention. Even the spatial theory of candidate-voter issue compatibility may be interpreted in terms of the changing context in which leadership attributions are made. American voters can engage in sufficient self-deception to judge a candidate whose attitudes are very proximate to their own as more competent and perhaps even more trustworthy. It is conceivable, too, that various emotional factors affect the voter's assessment of a candidate's leadership potential, and the resulting candidate evaluation proceeds to distort the voter's perception of the candidate's position on the issues. In this list of interactions we might mention the peculiar fact that excessive intelligence is evidently detrimental to election success despite its positive association with later assessments of presidential greatness. Given that a large intelligence gap between leader and possible followers renders the leader less comprehensible and that low comprehensibility tends to provoke negative reactions (Simonton 1985a), inordinate intelligence may undermine a candidate's perceived strength or goodness, competence or trustworthiness. Historians, who are more intelligent than the average American voter, would draw rather contrary inferences from the same datum.

When an incumbent seeks reelection, the same attributional criteria apply; this time, however, observers can judge demonstrated rather than promised performance (see Miller and Wattenberg 1985). That voters tend to reelect the wartime commander-in-chief may reflect, in part, the unusual impression left on leadership evaluations by the ability to command prodigious and lethal forces. Given the extreme salience of military events, and the exceptional hedonic value of their outcome (especially for those who are enlisted or have a family member enlisted in the armed services), this effect should also help carry the incumbent into a second term even if the peace treaty or truce is in effect by November, as was the case for McKinley. Wartime commanders-in-chief are given a unique opportunity to display strong, active, and, within the patriotic moralizing of any war, good leadership. These positive dispositional attributions ensue solely if the incumbent's performance passes muster. A mismanaged war can encourage unfavorable comparisons with the leader schema. Carter gained few points for his bungled raid on Iran in the general election a year later.

During peacetime, the material well-being of the typical citizen gains in importance, and so the judgments of the incumbent depend more on the most recent economic statistics. This is not to say that the average person is unashamedly a pocketbook voter, but merely that even the sociotropic citizen will attend to and recall the most salient and hedonically germane facts. Disposable income concretely affects the lifestyle people can afford, whereas other information (such as the money supply, exchange rates, and federal budget deficits) are far more abstract and distant in effect. Insofar as cognitive availability is a function of the temporal proximity of an event, the most recent condition of the economy will carry the most weight in the attributions, providing an incentive come election year for the incumbent to look strong, active, and competent in his management of the economy.

Economic and military information held constant, incumbents enjoy an edge over challengers, a political truth that can be subsumed under our theory. Besides any benefits accumulated from serving as the nation's sole commander-in-chief and principal executor of economic programs, the incumbent has abundant opportunities to stage dramatic events that underscore key leadership qualities. Special addresses before Congress, press conferences, speeches televised nationwide, White House bill-signing ceremonies, meetings with foreign dignitaries, and summit conferences with the mighty are just a few of the devices available for boosting the incumbent's leadership image. Only when the incumbent's seeming mismanagement of foreign and domestic affairs provides the challenger with ammunition to assault the president's image of power and control can the challenger entertain serious hopes of winning the election. It is insufficient for the challenger to claim that he or she will do a better job than the incumbent as long as the incumbent is viewed as doing an adequate job as the leader. The incumbent's presidential prestige will normally tip the scale in his favor.

The only potential exception to the incumbency advantage, besides apparent incompetence in handling foreign and domestic issues, is when a president enters office under circumstances that do not favor the accumulation of credit toward a positive leadership image. The disadvantage suffered by accidental and dark-horse presidents illustrates this exception. The absence of an unambiguous electoral mandate for the accidental president militates against his exercise of presidential authority, while the obscurity of the dark-horse incumbent means that a reputation for sound leadership must be established in a few short years before the time arrives for renomination and reelection. In these two instances, a challenger with considerably more experience and an established history of successful leadership will have a reasonable chance, in nomination or election, to unseat an incumbent who might otherwise be effective as an executive. Mark Twain said of one accidental president: "I am but one in 55,000,000; still, in the opinion of this one-fifty-five-millionth of the country's population, it would be hard to better President Arthur's Administration." Although there is some truth to this opinion, especially in light of the scandals that had sprung from Grant's administration some four years earlier, Arthur had insufficient opportunity to establish himself as a national figure, and thus had little support when he sought nomination for a second term.

Popularity in the Polls. The incumbent's approval ratings so closely parallel his election prospects that much of what has just been said pertains to any interpretation of why approval ratings fluctuate. In particular, the consequences of war and the economy are the same for an incumbent's standing with both survey respondents and voters, for all belong to the same class of political perceivers, with access to the same items of information. Even the incumbency advantage in the election has a counterpart in the opinion polls: the average approval rating across both time and incumbents tends to be respectable. Because reelection is a one-shot assessment, however, whereas the polls gauge the chief executive over many months, the research on presidential popularity has the power to isolate additional items that participate in the attributional process. An administration scandal (such as Watergate), which reflects directly on the incumbent's evaluated leadership, is one such item, and occasions in world affairs when citizens must rally around the flag (such as the Cuban missile crisis) provide another source of experiences both salient and, often, hedonically relevant. When these events receive considerable news coverage, their repercussions for leadership attributions should be all the more emphatic (see Iyengar et al. 1984). Furthermore, insofar as the mass media make the people aware of the results of past polls, such reporting may help maintain the autoregression observed in time series of approval ratings. The standing with the public that the incumbent exhibited in the last poll should influence the dispositional attributions made by the respondents in the next poll—just as the outcomes of previous primaries affect the leadership attributions made by voters in forthcoming primaries.

Probably the most important contribution made by empirical inquiries on this topic concerns the impact of time. Because an incumbent's competence in the White House should increase with practice and knowledge, the inexorable decay in the approval rating from poll to poll urges an attributional interpretation. It is probable that a president's standing with the public will regress toward the mean over time in the absence of events that uphold an image closer to the archetype. Dramatic happenings like reelection and international crises will revive the image with an injection of recent experiences relevant to gauging leadership, but that resuscitation can be merely temporary. As temporal distance decreases the cognitive availability of these events, the leadership attribution will lessen. This drop-off may be accentuated by the shift from pre- to postelection rhetoric, at least if we assume that the more simplistic campaign rhetoric approximates the vigor and immediacy expected of able leaders better than the cautious and compromising rhetoric used by the man in the Oval Office. In any event, according to the theoretical perspective put forward here, the persistent decline in an incumbent's popularity is an immediate psychological consequence of the loss of potency over time of facts that maintain a favorable leadership attribution. The decay curves in the polls reflect the similar decay curves in human memory.

Administration Performance. When we leave elections and polls to interpret actual executive behaviors, we switch to a new set of observers who are primarily responsible for the leader assessments. The observers whose opinions weigh most heavily are the representatives of the legislative branch. Most of the factors that affect the chief executive's performance vis-a-vis Congress can be interpreted as information sources for judging the incumbent as an able leader—a favorable assessment enabling him to exert his will over House and Senate. This power enhancement is manifested in the president's success in getting his legislative program past committee and floor votes. Incumbents who can boast an impressive approval rating in the opinion polls gain in apparent legislative authority, and accordingly can translate some of this prestige into a higher box score (although some members of the opposing party may take this as a call to practice obstructionism). Of far more crucial effect is the degree to which the incumbent's legislative success (judged against the chance baseline) depends on having his party control the two houses of Congress. A president who must face a Senate and a House organized by opponents will naturally look weak to the extent that the political context is allowed to influence the dispositional attributions; on the other hand, a president who enjoys comfortable majorities in both houses will appear strong, especially if his coattails swept a significant proportion of like-minded legislators into office (an item of immense hedonic relevance for the men and women in Congress).

Personal characteristics may also contribute to legislative success insofar as they expand the president's image as a leader among leaders. It is telling that Machiavellian personalities, although not necessarily more popular with the people, seem to score well with senators and representatives on Capitol Hill in terms of the number of bills pushed through. In the wheeling-and-dealing atmosphere of the legislative chambers, a shrewd, even sly chief executive may be more highly respected for competence. In any event, because the incumbent is probably engaged in self-attributions about his own leadership qualities on the basis of his performance, a feedback mechanism emerges. If much of this year's program gets nowhere, the incumbent becomes less ambitious the next year, ironically increasing the odds that he will raise expectations in the year after that. With time, an equilibrium should be reached in which the attributions of legislators and the self-esteem of the incumbent coincide fairly closely.

The empirical findings with respect to the regular veto and veto override can be explicated after the same pattern. Once again the amount of support the incumbent can summon in Congress is a central factor. The larger the number of political allies across Capitol Mall, the less often the president will have to resort to the veto to exert his will, and the less frequently Congress will overturn those vetoes it sees. The incumbent's prior experience in the national legislature may work in the same manner as the personality trait of Machiavellianism; by strengthening the president's image of competence, the incumbent may impress his desires upon the legislators before a bill is even passed, leaving the veto as a last resort only. On the other hand, another individual trait, presidential inflexibility, may lower the perceived competence of the incumbent as a legislative negotiator and compromiser, thereby encouraging members of Congress to overturn his vetoes; this inclination is aggravated if the senators and representatives belong to the opposing party.

Any situational circumstance that alters how closely the incumbent appears to approximate the ideal chief executive should reset the balance of power between the two branches of the federal government. Economic instability harms the incumbent's perceived value as a national leader, and so his vetoes are less likely to be sustained in Congress; military crises, in contrast, increase the president's apparent power and control, and his vetoes are correspondingly likely to be honored on Capitol Hill. In such instances as these, the members of Congress, like voters and survey respondents, presumably commit the fundamental attribution error, permitting situational factors to modify their evaluations of the head of state. The propensity of Congress to overturn vetoes after the midterm congressional elections illustrates another feature of this interpretation: because the midterm election gives all of the House members and one-third of the senators an endorsement from the voters, the incumbent's legislative position is weakened, for his mandate is then over two years old. The decreased temporal proximity of his electoral mandate gradually puts the incumbent on nearly the same shaky ground as the accidental president who has only a derivative mandate from the people. Finally, as we saw in the case of the legislative box score, the attributional process can generate a feedback loop: when an incumbent has vetoes overturned, that may subtract from his self-attributions of leadership, making him less willing to exploit the veto power later on.

Administration performance is a function of the leadership assessments made by the federal legislators, with an added provision for the incumbent's own self-attributions when we wish to address two-way causality or feedback loops. Nonetheless, senators and representatives are by no means the sole political observers whose judgments of the incumbent determine how he will exercise leadership. The high incidence of cabinet resignations suffered by accidental presidents might be partly ascribed to cabinet officials' failing to appreciate the incumbent's leadership qualifications; the trick of fate that triggered the vice-presidential succession may dominate the evaluations, the accidental president's real personal worth notwithstanding. By the same token, the fact that a Supreme Court justice may be more disposed to voluntarily offer the incumbent a vacancy if they share the same political affiliation may be interpreted in the same fashion, albeit more tenuously. Finally, we can speculate that the vulnerability to scandal of administrations headed by presidents high in affiliative motivation reflects the fact that appointees to high federal office may see such a need as a sign of an innate weakness that is easily taken advantage of.

The most significant audience, besides the United States Congress, perhaps consists of the other political leaders of the world. A prime portion of international affairs involves impression management, heads of state trying to portray themselves as strong, active, and good leaders, especially compared to world rivals and enemies (see Tetlock 1985). If the leader schema truly represents a universal set of criteria for judging the quality of political leadership, then all world leaders should be aiming at achieving the same image, for both domestic and foreign consumption, and the American president is a necessary participant in this game. For example, the shift in rhetoric occasioned by crises that end in military conflict may be seen as a maneuver by all parties involved to affirm forceful leadership, both as a reassurance to the people at home and as a warning to opponents abroad. Intellectually simplistic proclamations and propaganda project an image much closer to the ideal world leader than highly sophisticated reasonings. In moments of crisis, the resolutions of Macbeth are preferred to the soliloquies of Hamlet.

The link between presidential motivation and several events in international relations may exemplify this schema-relevant posturing. Assessments of power motivation have relied exclusively on content analyses of the inaugural addresses that launch each president's term in office. Yet these speeches are given in a specific political context, and are addressed to a wider audience than the American public attending the ceremonies; modern presidents must have an eye on foreign leaders, too. Consequently, when the times turn more vicious, and the use of military might becomes a prospect to be seriously considered, the president may attempt to present himself to the world and the nation as a powerful and determined leader, adjusting the rhetorical imagery of the inaugural accordingly. If the political context later compels the commander-in-chief to actually order American armed forces into action, a spurious correlation would result between power motivation and the president's propensity for military intervention, war, and even territorial acquisition. If the diplomatic zeitgeist favors a more conciliatory approach to the community of nations, the new chief executive may downplay the power motive, thereby producing spurious negative association between power motivation and arms limitation agreements. If this interpretation is justified, foreign policy decisions are determined more by situational than by individual factors, but because the situational forces shape both inaugural rhetoric and subsequent international events, individual characteristics are made to look as if they had some influence on the incumbent's performance in world affairs.

Historical Greatness. Given that the attributional model presented in this chapter is largely an extension of that presented in the last chapter, the implications for our understanding of historical greatness are essentially the same, and consequently I need not repeat myself here. I will instead confine discussion to three brief points.

First, as mentioned earlier, what is salient to a voter, survey respondent, or political colleague is not necessarily salient to historians some time in the future. This lessens the correspondence between historical greatness and the other criteria of presidential success. For example, while the state of the economy leaves an imprint on the attributions that underlie the first three success criteria, it is much less relevant to assessments of greatness. In the long run, the ups and downs in prices or unemployment have little consequence in comparison to wars and assassinations that permanently alter the path of history. Another datum, however, is just as salient to historians as it is to contemporaries, namely, that the leader being evaluated was or is a president of the United States. This introduces a positivity bias into any assessment: the occupant of the White House is presumed competent and trustworthy unless proven otherwise. Hence, historians in almost every published rating list more presidents as great, near great, and above average than as failure, near failure, and below average. This tendency is the historical analogue of the incumbency advantage on election day and the respectable average approval ratings of incumbents in the Gallup polls.

Second, the temporal remoteness of many key events of earlier administrations leave these events without effect on the historians' opinions of presidential leadership. It is probable that most historians are unaware of the legislative box scores that can be claimed by the incumbents in all but the most recent administrations, so it comes as no surprise that this performance variable has no influence on the overall assessments. Even in those rare instances where the historians have some awareness of legislative success rates, the fundamental attribution error may make them less likely to consider significant situational constraints, such as the amount of control held by the president's party. And, as noted in chapter 4, without a proper baseline, certain incumbents tend to be overrated, and others underappreciated. It is unlikely that the appropriate baseline is intuitively calculated by those who rate the presidents.

Third, hedonic relevance may determine which articles of information feature the most cognitive availability and hence exert the greatest influence on the leadership attributions. It may seem strange to employ this term for historians' judgments, but facts that are dramatic, that make exciting historical narratives, are more valuable to historians as lecturers and authors than boring statistics that might be far more germane to scoring leadership. Recounting battles and assassinations is much more fun than counting vetoes, overrides, the passage of administration-sponsored bills, and the approval of appointees to the cabinet and Supreme Court. As a consequence, a president's military prowess as war hero and commander-in-chief as well as his murder by an assassin, whether or not these facts are relevant, sway the historians' evaluations, whereas his legislative actions are demonstrably less pertinent, their superior prima facie validity notwithstanding. The curious finding that the greatest presidents tend to be those who are either very pragmatic and flexible or very idealistic and inflexible lends support to this interpretation. Historians above all else seem to want something interesting to talk about; to "make history" is, in part, to offer historians exciting stories—and blandness, no matter how competent, is of little use to the storyteller (see Simonton 1984d).

Summary

The above points do not exhaust all that might be said in light of the theoretical scheme. Yet I think it wise not to force the theory to explain more than can reasonably be expected. The principal goal of this book is to bring together the interdisciplinary, empirical research on the four criteria of presidential success, without concern for whether all findings could be subsumed under a single overarching theory. If a finding appeared both quantitative and nomothetic, and particularly if it had implications for understanding the comparative importance of individual and situational variables in the manifestation of political leadership, that finding was recounted, its compatibility with the present theory notwithstanding. Had my purpose been merely to offer and defend a theoretical position, many recalcitrant facts could have quietly vanished.

At this point the theory is little more than an interpretative scaffolding, one that I believe has immense potential for supporting a full-fledged account of many diverse facets of presidential success. Whatever future modifications may bring to the theory, the following tenets are fundamental: the respect or disrespect shown toward a president—whether registered in the voting booth, opinion polls, national and foreign capitals, or history books—tells us at least as much about how people observe political actors as about how those actors actually perform as leaders. John F. Kennedy rightly observed that "a nation reveals itself not only by the men it produces but also by the men it honors, the men it remembers." The four perspectives on presidential success divulge how various types of assessors judge a given political leader fits an idealized schema or archetype. Voters and survey respondents, historians, and fellow politicians (both domestic and foreign) are all governed by the same cognitive heuristic, but each class of observers has access to different information, and assigns that information different weight according to differences in salience, temporal proximity, and hedonic relevance. Individual and situational variables figure in these calculations insofar as they generate memorable events that seem germane to the abstract leader schema. All observers give insufficient care to how much the president should be held personally responsible for the facts affecting the assessments—even chance occurrences carry weight in these supposedly dispositional evaluations—as long as those facts appear representative of effective leadership.

In extreme instances, indeed, the perceived success of a president may have little to do with his innate ability as a leader. If the circumstances are fortuitously right, and a favorable leadership assessment results, the recipient of this gratuitous attribution may emerge victorious in the election, receive a resounding approval rating in the opinion polls, see administration bills passed and vetoes sustained, and perhaps go down in history as a great leader. Shakespeare wrote in *Twelfth Night* that "some are born great, some achieve greatness, and some have greatness thrust upon them" (act 2, sc. 5); on occasion the last of the three alternatives best describes the fate of a president. As the author of Ecclesiastes wrote, "The race is not to the swift, nor the battle to the strong, nor bread to the wise, nor riches to the intelligent, nor favor to the man of skill; but time and chance happen to them all" (9:11). This is not to say that assessments of leadership are utterly capricious, that no president deserves the approbations or condemnations he receives, but only that the nexus between act and attribution is a thin thread easily twisted, and sometimes altogether broken.

PRACTICAL APPLICATION

Theoretical questions aside, do the empirical results reported in this book have any practical value? Can they help us increase the odds of having successful leaders in the executive office? The proven capacity to predict the various criteria of success would seem to provide an affirmative answer, at least insofar as half the battle in having power over political events is predicting the repercussions of various choices. Because in a democratic country people select, they necessarily choose largely according to their expectations. Because delegates to national conventions seek candidates who will sweep the party to victory in November, predicting who has the highest likelihood of election success is tantamount to recommending a candidate. An informed voter could use empirical data to control better which policies will rule the country. Unfortunately, four obstacles block the full exercise of personal control over national politics.

In the first place, we may desire a president who is successful by more than one criterion, and these criteria might not have compatible antecedents. If we wish to place in office a president with a favorable disposition toward peace-building agreements with other nations, an affiliation-motivated executive may be a reasonable choice, but that very choice may carry with it an increased risk of scandal in the administration. Tradeoffs must be weighed in any application of useful knowledge, exchanges that require value judgments going beyond considerations of objective fact.

Second, in a democracy, many different individuals are capable of utilizing information—voters, congressional legislators, the chief executive, and others—and these persons will have distinct and often inconsistent interests to consider. An incumbent up for reelection may manipulate the real disposable income per capita with a hopeful eye on election day even if in the long run the material well-being of the average American citizen is compromised in the process. And a president willing and able to capture a second term with this trick may not be the best executive to lead the country anyway. More generally, applicable scientific knowledge can become part of the arsenal of one's rivals and adversaries as well as one's friends and allies in the political system.

Third, to the extent that the theory presented in the previous section proves justified, a significant portion of political leadership entails an attributional process with many pitfalls between fact and judgment. It is in no one's power to oblige observers to make their leadership schema more sophisticated, nor can anyone force observers of American politics to utilize information in a more rational fashion. Simplistic and uninformed attributions of leadership may always be with us.

Fourth, chance still intrudes upon the course of human events, and its randomness vitiates the reliability of personal control. America, for all its power, is at the mercy of events that originate almost anywhere on the globe. An incumbent may receive an unexpected boost from an international crisis not of his choosing, or suffer loss of reputation because of economic backsliding precipitated by decisions made in foreign capitals. Eight times in American history an unanticipated death has brought an accidental president into the limelight, deflecting the presidency along a new path. Thus, while expertise can raise or lower the odds of certain events happening, we are still playing a game of cards, not chess.

A scan of American history reveals how lucky the United States has been in getting able leaders to serve in the highest office in the land. The overwhelming majority of presidents have been competent politicians, and a half-dozen or so can be counted as great men. Any nation would be proud to claim a Washington or Lincoln as its own. Despite the occasional occurrence of an inferior or failed presidency, Americans have never had to endure evil, cruel, tyrannical, or otherwise truly bad leaders (see also Simonton 1983b, 1984d). Both Grant and Harding were basically decent men, each with his own admirable qualities; both were utterly out of their element in the presidency. What Alice Roosevelt Longworth ungraciously said of one might be applied to both men: "Harding was not a bad man. He was just a slob." However contemporaries might have ranted and raved about Nixon, or FDR, or Lincoln, no power-seeking dictator has ever managed to take the reins from the hands of the American people. This luck in the succession of presidents, of course, was probably aided by the wise design of the Constitution as well as by a citizenry that is unshakably committed to democratic procedures. In the future, this luck may be improved upon still further. As more empirical data on presidential success accumulate, our adeptness at prediction, the depth of our theoretical understanding, and the scope of events under our control should expand. If the institution of the presidency survives long enough, we may eventually reach the point where we can guarantee that only wise and honest leaders make decisions for us in the Oval Office. Not only may we systematically avoid more Grants and Hardings, but we may even increase the probability of more Washingtons and Lincolns.

BIBLIOGRAPHY

Abelson, Robert P.; Kinder, Donald R.; Peters, Mark D.; and Fiske, Susan T. 1982. "Affective and Semantic Components in Political Person Perception." *Journal of Personality and Social Psychology* 42:619–30.

Abramowitz, Alan I. 1985. "Economic Conditions, Presidential Popularity, and Voting Behavior in Midterm Congressional Elections." *Journal of Politics* 47:31–43.

Abramowitz, Alan I., and Stone, Walter J. 1984. *Nomination Politics.* New York: Praeger.

Adorno, Theodor W.; Frenkel-Brunswik, Else; Levinson, Daniel J.; and Sanford, R. Nevitt. 1950. *The Authoritarian Personality.* New York: Harper and Row.

Aldrich, John H. 1980. *Before the Convention.* Chicago: University of Chicago Press.

Alker, Henry A. 1981. "Political Creativity." In *Review of Personality and Social Psychology,* vol. 2, ed. Ladd Wheeler. Beverly Hills: Sage Publications.

Amlund, Curtis. 1964. "President-Ranking: A Criticism." *Midwest Journal of Political Science* 8:309–15.

Anderson, Norman H. 1973. "Information Integration Theory Applied to Attitudes about U.S. Presidents." *Journal of Educational Psychology* 64:1–8.

Archer, J. Clark; Murauskas, G. Thomas; Shelley, Fred M.; White, Ellen R.; and Taylor, Peter J. 1985. "Counties, States, Sections, and Parties in the 1984 Presidential Election." *Professional Geographer* 37:279–87.

Armbruster, Maxim E. 1982. *The Presidents of the United States and their Administrations from Washington to Reagan.* 7th ed., rev. New York: Horizon Press.

Atkin, Charles K. 1969. "The Impact of Political Poll Reports on Candidate and Issue Preference." *Journalism Quarterly* 46:515–21.

Axelrod, Robert. 1986. "Presidential Election Coalitions." *American Political Science Review* 80:281–84.

Aydelotte, William O. 1971. *Quantification in History.* Reading, Mass.: Addison-Wesley.

Bailey, Thomas A. 1966. *Presidential Greatness.* New York: Appleton-Century.

———. 1980. *The Pugnacious Presidents.* New York: Free Press.

———. 1981. *Presidential Saints and Sinners.* New York: Free Press.

Barber, James David. 1965. *The Lawmakers.* New Haven: Yale University Press.

———. 1977. *The Presidential Character.* 2d ed. Englewood Cliffs, N.J.: Prentice-Hall.

Barry, Herbert III. 1979. "Birth Order and Paternal Namesake as Predictors of Affiliation with Predecessor by Presidents of the United States." *Political Psychology* 1:61–66.

———. 1983–84. "Predictors of Longevity of United States Presidents." *Omega* 14:315–21.

Bartels, Larry M. 1985a. "Expectations and Preferences in Presidential Nominating Campaigns." *American Political Science Review* 79:804–15.

———. 1985b. "Resource Allocation in a Presidential Campaign." *Journal of Politics* 47:928–36.

Bass, Bernard M. 1981. *Stogdill's Handbook of Leadership.* New York: Free Press.

Beard, George M. 1874. *Legal Responsibility in Old Age.* New York: Russell.

Berkowitz, William R.; Nebel, Jeffrey C.; and Reitman, Jonathan W. 1971. "Height and Interpersonal Attraction: The 1969 Mayoral Election in New York City." *Proceedings of the 79th Annual Convention of the American Psychological Association* 6:281–82.

Block, Jack. 1961. *The Q-Sort Method in Personality Assessment and Psychiatric Research.* Springfield, Ill.: Thomas.

Blondel, Jean. 1980. *World Leaders.* Beverly Hills: Sage Publications.

Bloom, H. S., and Price, H. Douglas. 1975. "Voter Response to Short-Run Economic Conditions: The Asymmetrical Effect of Prosperity and Recession." *American Political Science Review* 69:1240–54.

Boller, Paul F. 1981. *Presidential Anecdotes.* New York: Oxford University Press.

Bond, Jon R., and Fleisher, Richard. 1984. "Presidential Popularity and Congressional Voting: A Reexamination of Public Opinion as a Source of Influence in Congress." *Western Political Quarterly* 37:291–306.

Boor, Myron, and Fleming, Jerome A. 1984. "Presidential Election Effects on Suicide and Mortality Levels Are Independent of Unemployment Rates." *American Sociological Review* 49:706–07.

Born, Richard. 1984. "Reassessing the Decline of Presidential Coattails: United States House Elections from 1952–80." *Journal of Politics* 46:60–79.

Brams, Steven J., and Davis, Morton D. 1974. "The $\frac{3}{2}$'s Rule in Presidential Campaigning." *American Political Science Review* 68:113–34.

Brent, Edward, and Granberg, Donald. 1982. "Subjective Agreement with the Presidential Candidates of 1976 and 1980." *Journal of Personality and Social Psychology* 42:393–403.

Brody, Richard A., and Page, Benjamin I. 1975. "The Impact of Events on Presidential Popularity: The Johnson and Nixon Administrations." In *Perspectives on the Presidency,* ed. Aaron Wildavsky. Boston: Little, Brown.

Brody, Richard A., and Sigelman, Lee. 1983. "Presidential Popularity and Presidential Elections: An Update and Extension." *Public Opinion Quarterly* 47:325–28.

Brown, Stuart Gerry. 1966. *The American Presidency.* New York: Macmillan.

Brown, Thad A., and Stein, Arthur A. 1982. "Review Article: The Political Economy of National Elections." *Comparative Politics* 14:479–97.

Browning, Robert X. 1985. "Presidents, Congress, and Policy Outcomes: U.S. Social Welfare Expenditures, 1949–77." *American Journal of Political Science* 29:197–216.

Bruhn, A. Rahn, and Bellow, Sheri. 1984. "Warrior, General, and President: Dwight David Eisenhower and his Earlier Recollections." *Journal of Personality Assessment* 48:371–77.

Buchanan, Bruce. 1978. *The Presidential Experience.* Englewood Cliffs, N.J.: Prentice-Hall.

Burns, James MacGregor. 1978. *Leadership.* New York: Harper and Row.

Campbell, James E. 1983. "Ambiguity in the Issue Positions of Presidential Candidates: A Causal Analysis." *American Journal of Political Science* 27:284–93.

———. 1985. "Explaining Presidential Losses in Midterm Congressional Elections." *Journal of Politics* 47:1140–57.

Carpini, Michael X. 1984. "Scooping the Voters? The Consequences of the Networks' Early Call of the 1980 Presidential Race." *Journal of Politics* 46:866–85.

Carter, John. 1984. "Early Projections and Voter Turnout in the 1980 Presidential Election." *Public Choice* 43:195–202.

Caruth, Gorton, ed. 1979. *The Encyclopedia of American Facts and Dates*. 7th ed. New York: Crowell.

Cattell, James McKeen. 1903. "A Statistical Study of Eminent Men." *Popular Science Monthly* 62:359–77.

Cattell, Raymond B., and Adelson, Marvin. 1951. "The Dimensions of Social Change in the U.S.A. as Determined by P-Technique." *Social Forces* 30:190–201.

Cell, Charles P. 1974. "Charismatic Heads of State: The Social Context." *Behavior Science Research* 9:255–305.

Chappell, Henry W., Jr., and Keech, William R. 1985. "A New View of Political Accountability for Economic Performance." *American Political Science Review* 79:10–27.

Chesen, Eli S. 1973. *President Nixon's Psychiatric Profile.* New York: Weyden.

Chicago Tribune Magazine, 10 January 1982, 8–13, 15, 18, as cited in Murray and Blessing (1983).

Colantoni, Claude S.; Levesque, Terrence J.; and Ordeshook, Peter C. 1975. "Campaign Resource Allocations under the Electoral College." *American Political Science Review* 69:141–54.

Coleman, Stephen. 1985. "The Human Brain, Social Conformity, and Presidential Elections." *Journal of Mathematical Sociology* 11:95–130.

Copeland, Gary W. 1983. "When Congress and the President Collide: Why Presidents Veto Legislation." *Journal of Politics* 45:696–710.

Costantini, Edmond, and Craik, Kenneth H. 1980. "Personality and Politicians: California Party Leaders, 1960–1976." *Journal of Personality and Social Psychology* 38:641–61.

Cox, Catherine. 1926. *The Early Mental Traits of Three Hundred Geniuses.* Stanford: Stanford University Press.

Current Biography. 1940–1983. New York: Wilson.

Donley, Richard E., and Winter, David G. 1970. "Measuring the Motives of Public Officials at a Distance: An Exploratory Study of American Presidents." *Behavioral Science* 15:227–36.

Edwards, George C. III. 1985. "Measuring Presidential Success in Congress: Alternative Approaches." *Journal of Politics* 47:667–85.

Edwards, George C. III, and Wayne, Stephen J. 1985. *Presidential Leadership.* New York: St. Martin's Press.

Elder, Robert E., and Holmes, Jack E. 1985. "U.S. Foreign Policy Moods, Institutional Change, and Change in the International Economic System." Paper presented at the meeting of the American Political Science Association, New Orleans, August.

Elms, Alan C. 1976. *Personality in Politics.* New York: Harcourt Brace Jovanovich.
Encyclopaedia Britannica. 15th ed. Chicago: Encyclopaedia Britannica.
Erikson, Robert. 1976. "The Influence of Newspaper Endorsements on Presidential Elections." *American Journal of Political Science* 20:207–33.
Etheredge, Lloyd S. 1978a. "Personality Effects on American Foreign Policy, 1898–1968: A Test of Interpersonal Generalization Theory." *American Political Science Review* 78:434–51.
———. 1978b. *A World of Men: The Private Sources of American Foreign Policy.* Cambridge, Mass.: MIT Press.
Evered, Roger. 1983. "Who's Talking about the Future? An Analysis of the U.S. Presidents." *Technological Forecasting and Social Change* 24:61–77.
Feldman, Paul, and Jondrow, James. 1984. "Congressional Elections and Local Federal Spending." *American Journal of Political Science* 28:147–64.
Finer, Herman. 1960. *The Presidency.* Chicago: University of Chicago Press.
Fiorina, Morris P. 1981. *Retrospective Voting in American National Elections.* New Haven: Yale University Press.
Fiske, Susan T., and Taylor, Shelly E. 1984. *Social Cognition.* Reading, Mass.: Addison-Wesley.
Fogel, Robert W. 1975. "The Limits of Quantitative Methods in History." *American Historical Review* 80:329–50.
Foster, Carroll B. 1984. "The Performance of Rational Voter Models in Recent Presidential Elections." *American Political Science Review* 78: 678–90.
Freud, Sigmund, and Bullitt, William C. 1967. *Thomas Woodrow Wilson.* Boston: Houghton Mifflin.
Gans, Daniel J. 1985. "Persistence of Party Success in American Presidential Elections." *Journal of Interdisciplinary History* 16:221–37.
Gelineau, Elaine P., and Merenda, Peter F. 1978. "Students' Perceptions of Jimmy Carter and the Ideal Self." *Perceptual and Motor Skills* 46: 1183–90.
———. 1980. "Students' Perception of Jimmy Carter, Ted Kennedy, and the Ideal President." *Perceptual and Motor Skills* 51:147–55.
———. 1981. "Students' Pre-Election Perceptions of Jimmy Carter and Ronald Reagan." *Perceptual and Motor Skills* 52:491–98.
George, Alexander L., and George, Juliette L. 1956. *Woodrow Wilson and Colonel House.* New York: Day.

Glass, David P. 1985. "Evaluating Presidential Candidates: Who Focuses on Their Personal Attributes?" *Public Opinion Quarterly* 49:517–34.

Goertzel, Victor, and Goertzel, Mildred George. 1962. *Cradles of Eminence.* Boston: Little, Brown.

Goertzel, Mildred George; Goertzel, Victor; and Goertzel, Ted George. 1978. *Three Hundred Eminent Personalities.* San Francisco: Jossey-Bass.

Goggin, Malcolm L. 1984. "The Ideological Content of Presidential Communications: The Message-Tailoring Hypothesis Revisited." *American Politics Quarterly* 12:361–84.

Gough, Harrison G., and Heilbrun, Alfred B., Jr. 1965. *The Adjective Check List Manual.* Palo Alto, Calif.: Consulting Psychologists Press.

Granberg, Donald, and Brent, Edward. 1983. "When Prophecy Bends: The Preference-Expectation Link in U.S. Presidential Elections, 1952–1980." *Journal of Personality and Social Psychology* 45:477–91.

Green, Thomas M., and Pederson, William D. 1985. "The Behavior of Lawyer-Presidents: A 'Barberian' Link." *Presidential Studies Quarterly* 15:343–52.

Grush, Joseph E. 1980. "Impact of Candidate Expenditures, Regionality, and Prior Outcomes on the 1976 Democratic Presidential Primaries." *Journal of Personality and Social Psychology* 38:337–47.

Grush, Joseph E.; McKeough, Kevin L.; and Ahlering, Robert F. 1978. "Extrapolating Laboratory Exposure Research to Actual Political Elections." *Journal of Personality and Social Psychology* 36:257–70.

Hammond, Thomas H., and Fraser, Jane M. 1983. "Baselines for Evaluating Explanations of Coalition Behavior in Congress." *Journal of Politics* 45:635–56.

———. 1984. "Judging Presidential Performance on House & Senate Roll Calls." *Polity* 16:624–46.

Hargrove, Erwin C. 1966. *Presidential Leadership.* New York: Macmillan.

Hart, Roderick P. 1984. *Verbal Style and the Presidency.* New York: Academic Press.

Hayes, Stephan L.; Shull, Steven A.; Howell, Susan E.; and Flaxbeard, John M. 1984. "Presidential Support among Senatorial Leaders and Followers." *American Politics Quarterly* 12:195–209.

Heller, Francis. 1960. *The Presidency.* New York: Random House.

Hermann, Margaret G., ed. 1977. *The Psychological Examination of Political Leaders.* New York: Free Press.

Hermann, Margaret G., ed. 1986. *Political Psychology.* San Francisco: Jossey-Bass.

Herring, E. Pendleton. 1940. *Presidential Leadership.* New York: Rinehart.

Hibbing, John R., and Brandes, Sara L. 1983. "State Population and the Electoral Success of U.S. Senators." *American Journal of Political Science* 27:808–19.

Hibbs, Douglas A. 1974. "Problems of Statistical Estimation and Causal Inference in Time-Series Regression Models." In *Sociological Methodology 1973–1974,* ed. Herbert L. Costner. San Francisco: Jossey-Bass.

———. 1979. "The Mass Public and Macroeconomic Performance: The Dynamics of Public Opinion toward Unemployment and Inflation." *American Journal of Political Science* 23:705–31.

———. 1982a. "The Dynamics of Political Support for American Presidents among Occupational and Partisan Groups." *American Journal of Political Science* 26:312–32.

———. 1982b. "Economic Outcomes and Political Support for British Governments among Occupational Classes: A Dynamic Analysis." *American Political Science Review* 76:259–79.

———. 1982c. "More on Economic Performance and Political Support in Britain: A Reply to William R. Keech." *American Political Science Review* 76:282–84.

———. 1982d. "President Reagan's Mandate from the 1980 Elections: A Shift to the Right?" *American Politics Quarterly* 10:387–420.

Historical Figures Assessment Collaborative. 1977. "Assessing Historical Figures: The Use of Observer-Based Personality Descriptions." *Historical Methods Newsletter* 10:66–76.

Hoffer, Peter C. 1978. "Psychohistory and Empirical Group Affiliation: Extraction of Personality Traits from Historical Manuscripts." *Journal of Interdisciplinary History* 9:131–45.

Hook, Janet. 1986. "Hill Backing for Reagan Continues to Decline." *Congressional Quarterly* 44:68–74.

Houweling, Henk W., and Kuné, J. B. 1984. "Do Outbreaks of War Follow a Poisson-Process?" *Journal of Conflict Resolution* 28:51–61.

Houweling, Henk W., and Siccama, Jan G. 1985. "The Epidemiology of War, 1816–1980." *Journal of Conflict Resolution* 29:641–63.

Hoxie, Gordon. 1976. "Presidential Greatness." In *Power and the Presidency,* ed. Philip Dolce and George Skau. New York: Scribner's.

If elected . . . . 1972. Washington, D.C.: Smithsonian Institution Press.

Israel, Fred L., ed. 1965. *The Chief Executive.* New York: Crown.

Iyengar, Shanto; Kinder, Donald R.; Peters, Mark; and Krosnick, Jon A. 1984. "The Evening News and Presidential Evaluations." *Journal of Personality and Social Psychology* 46:778–87.

Janis, Irving L. 1972. *Victims of Groupthink.* Boston: Houghton Mifflin.

Jenkins, James J.; Russell, Wallace A.; and Suci, George J. 1958. "An Atlas of Semantic Profiles for 360 Words." *American Journal of Psychology* 71:688–99.

Johnson, Joel T.; Jemmott, J. B. III; and Pettigrew, Thomas F. 1984. "Causal Attribution and Dispositional Inference: Evidence of Inconsistent Judgments." *Journal of Experimental Social Psychology* 20:567–85.

Jones, Edward E., and Davis, Keith E. 1965. "From Acts to Dispositions: The Attribution Process in Person Perception." In *Advances in Experimental Social Psychology*, vol. 2, ed. Leonard Berkowitz. New York: Academic Press.

Jorgenson, Dale O. 1975. "Economic Threat and Authoritarianism in Television Programs: 1950–1974." *Psychological Reports* 37:1153–54.

Kallenbach, Joseph. 1966. *The American Chief Executive*. New York: Harper and Row.

Kane, Joseph Nathan. 1974. *Facts about the Presidents*. 3d ed. New York: Wilson.

———. 1977. *Facts about the Presidents: Supplement to the Third Edition*. New York: Wilson.

Kearns, Doris. 1976. *Lyndon Johnson and the American Dream*. New York: Harper and Row.

Keech, William R. 1982. "Of Honeymoons and Economic Performance: Comment on Hibbs." *American Political Science Review* 76:280–81.

Keller, Robert R., and May, Ann Mari. 1984. "The Presidential Political Business Cycle of 1972." *Journal of Economic History* 44:265–71.

Kenny, David A. 1979. *Correlation and Causality*. New York: Wiley.

Kenski, Henry C. 1977. "The Impact of Economic Conditions on Presidential Popularity." *Journal of Politics* 39:764–73.

Kernell, Samuel. 1978. "Explaining Presidential Popularity: How Ad Hoc Theorizing, Misplaced Emphasis, and Insufficient Care in Measuring One's Variables Refuted Common Sense and Led Conventional Wisdom Down the Path of Anomalies." *American Political Science Review* 72:506–22.

Kernell, Samuel, and Hibbs, Douglas. 1981. "A Critical Threshold Model of Presidential Popularity." In *Contemporary Political Economy*, ed. Douglas Hibbs and Heino Fassbender. Amsterdam: North Holland.

Kernell, Samuel; Sperlich, Peter W; and Wildavsky, Aaron. 1975. "Public Support for Presidents." In *Perspectives on the Presidency*, ed. Aaron Wildavsky. Boston: Little, Brown.

Kessel, John. 1980. *Presidential Campaign Politics*. Homewood, Ill.: Dorsey Press.

Kick, Edward L. 1983. "World-System Properties and Military Intervention-Internal War Linkages." *Journal of Political and Military Sociology* 11:185–208.

Kiewiet, D. Roderick. 1983. *Macroeconomics & Micropolitics.* Chicago: University of Chicago Press.

Kimmitt, J. S., and Haley, R. K. 1978. *Presidential Vetoes, 1789–1971.* Washington, D.C.: Government Printing Office.

Kinder, Donald R. (1981). "Presidents, Prosperity, and Public Opinion." *Public Opinion Quarterly* 45:1–21.

Kinder, Donald R., and Fiske, Susan T. 1986. "Presidents in the Public Mind." In *Political Psychology,* ed. Margaret G. Hermann. San Francisco: Jossey-Bass.

Kinder, Donald R., and Kiewiet, D. Roderick. 1979. "Economic Discontent and Political Behavior: The Role of Personal Grievances and Collective Economic Judgments in Congressional Voting." *American Journal of Political Science* 23:495–527.

Kinder, Donald R.; Peters, Mark D.; Abelson, Robert R.; and Fiske, Susan T. 1980. "Presidential Prototypes." *Political Behavior* 2:315–38.

Knutson, Jeanne N., ed. 1973. *Handbook of Political Psychology.* San Francisco: Jossey-Bass.

Koenig, Louis W. 1975. *The Chief Executive.* 3d ed. New York: Harcourt Brace Jovanovich.

Kramer, Gerald H. 1971. "Short-Term Fluctuations in U.S. Voting Behavior, 1896–1964." *American Political Science Review* 65:131–43.

Kull, Irving S., and Kull, Nell M. 1952. *A Short Chronology of American History 1492–1950.* New Brunswick, N.J.: Rutgers University Press.

Kynerd, Tom. 1971. "An Analysis of Presidential Greatness and 'President Rating.'" *Southern Quarterly* 9:309–29.

Ladd, Everett Carll. 1985. "On Mandates, Realignments, and the 1984 Presidential Election." *Political Science Quarterly* 100:1–25.

Langer, William L. 1958. "The Next Assignment." *American Historical Review* 63:283–304.

Laski, Harold. 1940. *The American Presidency.* New York: Grossett and Dunlap.

Lee, Jong R. 1975. "Presidential Vetoes from Washington to Nixon." *Journal of Politics* 37:522–46.

Lehman, Harvey C. 1943. "The Longevity of the Eminent." *Science* 98:270–73.

———. 1953. *Age and Achievement.* Princeton, N.J.: Princeton University Press.

Leitner, L. M. 1983. "Construct Similarity, Self-Meaningfulness, and Presidential Preference." *Journal of Personality and Social Psychology* 45:890–94.

Lewis-Beck, Michael S. 1985. "Pocketbook Voting in U.S. National Election Studies: Fact or Artifact?" *American Journal of Political Science* 29:348–56.

Lewis-Beck, Michael S., and Rice, Tom W. 1983. "Localism in Presidential Elections: The Home State Advantage." *American Journal of Political Science* 27:548–56.

———. 1984. "Forecasting Presidential Elections: A Comparison of Naive Models." *Political Behavior* 6:9–21.

———. 1985. "Government Growth in the United States." *Journal of Politics* 47:2–30.

Lord, Robert G., and Alliger, George M. 1985. "A Comparison of Four Information Processing Models of Leadership and Social Perceptions." *Human Relations* 38:47–65.

Lowery, David, and Berry, William D. 1983. "The Growth of Government in the United States: An Empirical Assessment of Competing Explanations." *American Journal of Political Science* 27:665–94.

Machiavelli, Niccolo. 1513. *The Prince.* Trans. W. K. Marriott. Chicago: Encyclopaedia Britannica, 1952.

MacKuen, Michael B. 1983. "Political Drama, Economic Conditions, and the Dynamics of Presidential Popularity." *American Journal of Political Science* 27:165–92.

MacRae, Duncan. 1981. "On the Political Business Cycle." In *Contemporary Political Economy,* ed. Douglas Hibbs and Heino Fassbender. Amsterdam: North Holland.

Mahoney, John; Coogle, Constance L.; and Banks, P. David. 1984. "Values in Presidential Inaugural Addresses: A Test of Rokeach's Two-Factor Theory of Political Ideology." *Psychological Reports* 55:683–86.

Maranell, Gary M. 1970. "The Evaluation of Presidents: An Extension of the Schlesinger Polls." *Journal of American History* 57:104–13.

Maranell, Gary M., and Dodder, Richard. 1970. "Political Orientation and the Evaluation of Presidential Prestige: A Study of American Historians." *Social Science Quarterly* 51:415–21.

Margolis, Michael. 1985. "The 1984 Presidential Campaign and the Future of Election Studies." *Congress & the Presidency* 12:111–26.

Markus, Gregory B., and Converse, Philip E. 1979. "A Dynamic Simultaneous Equation Model of Electoral Choice." *American Political Science Review* 73:1055–70.

Marshall, Thomas R. 1984. "Issues, Personalities, and Presidential Primary Voters." *Social Science Quarterly* 65:750–60.

Matossian, Mary K., and Schafer, William D. 1977. "Family, Fertility, and Political Violence, 1700–1900." *Journal of Social History* 11:137–78.

Mazlish, Bruce. 1972. *In Search of Nixon.* New York: Basic Books.

McArthur, Leslie Z. 1981. "What Grabs You? The Role of Attention in Impression Formation and Causal Attribution." In *Social Cognition,* vol. 1, ed. E. Tory Higgins, C. Peter Herman, and Mark P. Zanna. Hillsdale, N.J.: Erlbaum.

McCauley, Clark, and Jacques, Susan. 1979. "The Popularity of Conspiracy Theories of Presidential Assassination: A Bayesian Analysis." *Journal of Personality and Social Psychology* 37:637–44.

Merenda, Peter F. 1964. "Perception of Role of the President." *Perceptual and Motor Skills* 19:863–66.

Merenda, Peter F., and Clarke, Walter V. 1968. "Technique for Prediction of Outcome of Election of National Leaders." *Perceptual and Motor Skills* 26:1003–09.

Merenda, Peter F.; Shapurian, Reza; Bassiri, Torab; and Clarke, Walter V. 1971. "Iranian Perceptions of the Reza Shah and President Johnson." *Perceptual and Motor Skills* 32:239–41.

Merenda, Peter F.; Shapurian, Reza; and Clarke, Walter V. 1974. "Pre-Election Public Image of Nixon and McGovern Given by English Students." *Perceptual and Motor Skills* 38:575–78.

Midlarsky, Manus I. 1984. "Preventing Systemic War: Crisis Decision-Making Amidst a Structure of Conflict Relationships." *Journal of Conflict Resolution* 28:563–84.

Miller, Arthur H., and Wattenberg, Martin P. 1985. "Throwing the Rascals Out: Policy and Performance Evaluations of Presidential Candidates, 1952–1980." *American Political Science Review* 79:359–72.

Miller, George A. 1956. "The Magical Number Seven, Plus or Minus Two: Some Limits on Our Capacity for Processing Information." *Psychological Review* 63:81–97.

Miller, Nancy L., and Stiles, William B. 1986. "Verbal Familiarity in American Presidential Nomination Acceptance Speeches and Inaugural Addresses." *Social Psychology Quarterly* 49:72–81.

Mills, Clarence A. 1942. "What Price Glory?" *Science* 96:380–81.

Monroe, Kristin. 1978. "Economic Influences on Presidential Popularity." *Public Opinion Quarterly* 42:360–69.

———. 1979. "Econometric Analyses of Electoral Behavior: A Critical Review." *Political Behavior* 1:137–73.

———. 1984. *Presidential Popularity & the Economy.* New York: Praeger.

Morris, Richard B., ed. 1976. *Encyclopedia of American History*. Bicentennial ed. New York: Harper and Row.
Morrow, Gary R.; Merenda, Peter F.; and Clarke, Walter V. 1974. "Perception of the Role of the President: A Nine-Year Follow-Up." *Perceptual and Motor Skills* 38:1259–62.
Mueller, John E. 1970. "Presidential Popularity from Truman to Johnson." *American Political Science Review* 64:18–34.
———. 1973. *War, Presidents and Public Opinion*. New York: Wiley.
Murphy, Arthur B. 1984. "Evaluating the Presidents of the United States." *Presidential Studies Quarterly* 14:117–26.
Murray, Henry A. 1938. *Explorations in Personality*. New York: Oxford University Press.
Murray, Robert K., and Blessing, Tim H. 1983. "The Presidential Performance Study: A Progress Report." *Journal of American History* 70:535–55.
Neustadt, Richard E. 1960. *Presidential Power*. New York: Wiley.
Nice, David C. 1984. "The Influence of War and Party System Aging on the Ranking of Presidents." *Western Political Quarterly* 37:443–55.
Nisbett, Richard E., and Wilson, Timothy D. 1977. "Telling More Than We Can Know: Verbal Reports on Mental Processes." *Psychological Review* 84:231–59.
Norpoth, Helmut. 1984. "Economics, Politics, and the Cycle of Presidential Popularity." *Political Behavior* 6:253–73.
Norrander, Barbara. 1986a. "Correlates of Vote Choice in the 1980 Presidential Primaries." *Journal of Politics* 48:156–66.
———. 1986b. "Selective Participation: Presidential Primary Voters as a Subset of General Election Voters." *American Politics Quarterly* 14:35–53.
Norrander, Barbara, and Smith, Gregg W. 1985. "Type of Contest, Candidate Strategy, and Turnout in Presidential Primaries." *American Politics Quarterly* 13:28–50.
Nunnally, Jum C. 1967. *Psychometric Theory*. New York: McGraw-Hill.
Oleszek, Walter. 1969. "Age and Political Careers." *Public Opinion Quarterly* 33:100–03.
Osgood, Charles E.; Suci, George J.; and Tannenbaum, Percy H. 1957. *The Measurement of Meaning*. Urbana: University of Illinois Press.
Owen, Guillermo. 1975. "Evaluation of a Presidential Election Game." *American Political Science Review* 69:947–53.
Padgett, Vernon, and Jorgenson, Dale O. 1982. "Superstition and Economic Threat: Germany 1918–1940." *Personality and Social Psychology Bulletin* 8:736–41.

Page, Benjamin I., and Jones, Calvin C. 1979. "Reciprocal Effects of Policy Preferences, Party Loyalties and the Vote." *American Political Science Review* 73:1071–89.
Page, Benjamin I., and Petracca, Mark P. 1983. *The American Presidency.* New York: McGraw-Hill.
Page, Benjamin I., and Shapiro, Robert. 1984. "Presidents as Opinion Leaders: Some New Evidence." *Policy Studies Journal* 12:649–61.
Peabody, Robert L.; Ornstein, Norman J.; and Rohde, David W. 1976. "The United States Senate as a Presidential Incubator: Many Are Called but Few Are Chosen." *Political Science Quarterly* 91:237–58.
Peskin, Allan. 1977. "President Garfield and the Rating Game: An Evaluation of a Brief Administration." *South Atlantic Quarterly* 76:93–102.
Poole, Keith T., and Rosenthal, Howard. 1984. "U.S. Presidential Elections 1960–80: A Spatial Analysis." *American Journal of Political Science* 28:282–312.
Porter, Carol A., and Suedfeld, Peter. 1981. "Integrative Complexity in the Correspondence of Literary Figures: Effects of Personal and Societal Stress." *Journal of Personality and Social Psychology* 40:321–30.
Quattrone, George A., and Tversky, Amos. 1984. "Causal Versus Diagnostic Contingencies: On Self-Deception and on the Voter's Illusion." *Journal of Personality and Social Psychology* 46:237–48.
Rabinowitz, George; Gurian, Paul-Henri; and MacDonald, Stuart Elaine. 1984. "The Structure of Presidential Elections and the Process of Realignment, 1944 to 1980." *American Journal of Political Science* 28: 611–35.
Rabinowitz, George, and MacDonald, Stuart Elaine. 1986. "The Power of the States in U.S. Presidential Elections." *American Political Science Review* 80:65–87.
Ringelstein, Albert C. 1985. "Presidential Vetoes: Motivations and Classification." *Congress & the Presidency* 12:43–55.
Rivers, Douglas, and Rose, Nancy L. 1985. "Passing the President's Program: Public Opinion and Presidential Influence in Congress." *American Journal of Political Science* 29:183–96.
Rohde, David W., and Simon, Dennis M. 1985. "Presidential Vetoes and Congressional Response: A Study of Institutional Conflict." *American Journal of Political Science* 29:397–427.
Rokeach, Milton. 1960. *The Open and the Closed Mind.* New York: Basic Books.
Rollenhagen, Rick E. 1984. "Explaining Variation in Concern about the Outcome of Presidential Elections, 1960–1980." *Political Behavior* 6:147–57.

Rosen, Benson, and Einhorn, Hillel J. 1972. "Attractiveness of the 'Middle of the Road' Political Candidate." *Journal of Applied Social Psychology* 2:157–65.

Rosenberg, Shawn W.; Bohan, Lisa; McCafferty, Patrick; and Harris, Kevin. 1986. "The Image and the Vote: The Effect of Candidate Presentation on Voter Preference." *American Journal of Political Science* 30:108–27.

Rosenstone, Steven J. 1983. *Forecasting Presidential Elections.* New Haven: Yale University Press.

Ross, Lee. 1977. "The Intuitive Psychologist and his Shortcomings: Distortions in the Attribution Process." In *Advances in Experimental Social Psychology,* vol. 10, ed. Leonard Berkowitz. New York: Academic Press.

Rossiter, Clinton L. 1956. *The American Presidency.* New York: Harcourt Brace.

Sales, Stephen M. 1972. "Economic Threat as a Determinant of Conversion Rates in Authoritarian and Non-Authoritarian Churches." *Journal of Personality and Social Psychology* 23:420–28.

Salwen, Michael B. 1985. "The Reporting of Public Opinion Polls during Presidential Years, 1968–1984." *Journalism Quarterly* 62:272–77.

Schlesinger, Arthur M. 1948. "Historians Rate the U.S. Presidents." *Life* 25 (November 1):65–66, 68, 73–74.

———. 1949. *Paths to the Present.* New York: Macmillan.

———. 1962. "Our Presidents: A Rating by 75 Historians." *New York Times Magazine* (July 29), pp. 12–13, 40–41, 43.

Schroder, Harold M.; Driver, Michael J.; and Streufert, Siegfried. 1967. *Human Information Processing.* New York: Holt, Rinehart, and Winston.

Schubert, Glendon. 1983. "Aging, Conservatism, and Judicial Behavior." *Micropolitics* 3:135–79.

Senter, Richard, Jr.; Reynolds, Larry T.; and Gruenenfelder, David. 1986. "The Presidency and the Print Media: Who Controls the News?" *Sociological Quarterly* 27:91–105.

Shyles, Leonard C. 1983. "Defining the Issues of a Presidential Election from Televised Political Spot Advertisements." *Journal of Broadcasting* 27:333–43.

———. 1984a. "Defining 'Images' of Presidential Candidates from Televised Political Spot Advertisements." *Political Behavior* 6:53–63.

———. 1984b. "The Relationships of Images, Issues and Presentational Methods in Televised Spot Advertisements for 1980's American Presidential Primaries." *Journal of Broadcasting* 28:405–21.

Sigelman, Lee. 1979. "Presidential Popularity and Presidential Elections." *Public Opinion Quarterly* 43:532–34.

Sigelman, Lee, and Knight, Kathleen. 1983. "Why Does Presidential Popularity Decline? A Test of the Expectation/Disillusion Theory." *Public Opinion Quarterly* 47:310–24.

———. 1985a. "Expectation/Disillusion and Presidential Popularity: The Reagan Experience." *Public Opinion Quarterly* 49:209–13.

———. 1985b. "Public Opinion and Presidential Responsibility for the Economy: Understanding Personalization." *Political Behavior* 7:167–91.

Simonton, Dean Keith. 1975. "Sociocultural Context of Individual Creativity: A Transhistorical Time-Series Analysis." *Journal of Personality and Social Psychology* 32:1119–33.

———. 1976. "Biographical Determinants of Achieved Eminence: A Multivariate Approach to the Cox Data." *Journal of Personality and Social Psychology* 33:218–26.

———. 1979. "Multiple Discovery and Invention: Zeitgeist, Genius, or Chance?" *Journal of Personality and Social Psychology* 37:1603–16.

———. 1980. "Land Battles, Generals, and Armies: Individual and Situational Determinants of Victory and Casualties." *Journal of Personality and Social Psychology* 38:110–19.

———. 1981a. "The Library Laboratory: Archival Data in Personality and Social Psychology." In *Review of Personality and Social Psychology*, vol. 2, ed. Ladd Wheeler. Beverly Hills: Sage Publications.

———. 1981b. "Predicting Presidential Greatness with Historical Data: Challenges and Difficulties." In Testing the Limits of Measurement in Political Psychology, chaired by Henry A. Alker, a symposium presented at the meeting of the International Society of Political Psychology, Mannheim, June.

———. 1981c. "Presidential Greatness and Performance: Can We Predict Leadership in the White House?" *Journal of Personality* 49:306–23.

———. 1983a. "Formal Education, Eminence, and Dogmatism: The Curvilinear Relationship." *Journal of Creative Behavior* 17:149–62.

———. 1983b. "Intergenerational Transfer of Individual Differences in Hereditary Monarchs: Genes, Role-Modeling, Cohort, or Sociocultural Effects?" *Journal of Personality and Social Psychology* 44:354–64.

———. 1983c. "Psychohistory." In *The Encyclopedic Dictionary of Psychology*, ed. Rom Harré and Roger Lamb. Oxford: Blackwell.

———. 1984a. "Creative Productivity and Age: A Mathematical Model Based on a Two-Step Cognitive Process." *Developmental Review* 4:77–111.

———. 1984b. *Genius, Creativity, and Leadership*. Cambridge, Mass.: Harvard University Press.

———. 1984c. "Leader Age and National Condition: A Longitudinal Analysis of 25 European Monarchs." *Social Behavior and Personality* 12:111–14.

———. 1984d. "Leaders as Eponyms: Individual and Situational Determinants of Monarchal Eminence." *Journal of Personality* 52:1–21.

———. 1985a. "Intelligence and Personal Influence in Groups: Four Nonlinear Models." *Psychological Review* 92:532–47.

———. 1985b. "The Vice-Presidential Succession Effect: Individual or Situational Determinants?" *Political Behavior* 7:79–99.

———. 1986a. "Biographical Typicality, Eminence, and Achievement Style." *Journal of Creative Behavior* 20:14–22.

———. 1986b. "Dispositional Attributions of (Presidential) Leadership: An Experimental Simulation of Historiometric Results." *Journal of Experimental Social Psychology,* in press.

———. 1986c. "Presidential Greatness: The Historical Consensus and Its Psychological Significance." *Political Psychology* 7:259–83.

———. 1986d. "Presidential Inflexibility: Two Individual-Situational Interactions." *Journal of Personality,* in press.

———. 1986e. "Presidential Personality: Biographical Use of the Gough Adjective Check List." *Journal of Personality and Social Psychology* 51: 149–60.

———. 1986f. "Supreme Court Vacancies as Individual Choices." Unpublished manuscript, University of California, Davis.

Smith, Marshall S.; Stone, Philip J.; and Glenn, Evelyn N. 1966. "A Content Analysis of Twenty Presidential Nomination Acceptance Speeches." In *The General Inquirer: A Computer Approach to Content Analysis,* ed. Philip J. Stone, Dexter C. Dunphy, Marshall S. Smith, and Daniel M. Ogilvie. Cambridge, Mass.: MIT Press.

Sokolsky, Eric. 1964. *Our Seven Greatest Presidents.* New York: Exposition Press.

Sorokin, Pitirim A. 1925. "Monarchs and Rulers: A Comparative Statistical Study. I." *Social Forces* 4:22–35.

———. 1926. "Monarchs and Rulers: A Comparative Statistical Study. II." *Social Forces* 4:523–33.

Stewart, Louis H. 1977. "Birth Order and Political Leadership." In *The Psychological Examination of Political Leaders,* ed. Margaret G. Hermann. New York: Free Press.

Stiles, William B.; Au, Melinda L.; Martello, Mary Ann; and Perlmutter, Julia A. 1983. "American Campaign Oratory: Verbal Response Mode Use by Candidates in the 1980 American Presidential Primaries." *Social Behavior and Personality* 11:39–43.

Stimson, James A. 1976. "Public Support for American Presidents: A Cyclical Model." *Public Opinion Quarterly* 40:1–21.
Stoll, Richard J. 1984. "The Guns of November: Presidential Elections and the Use of Force, 1947–1982." *Journal of Conflict Resolution* 28: 231–46.
Stone, Walter J. 1986. "The Carryover Effect on Presidential Elections." *American Political Science Reveiw* 80:271–79.
Stone, Walter J., and Abramowitz, Alan I. 1980. "Winning May Not Be Everything, but It's More than We Thought: Presidential Party Activists in 1980." *American Political Science Review* 77:946–56.
Stovall, James Glen. 1984. "Incumbency and News Coverage of the 1980 Presidential Election Campaign." *Western Political Quarterly* 37:621–31.
———. 1985. "The Third-Party Challenge of 1980: News Coverage of the Presidential Candidates." *Journalism Quarterly* 62:266–71.
Suedfeld, Peter. 1980. "Indices of World Tension in the Bulletin of the Atomic Scientists." *Political Psychology* 2:114–23.
Suedfeld, Peter, and Rank, A. Dennis. 1976. "Revolutionary Leaders: Long-Term Success as a Function of Changes in Conceptual Complexity." *Journal of Personality and Social Psychology* 34:169–78.
Suedfeld, Peter, and Tetlock, Philip E. 1977. "Integrative Complexity of Communications in International Crises." *Journal of Conflict Resolution* 21:169–84.
Suedfeld, Peter; Tetlock, Philip E.; and Ramirez, Carmenza. 1977. "War, Peace, and Integrative Complexity." *Journal of Conflict Resolution* 21: 427–42.
Taagepera, Rein, and Colby, Benjamin N. 1979. "Growth of Western Civilization: Epicyclical or Exponential?" *American Anthropologist* 81: 907–12.
Taylor, Tim. 1972. *The Book of Presidents.* New York: Arno Press.
Tetlock, Philip E. 1979. "Identifying Victims of Groupthink from Public Statements of Decision Makers." *Journal of Personality and Social Psychology* 37:1314–24.
———. 1981a. "Personality and Isolationism: Content Analysis of Senatorial Speeches." *Journal of Personality and Social Psychology* 41:737–43.
———. 1981b. "Pre- to Postelection Shifts in Presidential Rhetoric: Impression Management or Cognitive Adjustment." *Journal of Personality and Social Psychology* 41:207–12.
———. 1983. "Cognitive Style and Political Ideology." *Journal of Personality and Social Psychology* 45:118–26.
———. 1984. "Cognitive Style and Political Belief Systems in the British

House of Commons." *Journal of Personality and Social Psychology* 46: 365–75.

———. 1985. "Integrative Complexity of American and Soviet Foreign Policy Rhetoric: A Time-Series Analysis." *Journal of Personality and Social Psychology* 49:1565–85.

Tetlock, Philip E.; Bernzweig, Jane; and Gallant, Jack L. 1985. "Cognitive Style as a Predictor of Ideological Consistency of Voting." *Journal of Personality and Social Psychology* 48:1227–39.

Tetlock, Philip E.; Hannum, Kristen A.; and Micheletti, Patrick M. 1984. "Stability and Change in the Complexity of Senatorial Debate: Testing the Cognitive versus Rhetorical Style Hypothesis." *Journal of Personality and Social Psychology* 46:979–90.

Thomas, Dan B.; Sigelman, Lee; and Baas, Larry R. 1984. "Public Evaluations of the President: Policy, Partisan, and 'Personal' Determinants." *Political Psychology* 5:531–42.

Thorndike, Edward L. 1936. "The Relation between Intellect and Morality in Rulers." *American Journal of Sociology* 42:321–34.

———. 1950. "Traits of Personality and Their Intercorrelations as Shown in Biography." *Journal of Educational Psychology* 41:193–216.

Tolstoy, Leo. 1865–1869. *War and Peace.* Trans. L. Maude and A. Maude. Chicago: Encyclopaedia Britannica, 1952.

Tufte, Edward R. 1978. *Political Control of the Economy.* Princeton, N.J.: Princeton University Press.

Tversky, Amos, and Kahneman, Daniel. 1974. "Judgment under Uncertainty: Heuristics and Biases." *Science* 185:1124–31.

———. 1982. "Judgments of and by Representativeness." In *Judgment under Uncertainty,* ed. Daniel Kahneman, Paul Slovic, and Amos Tversky. New York: Cambridge University Press.

Tyler, Tom R. 1982. "Personalization in Attributing Responsibility for National Problems to the President." *Political Behavior* 4:379–99.

Ulmer, S. Sidney. 1982. "Supreme Court Appointments as a Poisson Distribution." *American Journal of Political Science* 26:113–16.

United States Statutes at Large. 1845–1982. Washington, D.C.: Government Printing Office.

Wagner, Joseph. 1983. "Media Do Make a Difference: The Differential Impact of Mass Media in the 1976 Presidential Race." *American Journal of Political Science* 27:407–30.

Walberg, Herbert J.; Rasher, Sue Pinzur; and Parkerson, Joann. 1980. "Childhood and Eminence." *Journal of Creative Behavior* 13:225–31.

Walker, Stephan G., and Falkowski, Lawrence S. 1984. "The Operational

Codes of U.S. Presidents and Secretaries of State: Motivational Foundations and Behavioral Consequences." *Political Psychology* 5:237–66.
Wallace, Myles S., and Warner, John T. 1984. "Fed Policy and Presidential Elections." *Journal of Macroeconomics* 6:79–88.
Wasserman, Ira M. 1983. "Political Business Cycles, Presidential Elections, and Suicide and Mortality Patterns." *American Sociological Review* 48:711–20.
Weber, Paul J. 1984. "The Birth Order Oddity in Supreme Court Appointments." *Presidential Studies Quarterly* 14:561–68.
Webster's Guide to American History. 1971. Springfield, Mass.: Merriam.
Wendt, Hans W., and Light, Paul C. 1976. "Measuring 'Greatness' in American Presidents: Model Case for International Research on Political Leadership?" *European Journal of Social Psychology* 6:105–09.
Wendt, Hans W., and Muncy, Carole A. 1979. "Studies of Political Character: Factor Patterns of 24 U.S. Vice-Presidents." *Journal of Psychology* 102:125–31.
West, Darrell M. 1980. "Cheers and Jeers: Candidate Presentations and Audience Reactions in the 1980 Presidential Campaign." *American Politics Quarterly* 12:23–50.
———. 1983. "Constituencies and Travel Allocations in the 1980 Presidential Campaign." *American Journal of Political Science* 27:515–28.
Whitney, David C. 1982. *The American Presidents*. 5th ed. Garden City, N.Y.: Doubleday.
Willner, Ann R. 1984. *The Spellbinders*. New Haven: Yale University Press.
Winter, David G. 1973. *The Power Motive*. New York: Free Press.
———. 1985. "Leader Appeal, Leader Performance and the Motive Profiles of Leaders and Followers: A Study of American Presidents and Elections." Unpublished manuscript, Wesleyan University.
Winter, David G., and Stewart, Abigail J. 1977. "Content Analysis as a Technique for Assessing Political Leaders." In *The Psychological Examination of Political Leaders*, ed. Margaret G. Hermann. New York: Free Press.
Woods, Frederick A. 1906. *Mental and Moral Heredity in Royalty*. New York: Holt.
———. 1909. "A New Name for a New Science." *Science* 30:703–04.
———. 1911. "Historiometry as an Exact Science." *Science* 33:568–74.
———. 1913. *The Influence of Monarchs*. New York: Macmillan.
Zeidenstein, Harvey G. 1985. "Presidents' Popularity and Their Wins and Losses on Major Issues in Congress: Does One Have Greater Influence over the Other?" *Presidential Studies Quarterly* 15:287–300.

INDEX